# Unlocked

# Unlocked

## Portraits of a Pandemic

A. J. Stone

KETTLE PRESS

First published in 2023 by Kettle Press
www.kettlepress.co.uk

ISBN 978 1 7392025 0 7

Printed and bound in Great Britain by
York Publishing Services

Cover design by Björn Bauer

For Nick

# Contents

Some names and details in the interviews have been changed to protect individual identities. I also gave all interviewees the opportunity to view their chapter prior to publication as I did not want anyone to regret the stories they had shared. As it turned out, only two interviewees chose to make any changes, and in both these instances it was just a matter of removing a couple of identifying sentences.

# Introduction

I went from labour ward to funeral parlour, temple to pub, to find out about people's experiences of living through England's mandatory lockdowns. Everyone had their own story, and this book presents the tale of the pandemic through the voices of thirty-three of the people I encountered.

My own experience had been dominated by my then four-teen-year-old daughter who had been diagnosed with anorexia nervosa and signed off school ten days before the first lockdown. Having been sucked into the vortex of an eating disorder, she was suffering physically and psychologically. Hiding beneath baggy clothing, her desire to disappear was threatening to overwhelm any instinct to survive.

When England's national lockdown began, her absence from school blended in with everybody else's. For her it was a blessing as it removed all the tension of being different, standing out, missing. Having my daughter at home 24/7 meant her anorexia was also home at all times. Her struggle was shared by all in my household, though as my husband and son were working full-time, I was her main supporter and challenger during the day.

My daughter and I settled into a routine. In the mornings, she would do the remote work sent through by her school while I worked, then we would spend the afternoons sewing, giving new life to old clothes, piecing together, stitching and unstitching.

The days were punctuated by the regular snacks and meals prescribed by her eating plan; food is an anorexic's medicine, while also being what they most fear. Lockdown meant I was constantly present to put up a persistent fight against the voice in her head that raged against every mouthful. By this time, I had worked out most of her tricks of slipping food onto my plate, up her sleeve, into a pocket. Refeeding is not an easy journey: she fought hard and calculated secretly; could the calories she'd just consumed after a two-hour battle with me be somehow nullified by a sneaky midnight workout? But slowly, during the turmoil and the quiet of lockdown, she regained weight, and, with it, her life.

During the first lockdown, I read an article by Arundhati Roy in which she wrote, 'Historically, pandemics have forced humans to break with the past and imagine their world anew. This one is no different. It is a portal, a gateway between one world and the next.'[1]

Given my own experiences, I was curious to explore this idea further and began to look for people to interview. Needing a geographical area to contain the project, I chose Swindon because the town is often considered a benchmark for the national mood: it is regarded as being as representative as any one place can be of the rest of England.[2]

As it was lockdown when I began this project, I conducted most of the interviews over Zoom and soon found it had its advantages. People could be in their own homes, but without

---

1 Arundhati Roy, 'The pandemic is a portal', *Financial Times*, 3 April 2020.

2 According to data from the Office for National Statistics and the British Social Attitudes Survey, Swindon has average earnings, employment, house prices, attitudes, ethnic mix and life expectancy. For over forty years the MP that wins in Swindon has come from the party that goes on to form the government.

any pressure to tidy up or host. With no travel for either party, it allowed some flexibility over timing; parents with young or special needs children took advantage of this, messaging me spontaneously to see if I could speak when they suddenly found a moment's peace. And, while Zoom might make us feel at one remove compared to an in-person meeting, this was not necessarily a bad thing as it meant I could slip more easily into the background. Sometimes people chatted as if I was barely there. Indeed, one young woman said that she had basically told me her life story because she felt like she had been sitting in her room talking to herself.

The collage of portraits I created from these interviews provides a nuanced reply to Arundhati Roy's thesis about the pandemic being a portal into a new world. For myself, despite the isolation and anxiety of caring for my daughter, I can look back on a precious, unhurried time of togetherness that formed an integral part of her recovery. Now, as we return to our busy lives and my daughter flits from one social to another and my son is barely home, I sometimes miss the times we had together as a family and hanker after plan-free weekends. This is just my story, and, of course, others have very diverse tales to tell of lockdown and its ongoing legacy.

# Laura Kirby-Deacon

## *How did we all just do that?*

I've worked in Swindon ICU for fourteen years, and I love being an ICU nurse – it's where my passion within nursing lies. I think having gone through my own significant bereavement, it struck a chord with me that, actually, we could probably change things and make things a lot better for people in end-of-life.

So, obviously, beginning of 2020, we got whiff that the dreaded C-word was heading our way. Initially, the fear factor kicked in, you know, you sort of put yourself first and think, well how's it going to affect me? How will it affect my family? If it's that highly contagious, will I be bringing it home?

Then the adrenaline kicks in. I wouldn't say I'm an adrenaline junkie, but I thrive in stressful situations. So you throw yourself into preparing that, you know, we're going to be working beyond our normal capacity. We normally work on a one-to-one ratio within ICU – one patient to one nurse – but this was probably going to be a lot bigger than all the staff we had on the unit. So, we frantically started preparing and thinking about how we were going to get staff redeployed to us on ICU so that they could receive the necessary training to help support the intensive-care nurses. I threw myself into that because that's my job, educating people – I'm one of the practice educators on the unit. Then we just waited, and, slowly but surely, our twelve-bed unit started filling up. I think at our peak we were at twenty-six or twenty-seven patients in one go. The trust allocated us main recovery within theatres so that we could accommodate the number of patients we were receiving.

At the very beginning there was an incident that sticks in my mind where a nurse was looking after a guy who, we all knew deep down, probably wasn't going to survive. Because he had a bit of pneumonia we then had to think, is this potentially a Covid patient? Test results were slow to come through in the early stages of the pandemic, so we had to take the necessary precautions, and sadly his family couldn't come in to be with him. Myself and another colleague supported this nurse in FaceTiming his family while we de-escalated his care. They managed to have four or five people on this FaceTime; they were all saying their goodbyes as he sadly passed away in front of them. And it just hit me like a bolt out of nowhere that, before long, this was going to be absolutely huge. The poor nurse was like, 'This is the hardest thing that I've ever had to do in my career.' My other colleagues came out and said, 'We're going to be faced with this on a daily basis now.'

I think the family took comfort in the fact that we were there with him while he died, but we're strangers at the end of the day. I just thought, there's got to be something else that we can do, and that's where my knitted hearts project came from. I was flicking through social media and I saw a pattern for knitted hearts, and I thought, I wonder if there's something we could do that would be something that the public could give and something to connect families with their loved ones. So, I saw this pattern for knitted hearts, and I like to have a go at knitting and crocheting, but I wouldn't say my skills are that great. I thought, I'll just put a thing out on my social media and see if a few of my friends who I know are crafty could just knit me up, like, fifty pairs of hearts. I put a pattern out and explained what they were for, you know, the idea being that we'd have two knitted hearts, one would stay with the patient and the other one we would post out to the family, so it's a way of connecting them together. And then, within an hour all my friends had shared the post. Within three hours I was like, oh my god, I'm going to have thousands of knitted hearts before long!

I phoned the charity Brighter Futures at our hospital, and we came up with a way of how we could manage it – they basically took over delivery of the hearts. We had thousands, absolutely thousands! They were knitted, they were sewed, they were crocheted. We had wooden hearts. You name it, we've had some amazing stuff. We had many sets of hearts that were very similar, so it meant that instead of just the next of kin having a heart, we'd give it to the children and the grandchildren, so they all had something to connect them together.

Then, I had a message from one of the chief nurses saying, 'It's a great project, Laura, but can you tell your knitters to stop knitting because the hospital is absolutely overrun with knitted hearts!' So we started sending them out to nursing homes – all the nursing homes in Swindon got huge sackfuls.

Before long, other hospitals were messaging saying, can we pick up on this? I was all for it, absolutely. If we can not only knit these families together, but knit the hospitals together, then what a great way of coming together in amongst all this. I didn't expect it to become as big as it has. I've had messages from Australia. I've made friends with a lovely lady in Canada – it's huge in Canada!

It was something that we could do that was very simple in a highly driven area. I know it sounds as sad as it is, but trying to create lots of little memories for families is really difficult when you're absolutely overwhelmed with the workload. So having something as simple as these two little hearts, yeah, it's used all around the hospital now, not just for ICU. I think it will be something that we carry on with now for the rest of our days within nursing. And Covid gave us that, so a small little positive, I suppose.

During the first wave, ethically, we struggled with the fact that families couldn't come in. This time around, we do advocate for families coming in if we know their loved one is dying, but obviously, if they're at home isolating, they can't come in. So if they're coming in for Covid patients, they have to wear a helmet, because they've not been fit tested for the masks. It's a welder's helmet, actually. So we get them all gowned up and stuff. The bed space, it's open, it's like an old traditional Nightingale unit, but there are curtains around the bed space. At the end of the day, we're trying to do the best job out of what we've got. I think people are just thankful that they can get that opportunity this time, because the first time we weren't allowing anyone in.

We're used to quite traumatic deaths, but these patients dying of Covid has just overwhelmed us. We've had some young people die; we've seen families within ICU, you know, a couple of people from the same family. The fact that you're on FaceTime with the family, that's really hard, really hard. Every day you're phoning somebody different so they can say their last goodbyes.

For me, one guy sticks out in my mind, and it wasn't so long ago. He came to us, and he was awake and I was working with him most of the day. And at the end of the day, I said to him, 'You do realise that by tonight, you could possibly end up being placed onto a ventilator to help support your breathing?' And he said he'd lost his wife earlier on in the year from something else and they had a daughter at home. He was like, 'I haven't made any provisions for things at home if I were to die.' And I said to him, 'You're not going to achieve that tonight, you know, I think you just have to put yourself first.'

I'd been speaking to his sister, and I said, 'Why don't you phone your sister up?' So he was on the phone to his sister and I could overhear him; he was, like, the mortgage can be paid off from this, and he was talking about what to do with the business. It was a very frank, matter-of-fact conversation and that really struck me, and I said to him, 'I've got a day off, but when I come in the following day, I'll come and look you up and see how you're doing.' And he was just very thankful, like, 'You've been amazing today, you've been very patient and thank you for everything.'

And then when I came on a day or so later, he sadly arrested and died. I was in charge that day, and I think I just cried all day long. Things build up, and, for me, that was the straw that broke the camel's back. One of the consultants came up to me and he was like, 'Can you help me do up my PPE?' I was doing up his gown, and he said, 'The great thing about wearing PPE is that you can give people really good hugs.' He just pulled me into his arms and gave me the biggest hug, and I was like, 'Please don't do that because you're going to set me off again.'

I spoke to the man's sister a couple of days later and we were both just crying down the phone. He was a lovely guy. I got to see him while he wasn't intubated and he was able to converse with me; you sort of develop that rapport. It's almost better if you, literally, like, intubate them straight away because you don't develop that familiarity with people. Yeah, that, for me, that really took the wind out of my sails. I think it was particularly difficult because I knew his wife had died, so they were trying to come to terms with that and then, sadly, his daughter got Covid and brought Covid into the house. That's how the man got Covid. For me, that's a family that will stick in my mind, and I don't think I'll ever forget that.

In the beginning, we were all running on adrenaline; the novelty of doing it drives you forward. This time around, I don't know what we are running on. Coffee? Red Bull? You just go on to autopilot, you just function: you go in, you do your job, you come home, have something to eat and you go back in. I'm full-time, so I do thirty-six hours a week, but in the first wave I was probably working double that. If you've got a really sick patient and things are happening, you can't say, 'Right, it's clocking-off time now, I'm going.' You do end up going home late and working extra days because the staffing is so tight. But this time around, I'm probably averaging forty to fifty hours a week, because I recognise that, actually, I can't sustain working those hours.

You get tired, really tired. You get quite fatigued in the PPE, and sometimes you can be in it for hours. You're physically on your feet all day, and we prone these patients, so that's really hard going physically, rolling these patients – you're doing one after the other after the other after the other. It's not just a case of going in and flipping somebody over; when you're sedated, you're literally dead weight. It's heavy to do, especially with all the paraphernalia that comes along with ICU – all the lines and the drips and what have you.

The fact that we've been going at it for over a year has been relentless, and obviously in the first wave all other services had stopped so we didn't see our normal ICU patients, the post-ops. And I think people were too frightened to go out first time around, and they were very reluctant to come into hospital for any reason. But this time, I wouldn't say we've had as many as our normal ICU, but we have had more than the first time.

We're really short-staffed and the workload is immense, so people just come in and do what they have to do. I see people struggling, and, you know, what can you do? I think people are frightened of talking about it, because once you start talking, you're then frightened that you're going to open the floodgates and you don't want to let your team down. We're an amazing team, absolutely phenomenal team. If I was going to do this with anyone, I'm glad I've done it with these people. Everyone's got each other's backs. We pride ourselves on that, probably a little bit too much, because we're trying to put everybody first before ourselves, but it's the nature of our work, I suppose. So, yeah, it's taken its toll and I think we can see that now.

As senior members of the team, not only are we supporting patients, relatives and families, but we're also supporting staff, and, actually, who do we get to lean on? You know, apart from coming home and having a glass of wine at night. And it's really hard because, like, my husband, he understands, he sees what I'm going through, but I think unless you're in it, you don't actually get the full effect of it. You come home and say, 'We've had another death today.' It's really hard to explain the emotional impact that it has on you.

My husband will grumble about wearing a mask all day, and he's a builder so he works outside, so he comes home, he cranks the fire on because he's been cold all day. I've been sweating my backside off in plastic aprons and really tight-fitting masks and stuff, and I just want to come home, have a cold beer and sit in a cold room.

I get very frustrated when I go to the supermarket, and I sometimes wish people could come and walk a shift in my shoes, see what I see, experience what I experience on a daily basis. Obviously, some shifts are worse than others, but when it's at its worst I just wish they had that insight. But I've always said, I think until it affects you directly, people just don't understand. I lost a child and people can say they're sorry, but until they've been through it themselves, they just can't empathise. So, yeah, you get frustrated, but I think you can either let it eat you up and make you angry or just, you know, everyone's entitled to their opinion. But I do wish I could wear a secret little camera and then just pop the recording in their pocket and say, 'Listen to what I've had to say and do today.'

I'm working every day, so I haven't had the luxury of discovering nature and going out for nice long walks and getting fit and healthy. I'm surviving on coffee and whatever's there to eat. Everybody was decorating their houses and decluttering, and I look around and think, oh my god, they've all got nice houses, nice gardens, and mine looks like Beirut!

I've got an allotment, and, obviously, I couldn't get up there last year. Then my husband said to me, 'Right, we're going to go up, we're going to tackle it.' I was like, 'I can't, I just can't face it.'

When I received it, it was so overgrown, and I had worked so hard by myself to get it to where it was, and I just knew that I was going to be going back to square one. But, this day, my husband took me up there and it was really funny because it was right at the end and we were walking down, and I said to my husband, 'Why are all these people here? They should all be at home. They should all be social distancing.' I was doing my absolute nut.

Then they all started clapping, and I was like, 'What are they clapping at?' and looking behind me. And he's like, 'It's for you, you muppet.' They'd literally dug over my whole allotment, repainted the shed, created me a little seating area, planted me some veg. So, for me, that was just amazing and they've said to me now, you know, 'Don't worry, we'll dig it all over this spring.' When I did have a day off, that was my little sanctuary.

The NHS was dying a very slow death before Covid, and I think this has almost given rebirth to the NHS. It's called it back into the front of people's minds. Yeah, we are all on our knees, but actually I think the respect that the NHS has been given is very well deserved. Obviously, it's going through a negative phase with all these anti-Covid extremist people and whatnot. I struggle with that; I just think that's very sad. I just ignore it online. We're already sad; why would I want to make myself even sadder listening to that tosh? I know of an agency nurse, she works in another hospital, and she had a guy on her unit who was one of the protesters about the masks, anti-Covid and all that. Before he died, he said, 'If I knew what I know now back then, maybe I wouldn't have done what I did.' Hindsight's a wonderful thing though, isn't it?

*Afterword – one year later*[3]

I look back and think to myself, how did we all just do that? How did we survive the exhaustion, fatigue, the seriousness of how unwell patients really were? How did we watch patients die alone holding the hand of a nurse they had not even had a conversation with? Then to fill their bed with the next patient.

I'm incredibly proud of what I did and achieved. There are patients who have imprinted on me and I will always remember their story. I'm proud to have held the hands of those who have died alone. I'm proud of Swindon, of all the people who were frantically knitting hearts, which then became known worldwide.

The pandemic impacted me in a profound way. It nearly cost me my family. It's made me evaluate what I want out of life. Do I want to stay within critical care? I have moments where I think I've done my bit now, I need to think about doing something else. Then I'm like, critical care, if you cut me down

---

3 Some afterwords in this book come from further conversations with the interviewees, others from emails, texts or Messenger exchanges.

the middle, I'd have critical care running through my blood. So, I think at the moment while I'm still young and I'm fit, I'll be stuck there for another ten years.

I think making family time more of a priority will be the biggest thing, because obviously I didn't get that luxury during Covid. I worked relentlessly and, like I said, it took its toll on family life, on my marriage, but it's made me relook at things and you just have to work that little bit harder. It's easy for work to say, 'We're short today, can you work?' 'Yeah, yeah, I'll work.' But actually, there needs to come a time where you tell them 'No.'

# Rich Loveday

*The start of the pandemic,*
*that was a big trigger for me*

*8 March 2021*

I've lived in Swindon all my life, born and bred here. I work in the security industry and I run boxing events. Jeez, I used to box myself; I've had many, many fights. About six years ago, I decided to do events and sort of went from there, and it got quite successful. I mean, the events, some of them could be quite fruitful.

I'm a father of three children. Obviously, my children are my life. Me and their mother, we were together since we were very young, but unfortunately – I'm going to be honest – I was unfaithful back in 2016, and then I got with the lady, but we just recently broke up. My eldest daughter's with me. My two younger daughters live with their mum, but we talk every single day. I guess if it wasn't for my children and what I do with the boxing shows, I really and honestly would not be in a very good place. For me, it keeps me focused, it gives me a purpose. But this last year, this whole Covid thing, there's been times when, you know, I had not great thoughts.

How things started for me, going back, at school I did a lot of cross-country running. Actually, my biggest achievement was I represented England on a couple of occasions over cross-country. I did that when I was seventeen, and then, when I got to eighteen, I picked up some Achilles injuries, so I couldn't really run like I used to.

Then it was time to get a job, right? I went straight into retail. Then I got to about twenty, I started in security work. Now bearing in mind I was literally a couple of years out from being a distance runner, so I was still quite petite, I wasn't physically cut out for security. I remember my first job in security vividly, it was a supermarket called Kwik Save. I was a store detective, so basically you just had to deal with shoplifters. My very first shift, I came across this chap who had stolen some alcohol. I had to pluck the courage up to approach him, and I wasn't very successful. And so, over the weeks of trying to challenge people, I wasn't very good and people got away with things. So, I guess it was like a Rocky moment for me – I started going to a gym, started to do weights, and I got physically bigger and stronger. And then the tables turned and my confidence grew from there.

I began working in pubs and clubs, and you come across some colourful characters, especially when people are drunk or under the influence of other things, and so I found myself in situations … You know, sometimes you've got to get your hands dirty.

I fell into mixed martial arts – I watched it on TV and wanted to have a go. I had three professional cage fights, and that's how I started to box. I thought I'd have a couple of boxing bouts, but then it turned out I had over sixty-five, and a lot of that was in a short space of time. I would get offered a certain amount of money to have a boxing fight – it was quick, easy money for me. I was very fortunate, I never got seriously hurt. When I used to go to a show, you see your face on a poster, and I found it very exciting and you felt special.

I certainly fell in love with boxing, and that's why I still want to stay involved with the sport. I've met some very nice people, and also there are a couple of individuals that probably aren't so nice. But as a whole, it's a gentleman's sport. I was too old to pursue a career, like a professional career, and that's what got me to do events really. Jeez, 2015 was my first boxing event I promoted in Swindon.

I'm not going to blow my own trumpet, but I think I'm quite good at what I do with my events and in security. I like to call myself a law-abiding citizen, you know, and I detest bullying. My nickname is the Sheriff, people call me the Sheriff. It's a bit of a joke amongst fellow guys in the security industry. When I used to box, I was called the Tank.

Lockdown, I was fortunate, I could still work in security – one place that was open was, obviously, supermarkets. I tend to get sent to the places where there's problem stores, whether it's the store where the staff have been assaulted or there's a particular problem with persistent shoplifters – every single retailer has shoplifters, but I mean the places that have a bigger problem. Today I was in a place near Gloucester; the manager was threatened at the weekend and he had his tyres slashed. I was in Didcot only two weeks ago because there was an armed robbery – a gentleman went in there with a knife at seven o'clock in the morning. It's interesting, every day is interesting.

With the shoplifters, you have the drug addicts and then what I'd call the professional shoplifters who know how to work the system. Since the pandemic, it's more what I'd call 'normal' people, just because they can't afford to have the luxuries. They buy their bread or their milk, but they put the desirable goods into a bag or inside their pockets. I've seen a lot more of that. And it's sad to see. I can tell the difference; I can tell the people that are doing certain things because they can't afford it. But then there's a lot of people, you know, when they get away with certain things, people get greedy. They gamble. You know, if I win £100, that's not enough, I want £200. If I win

£10,000, that's not enough, I want £20,000. So if I nick a block of cheese and I've got away with it, I'll nick two next time, and that's what happens.

Our roles changed when Covid was at its peak. I think all retailers did it – you had a sort of queue monitor, you know, only a certain amount of people in the shop at a time. I did that. I actually quite enjoyed that because you can interact with people. Normally, I'm very solitary. A lot of people got used to queuing, giving people space and time when they're doing their shopping, but I'm finding, more recently, people are getting more impatient. I think they can see light at the end of the tunnel and they want to just get things going. You know, what I observe is customers arguing amongst themselves, whether someone's not wearing a mask, or they're too close to each other.

I'm going to be open and honest with you. I've had, um … From an early age, I started to gamble, and I was gambling an awful lot. It was always on the machines, you know, the flashing lights, money there and then. Then, when I started to promote my boxing shows, money would come in, I would gamble more because I had more money. I knew then that I had a problem.

I first sought help, jeez, this is going back, I was still with the children's mother, so around 2013 or 2014. I went to Gamblers Anonymous - we call it the fellowship. People say you're going to have this for the rest of your life, you've got that in you. So I had to put barriers in place. Any money I'd get, I'd give to, say, my daughter. I would take off gambling apps from my phone. I wouldn't carry money on me because I would go to a bookmaker. So all these things, I'd put things in place so I couldn't gamble.

Then the start of the pandemic, that was a big trigger for me. I look back and it's quite scary. I'll tell you what it was: it was the night I should have had a show. So last April [2020], it was going to be my most successful boxing show by far. It should have been on 4 April. I put a lot of work into it, and for me that was going to be my payday. I had three prizefighter tournaments all in one night; it's never been done locally before. I did the maths, the show was practically sold out and I thought, 4 April I can get myself financially stable.

So, what happened, all the tickets were out in circulation; half the ticket money came in, which I used to pay for the venue, the ring hire, the paramedics, sound and lighting, the furniture hire. The other half of the money wasn't handed in because it was still three weeks out from show time. And then Covid hit; the show wasn't happening. People then started to send me messages wanting their money back. It was very, very uncomfortable, because I had nothing. I had no money because I'd paid for the event. So I had some uncomfortable conversations. I was like, 'The show is going to happen when it's safe to do so.' I was one of these people that were like, 'Oh, Covid's not that serious, it'll pass in a month or two.'

I don't drink very much, I'm not a big drinker, but I had a, kind of, big drink that weekend that I should have had the show. And I started to gamble again. I couldn't go into the bookmakers, so it was on my phone. I look back and I think, sugar, it got me into a bigger mess than I was in. I was worried I couldn't generate money from my shows. I was trying to … It's hard looking back – I tried to, maybe, get some money through gambling. Yeah, not a good place. The money I wasted!

It went on … It was on and off until I stopped just before Christmas. I remember, Christmas is a family time and I wanted to buy presents – it was either gamble the little bit of money I had at Christmas or buy my children presents. It was children's presents all day long, but I was contemplating it, and that was a big moment for me.

I mean, listen, I'm talking now about my problems, jeez, people have lost their lives, you know, or family members, and

I'm talking about losing some money. That's nothing compared to what people have gone through, so I'm blessed: I woke up today, and I've got my children that love me, and I've got a job.

*22 March 2021*

I've got this behind-the-scenes show at the end of May – I've fourteen fights, that's twenty-eight boxers ready to go. I am working on another event two weeks after, so I'm very, very busy at the moment. I feel a bit of relief. With that said, I'm doing all these plans, but obviously, we are still in a lockdown, aren't we? It wouldn't surprise me if things got delayed. I mean, let's hope not. All I can do is make the plan, and if I have to put it back, I'll put it back. What happens on the government side is out of my hands, isn't it? I did all my crying and sleepless nights last year. I'm a bit thicker-skinned now.

You know, it wasn't until after we spoke – I know it was some weeks ago – I know we spoke a little while, but then I thought, blimey, actually it was very significant because I had some pretty bad times. I had weekends where I, sort of, had a drink, and I didn't want to talk to anybody. I mean, there were times when I would book myself a hotel in town on a Friday, and I would just stay there for the weekend. My oldest daughter was with me; I would say that I was going to a party or something. This was in between lockdowns, in the summer. I did that a couple of times, where I would just stay out for the weekend. I would be locked away.

I mean, I'm not a drinker. When I say drinking, you know, um … Oh, this is hard. I feel really uncomfortable saying, but it was cocaine. And that was something I'd never done before. My friends in their twenties and thirties, they will do it. I never associated with that, I really detested it. But last year, I did it. When I was doing it, I wasn't gambling. How weird because you're either gambling or you're spending money on that. That's not going to help you, but at the time … You know, when I was away, that Friday night, that Saturday night, I wasn't thinking or worrying about anything.

The dark times were after what I would call a bender. I mean, on a Monday I'm feeling awful. The comedown, you know? Like I say, I am really close to my children, but there were times when I had to message my youngest daughter, 'I won't be able to see you. I am not very well today.' I was saying not very well, but it's because of what I've done at the weekend. I did miss shifts, did sickies, but the horrible thing was lying, saying that I wasn't well, because I was getting fucked up on cocaine. That was not very nice. That hurt a lot. That's what made me feel … I think I'm a good dad, but that's not a good dad doing that. That was bad.

We spoke about the gambling; I turned back to my gambling because I was worried, and that, obviously, didn't help, because I got myself in a bigger hole. And it was at that time, I felt, shit – excuse my language – I felt, damn, there's no way out. I mean, I did reach out to some close friends for some help, financial help, but you've got to remember, back then, everyone else was watching their purse strings because of the uncertainty that we had. Even my parents, I went to them. They didn't say no, they wouldn't, but it was very uncomfortable. That wasn't a very good moment for me, having to ask for help.

I remember doing 1k in a day, thinking I could turn that, hopefully, into 3k or 4k. Then summertime, that was probably my darkest, because I had thought I could get this show on in the summer. Then summer fell flat on its face, and I was financially struggling. I mean, I was fortunate, I was working, but I didn't want to go to work. I was really, yeah, not in a good place. My children, they were the only thing that kept me alive, in all honesty. There were times when I was on my own, and I thought, jeez, thought of, um … I read about people that struggled mentally or, you know, have suicidal thoughts, and I've had friends that have had that, and I've helped them out. But then that was me, but I didn't want to reach out to anybody.

I mean, at the time, I had my partner, I did sort of talk to her briefly, but none of my friends knew, nor my children. No one knew. I just felt that it would have been easier just to … I didn't want to face … I'm not just talking about bills, they're easy – if you can't pay a water bill or, I don't know, a bloody credit card bill, you can pay the month after, it's not the end of the world. But, for me, I owed my parents money, and a few friends helped me out over the year, so I wanted to repay them and I couldn't, and that's what hurt me the most. Yeah, that was pretty tough.

I remember my mum and dad – my dad's a bit old-fashioned – saying, 'Work more.' I said, 'Dad, if I work seven days a week, fourteen-hour days, I'm not going to get myself out of this hole.' I actually needed thousands.

Like I say, I'm a law-abiding citizen, but I've done things for people, like if people are owed money, I've done some unofficial things where I've convinced people that they need to pay up … I even was thinking about … I needed money. So I mean, within boxing there's certain circles, I know these people could give me money, but I'll have to do something that is not legal. But you know, what scares me is that I've never been in prison in my life, I have never been in trouble. And I wouldn't. If I were in prison, I couldn't see my children. That's the thing that kept me: one, the children kept me not doing anything stupid with my own life; and two, kept me not doing anything stupid criminally. I was so close to making contact with people to try and get some money, and I look back and I think, why the hell did I even think that?

Jeez, what drives me on to do it? When I lose, then straight away my instant thought is, 'Damn, I've just lost!' I then think to myself, 'How can I replace that?' There was horse racing last week – Cheltenham was on. Horses don't do nothing for me, but I bet on a few horses, and I just did a little bit, you know, literally two or three pounds on a couple of horses. Didn't really excite me. So then I did twenty or thirty pounds on a horse, and then I did – you could do different combinations – so then it turned out to be fifty, sixty or seventy pounds. By the end of the week, I remember, I think I lost three or four hundred pounds. I didn't really have that money to lose, and I thought, sugar, I didn't even win anything, didn't get close. I always say to people I have lots of luck, but it's all bad. But then I think, well why do I do it then? If I know I'm not going to win, why do I do it? I mean, I have won before, don't get me wrong, I have had wins.

All I can do is put up barriers. I need to stop, that's it. Last week was a classic example; that's not the way to go for me because right now I am literally living on a budget. Today I had some expenses go into my account, so I transferred it to my daughter and it's safe. The good thing is I can't gamble today. One thing I learnt is just one step at a time, or one day at a time; but I bring that shorter, you know, like one hour at a time, because you can do a lot of damage in one hour if you're a gambler. I don't carry money on me, I don't have money in my account. If I do that, then I'm good. If I'm gambling, that's when I'm dangerous, because it could get me into trouble, and I don't want to get into trouble.

Yeah, so going back on the whole thing with Covid, this had a massive impact with the choices I was making, the gambling, the benders. But, listen, I can't blame. I'm a believer you're responsible for your own actions – if you choose to go rob a bank, then you've got to face the consequences; if you choose to drink a litre of vodka, you've got to face the consequence of feeling rough. I'll always say it is my fault. So I'm suffering now as a result of my actions. Yeah, in a way I should be grateful, because I'm glad I've got the chance to put things right and make the right choices, not behind a prison cell or anything. Looking back, a few years on, I'd like to think that I'd be debt-free, I'd repaid my friends and family, I am still organising great shows. And I would love not to be gambling.

*Afterword – one year later*

It's quite clear I had my struggles. Some of my close friends know, but a lot of people don't know what I was going through. But I've got no shame in that. And I'm climbing out of a hole now, and I'm peering over the top and I can see a future. Probably haven't got the strength to get my big belly out of the hole, but I'll get there!

I did a behind-closed-doors show last May. I hired a gym, because no venues were open because of the restrictions we had; we got everyone tested, there was no crowd, I had to segregate boxers when they got to the venue. So we did the show and it was live-streamed, pay to view; it was a bit of a gamble, it wasn't about making money, I wanted to keep boxing going.

Then when restrictions eased off, the show that I couldn't have due to the lockdown, I got that up and running back in August. That was with a crowd, I honoured all the tickets from the year before.

Then I bounced on, did a show in October and November, and now, the start of this year, I'm starting strong and positive. I just had a show three days ago – actually, two shows in two days. I achieved it, it was a success. And I've got my biggest show to date on 2 April, an anniversary to what we were talking about at the start of the pandemic.

I didn't actually attend the fellowship because of Covid. You couldn't get together, everything was done by Zoom and I'm not very technically minded. I'm not going to lie, I have gambled, but where I've been so busy I've not had much time to do that, so it's been good.

One thing I've learnt is you've just got to keep going. I'm still struggling financially, but I'm getting better. My parents did help me out as much as they could, and I'm still repaying them. I'm not flush, but I think if I can just get some successful shows this year, I'll be in a strong position. I've had to shuffle money around and ask people for some time to pay things back. I wasn't paying utility bills, that all mounted up, but things are more in control now. I just transferred some money to my daughter today – I can't just say I'm never going to gamble again; I need to treat myself like a little kid with how I manage money.

# Mazza Somers

*I was on my own, but I still dressed up*

*16 March 2021*

Just before we start, I've got a condition that makes my voice shake, so it's not that I'm really old and weak, it's just I have this condition and it changes to more wobbly or less wobbly. It's called dystonia. I'm having a gin and tonic while talking to you, because my consultant at the hospital said to me, 'If I put you on medication, you could have nasty side effects.' But he said, 'Alcohol can help.' Well, I nearly hugged him. So, I'm drinking a gin and tonic now, so that I don't shake too much when I'm talking. It does help; you have to wait a little while for it to get into your system and then it calms things down.

I was born about seventeen miles from here, and I left to work in London in the Post Office. There was another girl went up as well. We moved to a bedsit and my husband, John, was living upstairs with his mate. We shared a kitchen, and I would go up and pretend to wash a mug, hoping that he'd be in there. He was 6′2″, good looking, with auburn hair. He had this olive jumper, and I not only fell in love with him, I fell in love with his jumper!

He didn't tell me, but he was going out with a nurse from Romford hospital and me at the same time, waiting to see which one he liked best. And he chose me. That was 1960, so I was twenty-three. We were married after fifteen months. Then I was having a baby, and I didn't want to stay in London, so we moved down to live with my mum and dad.

A friend of John's phoned up to say he was giving up a pub where he was a tenant for Whitbread's. We went over and looked at the pub, and Whitbread's accepted us. We were there from 1967 to 1984. Then the land the pub was on – it was quite big – was being sold to a development company and we had to leave. We came to Wroughton from 1984 to 1992. Then John started working at The Beehive; he was there for nineteen years and he did the bar, he did the cellar, he did the orders, he did everything as if it was his own pub. And then he became ill and was diagnosed with lung cancer. He died in October 2009, and that's when I bought this flat.

There are thirty-four flats and a guest suite, and we're on three floors. I've got a one-bedroom flat, which suits me, and a large lounge-diner. It's just a nice place, with a laundry. We're retirement flats, and most people are ladies who have been widowed.

I'm great friends with Margaret, who lives next door to me, and another lady up the corridor on our floor called Sue. We call ourselves the Three Musketeers because we do things together, you know, we like the same things. We have a lot of laughs. I've lived here eleven years in May, and I've never had such close friends. To tell the truth, being in the pub trade, we didn't really make friends; when you're tenants, if some people think you're favouring some customers more than them, we felt we could cause a bit of a problem.

With Covid, to begin with, it was a bit of a novelty. Strange word to use, but we sort of laughed and joked about it, us people in here. But then it went on and on and on, and we're feeling it more now. For people who've become unwell, like had a stroke or their arthritis is hampering their movements, they have to have carers come in. Some of them, a member of their family is a carer and will come in. Sue has her daughter as a carer, but Margaret and I, we do our own thing. I'm self-sufficient.

Margaret and I, our doors are next door to one another, so what happened was, we would sit in our doorways with a chair holding the door back and we'd make ourselves a cup of tea and sit and chat that way, maybe three days a week. We've got a small garden here, and we've got some plastic chairs. We sat out in the garden last year. Some days Margaret would make tea and we'd bring cakes down.

In the lockdowns, my children would do my shopping for me, but I would just meet them downstairs at the door, take the shopping and give them cash. And that's been going on ever since it first started. I get a bit low because I can't see my family properly, but I put my shopping away, I make myself a cup of tea, sit on the settee and say to myself, 'I've got everything I need. This is my home, no one can take it away from me. It's all mine.' And I sit there trying to feel contented. I've got my lovely flat and, thank goodness, I've got everything I need in the way of food.

We have a lounge downstairs, but we can't use it at the moment because of Covid. I used to do the afternoon teas there on a Friday, and another lady did the coffee mornings on a Tuesday. Occasionally, we would have something like a Macmillan coffee morning, and afterwards I would entertain the people who were there.

The last one we did before lockdown was a coffee morning and I entertained, oh, I think it was about twenty-odd people. My favourite poet is Pam Ayres, and I've read some of hers downstairs, and they make everyone laugh. And I suddenly thought I would like to write poetry, and I had things buzzing through my head – phrases and what have you, words to use.

I make people laugh by reading my poems too, like this one called 'Too posh to poo':

*When I was young, maybe six or seven,*
*I had wondrous thoughts going on in my head.*
*I thought King George VI, and Elizabeth too, never*
    *ever went to the loo,*
*Never farted, never weed and certainly never did a poo.*
*So finally decided to ask my mum, she would know, I thought.*
*'Of course they do, you silly child,' she instantly replied.*
*And did they have the Daily Herald, Telegraph or Mail,*
*Torn into pieces, threaded onto string, and hanging*
    *on the nail in the loo?*

Well, when I was a child, you see, toilet rolls were rationed and everybody tore up newspaper in oblongs, put holes though them and hung them on a piece of string in the toilet.

I would like to read you another short poem. It's called 'Legs'.

*I always look forward to spring, summer and Easter if the*
    *forecast is good*
*'Cos lo and behold, first signs of warm sunshine, out come the*
    *guys in their shorts.*
*Strappy sandals with white socks, flip-flops and trainers*
    *everywhere to be seen.*
*The age range is varied, from young men to old, not perfect in*
    *every way,*
*Some legs are hairy, some have brown patches, some are lumpy*
    *and veiny,*
*I was walking behind a man I'll call Cecil, he of strappies and*
    *white socks.*
*I studied his legs really hard. Well, I declare, they're just*
    *like a map of Great Britain.*

> *On further perusal, 'Heavens above, I've just found a road*
> *to Carlisle!'*
> *My favourite legs come to Wimbledon each year, which I watch,*
> *but not for the tennis.*
> *Really fit guys with muscly legs, some hairy but beautifully*
> *tanned.*
> *These are the legs I love most of all, and not a lumpy vein in sight!*

We used to have card afternoons. I miss afternoons in the lounge, but we sort of wonder, if this never goes away and you still have to wear masks, whether those gatherings will ever really take off again. We've got a person here who's ninety-six, and she was always very sociable, and now she's scared. We've got several in their nineties.

When the Prime Minster and his colleagues speak and they bring out new rules, they don't say, 'Keep wearing your masks.' I think a lot of people relaxed those rules too soon – a lot of younger people aren't wearing them. There are some who say it's an infringement of their rights, and I think, well, what about our rights? We're trying to be protected from it, because we'll die if we get it. You know, it makes me cross. Lots of people are not here any more. At our age, we have all got a lot to lose. The younger people might get through it.

My mood has changed a bit since lockdown, and I don't feel so spirited as I did before. I'm going on all right, as you can tell, but I've lost a bit of something. With my poems, I just wanted to make people laugh. My mind was alive before lockdown, I could think of all sorts of things. I used to keep a little notebook and pen on the table, and I'd suddenly think of a phrase, and I'd write that down and then I'd think of something else. But that's not happening. I think because of my life being restricted, I've lost a little bit of spontaneity. It's gone on for so long, and

I sort of think, have I got stuck in my ways? Will I go out as often? Some days are hard, and all I want to do is sit down and watch television. I try not to do it, but there's a strong pull some days, to be honest.

I've been doing jigsaws, sorting photographs, paperwork. I do little jobs; I don't try and do everything all in one day, because I'm eighty-three. I always get dressed up, and I match my jewellery to my clothes. People are always saying how nice I look, which is good for me. Since John died, I've never ever worn black – I know he wouldn't want me to. I just always wear bright colours.

I've got Chanel perfume on. I've got three Chanel perfumes, and a Christian Dior one. I always wear perfume, because otherwise I wouldn't feel dressed. And if I haven't got earrings on, I think, oh my god! I have to go and put some on. It's a real regimental thing for me. If I know someone's coming in here, then I will put on make-up. Good Boots lipsticks. Bit of eye shadow – they have to be in a twist-up, like a lipstick, because my hand shakes, so it's a bit awkward.

There's a restaurant called Biplob,[4] and on Mother's Day last year the manager spoke to my daughter about doing something nice for his neighbours.[5] The back of his property backs onto our car park. So he sent around chicken korma, with pots of – oh, what's that dip with yoghurt and cucumber? And bags of poppadoms. Margaret and I took them round. Well, the following Thursday after Mother's Day, he got in touch with my daughter again and said, 'I want to continue.' So, the following

4 The next interview is with Biplob's manager, Rokib Ali.

5 On 22 March 2020 prime minister Boris Johnson announced: 'I am afraid that this Mothering Sunday the single best present that we can give – we who owe our mothers so much – is to spare them the risk of catching a very dangerous disease. The sad news is that means staying away.'

Thursday, we had twenty-five curries, some vegetarian, one gluten-free. And he's been doing it every week since that. And they're all free of charge. He said he lost his mother four or five years ago, and he still misses her so much. From then on, Margaret and I went round asking people, 'Would you like to have a chicken korma every Thursday?' We kept the same one because it's simpler. Margaret and I sit down in our lobby, and they come up the steps anytime between half five and six. Two guys come round carrying the bags and we have a little chat with them. We've got cards written out of the doors we've got to go to, but we know them off by heart.

Over Christmas, because they were able to open and do takeaways, I said to my daughter, 'It's been very, very kind of him doing it, but ask him if he would like to stop doing it now, because he's got to get his restaurant up and running.' So she sent that message back, and he came back with, 'I want to keep it going until this is all over.'

I can't bear thinking about what lockdown might have been for me if I wasn't here. I might have bought a bungalow or something. Or another flat that's in a block of, who the heck lives in all these flats? I'm lucky. I keep thinking, if I didn't live here, how much I would have lost. I would have lost a year of my life.

It's been really great talking; I've, sort of, come alive a bit. Well, I'm going up to Sue's now because Margaret's already gone up. We're going to have a cup of tea together. Sue sees her daughter, but she loves to get with us because she says you can't talk the same with your daughter as we three talk to one another. Margaret said she had a spell recently when she couldn't stop swearing, and she kept apologising. And I've had a bit of that, but I don't swear in front of them. But when something happens here, on my own, I sort of think to myself, if they could hear me now! Do you want to hear my favourite word? …. Bollocks! And that's how I'd sum up this year, yes, it's a load of …!

*Afterword – one year later*

I lost my brother to Covid in November, he was eighty. Their cleaner, although she always wore a mask and gloves, she somehow gave it to him and his wife. My brother was taken into hospital on the Friday, and he was dead by Monday. He'd had three vaccinations. It was very sad.

I got Covid. I was ill over Easter. Just before me, another lady got it, and a couple upstairs on the next floor, her and her husband had it. So it was a little cluster of us. I spent Easter in my flat. I was isolating on my own a good two to three weeks. I phoned the surgery to let them know I had Covid, and they said, 'Well, if you get breathless, ring again.' But I didn't need to.

Even though I had Covid, I got up in the morning, I suppose about 10am, and then I was up for the rest of the day. I was on my own, but I still dressed up. I didn't want to give in to it. I still put on my perfume and my jewellery to match whatever I was wearing.

Luckily, my daughter had taken me just before to a good butcher that she goes to, and then we went on and got about six bags of shopping. And I had bread and milk in the freezer. So I had plenty of food. I was quite content, to be honest. I would walk around, look at my lovely flat, and put my arms in the air – punch the air – and just think, how lucky I am!

# Rokib Ali

*We'd never done deliveries before*

*1 April 2021*

My mum died in Swindon, she died in 2010. I go to the grave-yard every week, just to visit her. I was forty days old when my dad died, so my mum was everything to me, like mum, dad, friend. I was born in Bangladesh. My dad used to stay in London, he used to work for an asbestos company and then he died from that. My mum stayed in Bangladesh until my grandparents died, then she decided to come over to London. Me and my sister went to secondary school in London, and I used to work part-time in a restaurant doing washing up because it was very difficult for my mum to manage. Then, at seventeen, I had to start work early, after GCSEs. London was too expensive and eventually I found a job in a restaurant in Swindon. They provided me with the bedsit as well – I could stay there free of charge. And that's how my single life began. So, I've been involved in Biplob since 1994. Eventually, I took over the partnership. I'm forty-six, and I'm still here.

When the pandemic started, in February [2020], I was actually on holiday, because I went to my motherland. My parents had a house there. I don't go there very often; it's not cheap going, but I want to keep that house. It's only a short visit, ten days, but on the way back, I was in transit in Qatar, and I've seen people are more careful. People are talking about it, 'There's a virus coming,' and they're quite serious. The first thing when I arrived in Qatar, I've been told I should wear a mask by the staff, so that's the first I had a glimpse of knowing how to wear the mask.

So, when I got back, I was worried and concerned, but wasn't expecting lockdown or anything. When we had the news we have to shut the restaurant, it was shocking. 'Really, oh god, what are we going to do and how are we going to manage it?' But we thought it's going to be a short time; I don't think anybody ever imagined it's going to be more or less a year of lockdowns. At the beginning, nobody had an idea, neither the government have any idea, where are we heading, how is it ending.

We had a running kitchen, so we managed to keep the takeaway going. Then the furlough scheme came, so we decided some of our staff were to furlough. Unfortunately, a few of them, like part-timers, we had to tell them, we're not going to be able to afford them any more. That was the hard part.

We'd never done deliveries before, but then we had calls from people saying, 'Do you do deliveries? We can't come out.' Then we decided to start doing deliveries. We work together with a company, they're involved in catering, they do the wedding services, so they had the drivers available. It is nothing similar to what we normally do, so it wasn't profitable, but my intention was to keep my name out there, because if we shut completely it would be difficult to come back. We decided to cut our opening hours and not to open on lunchtime, just to open from 5pm until 10pm for collection and delivery people. People staying at home, they're not going to have a late meal or anything, and also saving us the electricity and gas and things like that.

Then back in April [2020], we seen a lot of people are struggling, they're not going to be able to see their family, so we decided to start helping people out. We started with our neighbours, they're like, what do you call it? A nursing home, sort of place.[6] None of their family was able to come and see them, so, on their Mother's Day, we said, 'We like to give you a lunch from us.' They're waving at us, and, oh my god, every one of them was clapping at us, and it touched my heart. I just said, 'Well, listen, I will be coming.' So we decided we're going to carry on.

Today is Thursday, so I'm looking forward to going and seeing those neighbours today. It's not they can't afford a meal, it's for me to go and see them and take something for them, and how much they appreciate it. I find anywhere in the world, if I know there's some old people need help, I will always help them. My customers, the elders, they all call me 'son'. A handful of people, they treat me like their son. My next-door neighbour, they always call me, 'Hello, son, how are you doing?' They never call me by my name. I try to find my mum and dad through other people of the age they would be now, and that makes me happy. When I can make them smile, that's the greatest pleasure I get. And when I look at their faces, I always say, yeah, my mum was here, my mum do that.

After we started the curry night with the neighbours, the next thing, we heard a place in London, they're helping doctors, because the doctors are overworking, they don't have the time to go home, prepare the meal. So we started delivery to the Great Western Hospital. They are completely free of charge. We haven't charged any single penny to anyone. We extend ourselves to the police authority, ambulance; anybody wishing to have a meal or not able to cook, they just can pop around and take one, or call us and we'll deliver. We extended the service to our customers, so we turn up with the food on their doorstep and they're, like, shocked: 'Why are you giving us the food?'

---

6 The retirement flats where the previous interviewee, Mazza Somers, lives.

I said, 'Well, you used to come in and support us for the last twenty or thirty years, and this is the time for us to return and say thank you to you. This is the time we need to support you.'

At the beginning, we started with about fifty meals, then it reached up to, some weeks, two or three hundred meals we were giving away. I reckon we've done about, I don't know, about eight to ten thousand meals. In May and June, instead of going there five o'clock, we used to go there three o'clock, just to cook the extra meals going out to the hospital, going out to the people that are shielding. The amount of friends we made, it's unbelievable. People they wanted to talk to us, they want to tell us their stories, you know, telling me, 'Oh, I haven't seen my grandson.' 'I haven't seen my children for months.'

We are helping people with their shopping. They pay; they're like, 'Can you get me some milk?' or 'Can you get me some bread?' It's become a community service for a good three or four months for us. So I was really busy that time, helping. We've always been doing our best, with charity and helping people, but this pandemic, I find it's bringing people more together.

We're still doing it, actually, we haven't stopped. We have cut down, because a lot of people are saying, 'No, you've done enough and you have your business to look after, you cannot just be giving us food all the time.' But we're still doing it for people like our neighbours because they're always going to be vulnerable. I've had calls from America, because their relatives, their son, they're living abroad, and they're just calling me and they're saying, how can they thank me? They wanted to send me money for helping their families. We said, 'No, listen, we're not going to accept any money, it's our service and we wanted to put it back to Swindon, thank people.'

We had to work to protect ourselves as well. I lost my uncle in London. I lost a great friend from Swindon. Recently, in

January, I lost a colleague of mine – he worked at the restaurant – we worked together for ten years. He's from Goa. He was forty-seven. So that was shocking. He's Catholic. I led the funeral service because his wife and his family, they're in Goa. Nobody could come from Goa, and we're not allowed to send the body because he had Covid. On the service of his funeral, the priest said his prayer for Catholics only and they pray, and we just stay silent. Then we stand up, there are some memories, we pay respect, giving flowers.

It's very real, very real. I see it with my own eyes. I know more than a hundred people, personally, we lost to Covid. We have another colleague, he used to work with us, he died as well from Covid. My next-door neighbour, there's a couple live there, his wife, we lost her.

I have a relationship with customers, generation to generation, people are coming. And yesterday, I had sad news. It's a real shock, actually. I wasn't even able to work after that, I had to leave. His son committed suicide because of the Covid, because he lost his job. He was frustrated. It's been over a year.

I don't know more inside, but his dad called me, they treated me as family, they said, 'You are part of my family because we've been going there for over thirty years, and you know everything about our family, I thought you like to know, my son is no more.'

When I heard the news, I just sat in my car. It took me an hour to recover. Then I went to the mosque. I just stayed there and, you know, sat, cried. It's been a really, really difficult time. I just feel like if I sit down, then I'll just sit there, but I must go and do something. The only way I feel good is by helping people.

We also did a community service, because where I'm from, Bangladesh, they're very, very poor people. So we collected money as well, asking all the friends – everyone donated – we helped them with a couple of thousand pounds.

When I look back on this time, obviously, I'll be sad that we have lost so many people, but I would say we gain in the pandemic in two things: the family values, where we're spending a lot of time with our families; secondly, we think it's bringing communities together. With my daughters, they've never been involved in cooking, and now, being at home, I find they're baking cakes. We are all together, sitting together, sharing each other's news. I find this really good.

With the community, I mean, we learnt a lot from this pandemic. Before I would have hesitated to ask somebody how they are, but nowadays I do it more; I'm asking people personally, 'How have you been? Do you need any help, have you been okay?' And I want to carry on with this, because this is important. And especially the elders, I try to help them, because one day, I'm getting old, so I will be hoping somebody would do that to me in return.

Yes, I will remember this year this way. And we know that life, in a way, it's very short. We don't know when my time is going to come. You know, it could be tomorrow. That's one thing I learnt – just live today and do your best: look after the family, look after people as much as you can, and just try to be happy with whatever you have. And I know we could have money before, and now the money is very tight and we have to think about what we're going to spend. But one thing I will remember, in life we will always want – we will want a bigger house, maybe want a better car, better lifestyle.

I was pursuing wealth at times in my life; some of the time I wanted to do better, I wanted to live in a better home, and I worked hard for this. But now, I think I should not do this. This is not important. If I look at the amount of people that died, most of them died from the health condition – maybe their obesity or they have diabetes or that kind of problem. I think that should be our concern, how to keep yourself good and fit and well. What's important is your health and your well-being and being a kind human. That's more important than I would have a Mercedes in my driveway or have a bigger house.

# Rebecca Everett

*Covid regulations and being disabled
don't go hand in hand well*

*6 February 2021*

I've had an interesting journey over lockdown. We were plodding along quite happily and, yeah, everything was fine, and then something pretty drastic happened.

So, I'm thirty-five, married with three children. Before lockdown, I was working as a pastoral and safeguarding lead in a primary school. My husband, Aiden, works in a mainstream school – he works in their unit for physical disabilities. Our three children are all neurodiverse, so lots going on with those three. They are nine, ten, and the one sat opposite me is thirteen today. They all attend different schools, which can be a bit of a handful. We're a blended family – my oldest and youngest are mine from a previous marriage, and the middle one is my husband's from a previous relationship.

Before lockdown, we used to like going out on lots of big walks, me and Aiden in particular. The furthest we walked was forty-five miles, from our front door to Bath! We walked to Cheltenham, we walked to Oxford, we walked to Newbury. I think the longest walk was about fifteen hours, but that's without breaks. With breaks, it took us all day, twenty-four hours; we walked through the night. So, yeah, crazy walking family!

Initially in lockdown, it became very busy for Aiden and me at work because we're both key workers. It was me going into school to still do the pastoral stuff, especially with some of the more vulnerable children. I was part-time, luckily, and we decided to keep the children home, so we were trying to juggle the home learning with the working bit.

During that time frame I'd been, not keeping secret, but not really mentioning, that my vision had started to become blurred. I've always worn glasses since I was about two, always had really short-sighted eyes, but every year just got a new prescription, and sort of got on with it. I'd started to have headaches back in November [2019], so I went to the opticians thinking I need a new prescription, but the opticians saw something and referred me to the hospital. So, by the first lockdown in March [2020], I'd started to go to the hospital to have regular eye exams because they weren't sure exactly what they were seeing. April, May and June, I had further appointments.

I was working until ten or eleven o'clock at night because I needed to take that extra time to be able to see everything, and the laptop was just the hardest thing to manage – lifting it up to my face was the only way at one point I could actually see it, and then looking down at the keys to try and type. It's just not a way of working, but then we're human beings, you know, putting other people first. And I think when you have children, you're always the last to get to the doctor, you're always the last to look after yourself, and you're always the one pushing everybody else along when they're struggling.

It's something you take for granted, your sight, but I was starting to struggle with seeing anything. I couldn't see the television properly; we got a bigger TV, didn't work. I was like, hmm, okay, that's not good. And then it became a bit of a worry when I was driving, and I'm the only person that drove in our household, because my husband doesn't drive, well, didn't drive. I had noticed that I was missing things, and when I was driving my peripheral vision wasn't great so things like roundabouts I found really difficult. I'd be there for ages, waiting for it to be safe. My acuity levels – like the amount you can see – had been dropping so rapidly it was getting to the point where having my glasses on was no different to having my glasses off, and my prescription's minus seventeen in both eyes, so, you know, it was getting ridiculous.

I had to go to all the hospital appointments on my own all the way through because of Covid restrictions, which was terrifying, especially in August when I kind of had an inkling that there was something coming, but wasn't a hundred per cent sure. And that's when I got diagnosed with two progressive eye conditions, one called pathological myopia and one called myopic macular degeneration, and some very fast-growing cataracts – which have been extremely fast-growing – and, yeah, have taken away my vision.

When they gave me my diagnosis, they took away my driving licence. That was the 'oh my goodness' moment. And they're very much like, 'You can't drive from right now, like never again.' And then they register you – I'm registered partially sighted – and then they refer you to social services straight away. It was just a case of ringing my husband and saying, 'I can't drive and I can't pick the kids up from school.' Your life just changes from there on in.

The hospital referred me to a retina specialist to see if there were any treatment options. I saw him in September. I heard him say, 'No, we're really sorry, there's pretty much no treatment options.' I was on my own. I went to the toilet, and I just sobbed and sobbed and sobbed. I was in there for about an hour. Then I came out, I got on the bus and sobbed some more. I fell on the bus, and it was just awful. And that was it then, anxiety kicked in and I felt I can't go out on my own, I can't do this and it's going to get worse.

Yeah, so it's been a bit of a roller coaster. I'm eventually, probably, going to lose the majority of my beautiful vision, so it's kind of adapting to that loss over time. It's like a long-term bereavement, really, that keeps happening. You don't forget it's happening, but it just sort of creeps up on you, a bit more every time. Aiden's dad's got dementia, and I keep comparing myself to him at the moment, because your working memory, you do not realise how much you rely on sight for your memory. I can put something down and just walk away from it and just completely forget. And also, even to remember that you've started a job, even if it's just like the washing up or something, I forget it's there because I can't see it.

I use Alexa for a lot of prompting and I ask her the time and she's got my calendar on there, so I ask her what's going on each day, and she reads my emails to me. We've got one in every room. The loss of privacy is huge because Alexa reads everything out, my phone reads all my text messages, it reads everything.

I had to give up my job in September. I just couldn't do the job justice. I kind of need the time as well – you have to relearn to do absolutely everything, from making a cup of tea to walking down the street to even going to the toilet. Everything is different, like, everything is different.

The girls' schools contacted us straight away because I can't do the home learning with them, it's just too much. Their schools have been lovely and, you know, I feel really guilty sending them to school because I want the teachers to be safe and I want them to be okay, and I know from experience working in a school that, ideally, we would all keep them home and we would all stay safe and schools would be completely closed rather than actually open.[7] Well, they say they're closed when

---

7 Vulnerable children and those of key workers could attend school during lockdown. On 7 January 2021, a change in government rules meant that so too could children without laptops or room to study at home.

they're clearly not closed because, well, I think my littlest has got fifteen in her class and that's not closed, is it, really?

My husband's now a full-on carer, and it's the bit that I worry the most about. And, obviously, he's now the only breadwinner. Yeah, my husband's caring role is huge. I can't cook by myself, so he'll have a whole day at school and he'll come home and he'll have to help me make the lunch boxes for the kids, and he'll have to help me make dinner and do all the practical things. I can clean, but I don't do a very good job because I can't see what I miss. I try to be methodical about it and social services try and teach you how to do things, but, you know, it's just not quite right. I like things clean and tidy and a certain way, so Aiden will go over it afterwards for me, bless him.

He's now had to start driving again, after twelve years of not driving, to get the kids to school. I don't want to be a burden to him and I don't want our relationship to change in any way just because I can't see. I don't want him to think that I need looking after all the time. I'm very stubborn and I like to be independent.

I have to say, on the Covid front, things have been really difficult. I think Covid regulations and being disabled don't go hand in hand well. If I went to the shop, I can't do the social distancing, so it makes it really tricky. And I'd ordinarily ask somebody from the shop to help. Asda and Sainsbury's, in particular, do a service where they'll do a guided shop with anyone who's visually impaired, but they're not doing it at the moment because of Covid.

When they brought in the one shopper at a time, I can't do that, and we did have one person say, 'Why are you even bringing her out, and isn't she vulnerable?' And this was October when I was kind of like being a bit defiant because I'd just been diagnosed and I was very like, no, I'm going to do this for myself.

Now I'm just anxious all the time, to be honest. I'm anxious going outside. At home, although I can't see, it almost tricks you into thinking you can see because I know where everything is, and it's your most familiar place. It's stepping outside the front door into the world that isn't adapted for me that makes it hard. Nothing is set up for me to manage, so I need help. As I step out of the door, I almost feel that my eyes have worsened in a second. It's sort of overwhelming.

I had cane training and you learn routes with the cane trainer. It's so difficult. So I learnt the route to my daughter's school, which is normally a three or four-minute walk; for me it's ten to fifteen minutes because I'm slow and careful and there's a lot of footfall because it's a school walk. I don't go out unless it's to take my daughter to school. It took me ages to learn the route, just to make sure that it was safe. I'd really struggle with anything further.

We've had some problems getting benefits and stuff sorted, and when we had the assessment, my husband said to the lady, 'You know, there's an end date for Covid for everybody. There's no end date for my wife. She's been housebound and she's been stuck in and her social interaction is limited and she needs help with everything and that's never going to end.'

You know, he's been a big one for helping me to realise and accept and embrace the fact that I'm disabled now, and that that's not a bad thing, and he's wonderful at that. He's really positive and he's signed us up for, oh god, canoeing, double kayaking and a tandem in the summer. He's kind of like, 'No, we're going to be great, and we're going to do this and I'm going to talk you through everything that you're not seeing and you're not going to miss out on anything.'

The children have been registered as young carers. My son, he did say to me yesterday, 'It doesn't really make a difference to me if you're blind or not.' And I think for him, it's just your mum and you're always going to be a mum. To be honest with you, I don't think he'd notice if I came in with my knickers on my head! I really don't. I think it's a universal teenage thing, isn't it? My youngest is finding it tricky to not keep saying, 'Oh Mum, look at this, look at that.' Girls especially, I think they like to perform and show off and do their little dances, and it's difficult because she wants me to watch her all the time and I can't, obviously, see her doing it. I mean, I humour her and sort of sit there and go, 'Well done.' And I can film stuff on my phone, and then I can zoom in and magnify it and watch it back.

My mum was in quite a lot of denial to start with, and I think because they're genetic conditions and they're progressive, she did feel a lot like it was her fault. Obviously, it's totally not her fault, but I think she felt that she had some hand in that, I don't know why, but initially she didn't want to talk about it. Obviously, it was only phone contact because of Covid, and it's been really hard because they live in Somerset, my mum and my stepdad. Finally, in October [2020], we did see my mum, socially distanced, but I think seeing me with the cane was a bit much. She found that really difficult. I can talk to my mum on the phone and it's no different, but obviously when she sees me struggling with stuff – needing my husband to hold my arm, trying to eat and all the things that are a bit more difficult now – I think that all will take a lot of time to sink in. I think Covid's been a bit of a mask for that because she hasn't had to deal with it.

I caught Covid about two or three weeks ago. My middle daughter, we do have shared care so it was the other parents' year to have them at Christmas. We decided not to mix at Christmas, and the other parents decided that they would mix. Unfortunately, my middle daughter had come back on 28 December and was asymptomatic; her mum then rang us on 30 December and said, 'I've got Covid.' We were like, oh god. I didn't start getting symptoms until quite a while after, about seven days later. Then my son and youngest daughter caught it. Aiden, we think, had it, but was asymptomatic. He's a happy-go-lucky, plucky vegan; he was jumping up and down, and I was like, 'What are you made of?'

I was ill for the whole ten days. I had various different symptoms, started with a headache, then sore throat, and then on day four I lost my sense of taste and smell. At one point, I was just sat there thinking, I literally have two senses left – I've got touch and hearing, and that's it. And then I got restless legs, which was horrible, and that went on for about two or three days – it was all day and all night and it felt like they were on fire. Then I got stomach cramps on day eight or nine, then the shivers that was almost like I'd eaten gone-off rice or something. Then day eight, I thought I was better, and then day nine, I was floored again and back in bed with a headache and a little bit of a cough and a tight chest. Then day ten, absolutely fine, back to normal, taste came back, everything. It was unbelievable. I was like, what is going on here? It was a different symptom every day, and you just never knew whether you're coming or going, to be honest.

*12 March 2021*

We're all recovered from Covid and all healthy. Had my first vaccine, so that's really cool. I went to the museum, to STEAM, to have it; my husband took me.

I'm still walking my youngest to school. When I drop off, I don't really want to speak to anybody. I haven't seen anybody for so long because of Covid and I've gone blind during Covid, so nobody's seen me like this. It's the double shock of seeing me like this, but also me getting used to bumping into people that I've known for a long time. Occasionally, the parents that I do know will say hello. It's really hard because unless someone says my name first, I don't know they're talking to me, because they could be having a conversation with anybody. I'm so, so awkward. In a way, Covid's been lovely because I can just speak to people on the phone and that's okay, everyone's doing it and everyone's sort of in the same position.

I actually went to a shop for the first time in ages the other day. I could see a person and the outline of a trolley, and I said to Aiden, 'Oh, I'd better mind out the lady's way because she needs to stock the shelves.' And then I stood there afterwards, and I said, 'I just assumed that was a lady, I actually couldn't tell.' I'm going to have to stop gendering people because I could really offend somebody. It puts you off socially a little bit because you can't look at somebody's face like you normally would; I end up twiddling my thumbs and feeling very uncomfortable. Sometimes I don't even look at people any more because I don't know whether they find it off-putting because I'm, sort of, staring. It's weird. I don't know, I can't really explain it, it's just really bizarre.

We had an incident in half term. Me and my husband had some time on our own because the children had gone to their other parents, so we decided to do some bigger walks. We thought, we'll walk to Wroughton because it's still Swindon and it will get us out for a good long time. It's a ten or eleven-mile walk. I bought this thing called a ramble tag – it's a Velcro cuff, bit like what you get when you have your blood pressure taken. Aiden wraps it around his arm and then I get to hold on to it; it's got a handle. It's amazing how well it works because he'll move his arm in the direction that I need to go, and it automatically moves me. People don't notice the ramble tag, it just looks like we're linking arms, which is the beauty of it because it means you can blend in.

We set off, and this woman, she was jogging and she was coming up behind us, and she sort of was mumbling to herself that we should not be side-by-side because we were walking on the path. She said, 'There's a pandemic, don't you know? You're taking up the whole path.' Obviously, she couldn't see that I was blind, so I said, 'I'm really sorry, but I'm blind, so I need to hold on to my husband's arm.' And she started answering back and being quite rude. And then my husband got really cross and he was quite defensive of me and said, 'Well, you know, if she had a wheelchair you'd think differently, and you wouldn't be so, you know, ignorant.' And she spun around and came running at my husband and was really, really aggressive and started shouting in his face and saying that her child was in a wheelchair and how dare he be so insensitive and rude, and she was absolutely ranting. It was really uncomfortable and Aiden was getting angry, and I was pulling on his arm to shut up and stop antagonising her because it was making it worse. It was horrible and it really knocked me, and the whole walk, I was so nervous.

There's that age-old thing where people go, 'But you don't look blind.' People say, 'How many fingers am I holding up?' And you know, they do that whole thing with you like, 'How much can you see?' It's human nature and a lot of people have never met anybody that's blind. They want to know what it's like, how it feels. People almost demand to know. I've written a blog, so I kind of tend to say, 'If you're really interested in my condition and what I can see, you're welcome to have a look at the blog and read that.' I started it when I began losing my sight. It's getting harder to write in it because as things are progressing, my mental health has been … I'm not sleeping, and I have been feeling more down about my prospects. It's harder to write positive things, so I tend not to write too much unless there's going to be an element of positive in it. No one wants to read just constant moaning, do they?

There is a massive outpouring of grief. It was just sort of, I can't get out of bed, I don't want to get out of bed. You feel low, and then you realise you've got three children and you have to get out of bed because nobody's going to get them up for school and get their lunch boxes done and your husband's got to go to work because he's a key worker, and you've just got to keep going.

It's peaks and troughs, but there are still days where … I mean, I've been so lucky because we've got building work going on. We started our extension before lockdown and it's still ongoing, so it's lovely to have the builder in every day and have a little bit of conversation and I can't just go back to bed. I think if I hadn't had that, I probably would've had plenty of days where I just would have gone back to bed and cried.

There was a lot of denial, and there's still an element of that. At the beginning it was, it will be absolutely fine and there'll be treatment options. And there were lots of discussions about that with my parents, with my mum especially, you know, 'Oh, Becky, there's loads of advances in medicine, and don't be ridiculous, you'll be absolutely fine.' I'm thirty-five, I could have sixty years left, and I think to myself, I think you're prolonging the inevitable. I don't think my mental health could take that … I mean, they have said I will lose my central vision; there is no stopping the macular degeneration; there's nothing they can do. There's no treatment.

My perspective is that I've got to completely adapt my way of life and my habits and my house, so that I'm well equipped, because sixty years is a long time to be on the planet, and it's more time than I will have had with sight. I think that's something I have to be realistic about. There are plenty of people with sight loss who lead wonderful, accomplished, fantastic, brilliant lives. It's not a death sentence, it's not a terminal illness. I just want to accept it, I want to be able to put that denial to the side, and just crack on. It's the new part of who I am. I am now a blind person. It's part of my personality now. It's almost like having a personality transplant overnight. You have to do everything differently and you have to relearn things.

At the moment, I use what little vision I have, because that's what the ophthalmologist and retina specialist said: 'Persevere with what you've got and use it the most you possibly can.' So, you know, I will squint and get right up close to my cup of tea to make sure I put the right amount of milk in. Eventually, I won't be able to do that; I will have to taste it, or whatever it is. I put hair bobbles on my shampoo so that I know it's not the conditioner, because I can't read the labels, and I have to organise my cupboards so that I know where everything is, and you become very tidy.

My husband says there's nothing we can't do together, we just adapt stuff. He's amazing, he's just so wonderful. It's like, we are big board game fans, and we sold all the board games, and he bought adapted dice and adaptive cards and adaptive Uno, and we play different games now. He's researched it all on YouTube. And I mean, he was an absolutely voracious reader and had the biggest collection of *Star Trek* books you could ever wish to see – he's a huge Trekkie – I mean he must have had about 350-odd books of *Star Trek*. And he gave them all away. He said, 'That's it, I'm not reading any more.' And I said, 'But why, why are you not reading any more?' He said, 'I read when you were reading, it was something we did together.' He said, 'You can't do that any more, I'm not doing that any more and everything we do, we do it together.' So we bought Audible, and we do Audible together, and we listen to the stories together. He's just, honestly, I couldn't ask for anybody more wonderful, thoughtful.

We're very much a couple where we look after each other, and my sort of role in looking after him is slightly compromised, but I try and step up the emotional support, if that makes sense. I'm much more able to support him in that way, and I make sure he goes out regularly for walks by himself, so that he's got space, and I bought him some gym equipment because he likes exercising.

You have to look for the positives. I'm not judgemental in any which way about anybody's looks now, not that I was before, but I think it cements it even more so. I'm a lot less stressed about my appearance, because I can't see what I look like. I've been wearing more colourful, bright clothes and not worrying so much about what people might think. I've let my hair go a little bit greyer. It just doesn't matter; I can't see myself in the mirror.

On a jokey side, I'm quite looking forward to when restrictions are lifted, as I'm hoping to go to a couple of festivals this year. I've emailed a few and I've said, 'I'm blind, what have you got disabled-wise?' And they said, 'Oh, you can have a discounted ticket, your carer can go free and we're going to have a special area for disabled people, so you can have a little cordoned-off area.' And I think, bloody marvellous, why didn't I become blind earlier?

I'm so much at the beginning, so at the moment, obviously, the negatives far outweigh the positives. And I'm starting counselling on Tuesday, so I'm really looking forward to that. The RNIB[8] have just got back to me and said that they're near enough ready for me to have specific sight loss counselling, and then I'm paying for my own counselling, to just talk about all the other things like relationships and family and being a blind

---

8  Royal National Institute of Blind People.

mum. It's that bit of self-care, isn't it? Not putting your head in the sand and going, 'I'll be fine, I'll be fine.'

You know, I cry. I cry a lot at night and I don't sleep. Initially, I was coming downstairs and doing colouring, and then, obviously, that stopped because I couldn't see to do it. So, I was listening to music downstairs and then I thought, no, I need to be with Aiden and I need to go to bed at a normal time with him, so I tend to go to bed. But I have lots of nights where I will just sob. Like lie there and sob. It just comes over me in the night, and I'll wake up at different times. And Aiden's fast asleep, bless him, so it's not a bother, but he knows I'm there next to him and that I'm trying my best to cope. And sometimes he'll wake up and he'll hold my hand in the night just because he knows I'm struggling.

# Ian Surtees

*Swindon is one of those towns where it's a barometer*

*19 March 2021*

STEAM was Swindon's millennium project. Swindon's got a very rich railway heritage, and the museum tells that story – about the GWR[9] in Swindon, but also about the very big GWR network that covered a vast proportion of the UK in its heyday. Without the railways, there wouldn't be a Swindon. It's what Swindon is all about. My mum and dad and grandparents all worked at the Swindon railway works, so I've got a personal reason to want to see the museum succeed.

I've been at STEAM for a long time; I joined in 2002. I started off in events, and then got into income generation roles. Over the best part of twenty years, we've really grown the museum up into a big conferencing venue. We became one of the busiest conferencing and events venues in the region. So, pre-Covid, we were just in the throes of recruiting two new events and conferencing officers, because we had so much business.

Then, all of a sudden, the story started to come out about this virus. I think the first case in the UK was announced late in January 2020, and from that moment, our phone just started ringing and people started cancelling bookings. Every time I'd go out of the office and then come back into it, my colleagues would say we've had another one or another two or another

---

9 Great Western Railway.

three cancel, and then it was multiples. I was worried: you know, if we've got no bookings, what are we going to do? What's the future going to hold for STEAM, and how are we going to survive with no bookings?

Then, March 2020, we closed following the government's announcement. It felt really strange working at home. We'd never used Zoom or Teams or Skype, so overnight we had to become experts on virtual meetings. We launched a virtual tour of the museum in about April time – it was a project that we'd been working on previously, but it gave us the momentum to complete it. We were voted one of the best virtual tours in the UK within the heritage setting, so we were really chuffed with that. Absolutely thousands and thousands of people were using the virtual tour. We had a heat map of where people were logging on, and it was across the world. To see that you've got people in America and Australia and in China, in Europe, logging into our virtual tour! The Great Western Railway is loved throughout the world. Apart from the landscape it goes through, there are fond memories of the GWR being what they called the holiday line. People would often take the train down to the coast, down to Somerset, Devon, Cornwall. And it was a lot bigger back in the day: it would stretch all the way up to Liverpool. So you'd go from Paddington to Penzance, from Portsmouth up to Liverpool.

So yeah, the team were really busy during that first lockdown trying to engage with our customers and visitors in a digital way. It was a buzz, but even with that going on, in the back of my mind was, you know, how sustainable is this? We also worked hard on trying to develop our online shop and create products to sell, but nothing replaces having the museum.

When we reopened on 17 September [2020], we had all of our Covid measures in place: sanitisers, one-way systems, Perspex screens on our reception desk. We pride ourselves on being a hands-on museum, but a lot of the things that you would have touched, we took out. You had to bring the staff with you, because, you know, they were anxious about going back into STEAM, interacting with customers. It was quite a stressful time, really, to bring all those measures together.

I can't really put an exact figure on it, but you know, the Perspex screens were probably three or four thousand pounds. And then sanitiser, probably another two-and-a-half or three thousand. You're heading up towards ten thousand pounds of investment just to reopen. Then we had to close again on 5 November [2020]. We were in this kind of open, closed, open, closed situation.

When they started talking nationally about a new vaccine, there was a lot of speculation and talk about when it might happen and will it happen. And I always remember, at that point, talking to my wife about it and saying, do you know what, it'd be great if STEAM could have a role to play in this.

In November [2020], as luck would have it, I got a call from a chap who works for the Brunel Health Group. Quite an appropriate name given what STEAM does. He contacted me to say they are part of the local primary care network, they manage a lot of doctors' surgeries in Swindon. He said, 'We're looking at different options at the moment on how to do a vaccine rollout. Could we come up and have a look at STEAM as a possible venue?' I said, 'Absolutely, that'd be great!' So I was emailing and chasing, because I really wanted this to happen.

Eventually, we managed to set up a meeting on 23 November 2020 and the Brunel Health Group came down with some of their staff and looked around. We took them into our Great Western Hall, which is a massive, massive space. It's an old railway workshop with high roofs. It's one of our conferencing spaces; it is one of our core areas in STEAM.

I remember talking to the principal organiser at the Brunel Health Group about how the GWR was instrumental in providing a medical service for its workers way before the NHS. When the railway started in 1841 in Swindon, as soon as they started manufacturing and building wagons and locomotives, what happens is people get injured. So workers used to pay from their wages into the medical fund, which then purchased a medical theatre, a hospital, a dispensing chemist, a doctor and all these different services that they would need. And it grew and grew and grew, and then that service was available for their families. It was a real strong benefit for people to come and work for the GWR – you get a medic, when everybody else in Swindon didn't have access to a hospital or a doctor. The people that were involved in that medical fund were in communication with Aneurin Bevan, who was the creator of the NHS. It's well documented that the NHS was built on the GWR's model, not one hundred per cent, but it certainly influenced it.

As any good organiser would do, the Brunel Health Group were looking at different options. They said they'd need to get the NHS involved to approve it. There were a lot of obstacles. But I was so keen, I was so desperate to get it. Not from, necessarily, a commercial element, but from a community perspective – I just wanted to be part of it.

On 16 December [2020] we did our first vaccination. So not a lot of time really from when we first met them to when it happened. I'd be lying if I said I didn't have sleepless nights. It was a very busy time. I can't remember the exact number, but we're talking about quite a few hundred people who were booked in for the first vaccinations, that over-eighties bracket. And you know, the vaccine coming in for the first time, this much-talked-about Pfizer, it was so inspiring. People had dressed up; they hadn't been out of the house, a lot of them, since March;

this was a monumental moment for them. I remember a lot of them saying, this is our Christmas present. The weather was freezing, and it was just all the elements. It was unfortunate, the oldest age group coming out at the coldest time, but not a moan, not a groan, not a complaint. They were just so happy to be there and so positive. And you'd go home and watch it on the telly – they talk about the first vaccinations being done, and you think, yeah, this is going on in our building!

In the UK, you've got mass vaccination sites; STEAM isn't a mass vaccination site, but it's doing more vaccines per day than the mass vaccination sites. Just over a week ago, they did 3,300 on one day. It's all down to the people that are running it. So the two people that head up the Brunel Health Group, who set up the whole process, they come from a distribution and logistics background, so they've created a system which can process more people more efficiently. So a lot of the other sites have been coming to STEAM to see how they're doing it, to take that best practice back to their sites. For a long time, Swindon was the most vaccinated place in the world.

When you walk into the Great Western Hall, the first area that you go to is our registration tables. Once you've registered, you're then directed to one of ten lanes. At the top of the lane, we have the vaccination tables behind the screen. Sometimes you can have as many as seventeen vaccination tables, which are staffed by two clinicians. We've got some, best describe them as beds really; if anybody does feel unwell or faint or whatever, they have a screened-off area where people can be taken to – very rarely used, to be honest, we've not seen many major reactions at all.

Beyond the seating area is the vaccine preparation area, which is where you have two or three members of staff preparing the vaccines. And then they've got the stock cupboards where they keep all their essential supplies and PPE, which is quite mind-boggling, really, how much they've got. And then, the beauty of Great Western Hall is we've got a viewing gallery, which overlooks the whole space. So the viewing gallery has now been turned into a staff area, so they have tea and coffee there, have their lunch. It's also where their chief execs operate, so they sit up there and oversee the whole operation. There's a real buzz in there.

We've got hundreds and hundreds of volunteers that have come forward and help out on a daily basis with car parking or stewarding, and people are so proud to volunteer and be part of it. It's just a big team effort.

We would get onto site about seven o'clock and then we'd leave about half past eight at night; the day would go so quickly. I wanted to be at every session, to be there all day long, but it's not sustainable, so we've created a rota now. So I go in on a Thursday, as a rule, and I like that – the opportunity to go into work is just good. I'll open up the building, help set up a few of the critical things – turn the tea urn on, which is most important! And then, normally, about seven o'clock, the first staff start to arrive, and they set up their laptops and start preparing the vaccine. And then about eight o'clock, the first patients start arriving, and then it's constant all the way through, up until 6.30pm, all day long.

Financially, it's okay. You know, pre-Covid, we would earn far more income from conferences and events. This is a whole different world for us. There's a modest amount of income that comes from it, but it comes from the public purse, so it's kind of our money that's paying for this. But it's welcomed – it's the only booking that we have got.

Initially, we were contracted until the end of March, and then that contract was extended to the end of June, and now it has been extended to the end of September. We don't know exactly when it will come to an end, but there is a lot of talk about boosters. It's that, kind of, painting of the Forth Bridge, isn't it? By the time you've finished it, you've got to start all over again.

I think what we have proved is that we can do it. So I'm proud. I'm really proud of the coverage that we've had and the positive feedback. There won't be many people that haven't heard of us now. I think that was always something that I'd hoped for. It was great to be able to have everybody coming in; although they don't get to see the whole museum, they get to see a snippet of it. I hope people come back. I hope people remember us.

We are collating key objects to do with the vaccination clinic. We've got the first box that the first Pfizer vaccinations came in; we're also going to be collecting the last empty vials of the Pfizer and AstraZeneca vaccinations as well. And key literature. We've got photos, videos – we've had national press coverage. Hopefully, we will have time to properly curate those items and put them in the right location in the future.

It's been a roller coaster for me, for STEAM. You know, we opened and then we closed so many times, and we've tried to reach out to our customers with different social media and digital activities. I've never been busier, and that's the truth.

So, yeah, when the vaccine was first announced, my initial reaction was, how can we play our part in this whole operation? And fortunately that opportunity came up, and we grabbed it with both hands. That's our approach often to enquiries and events, just grab that opportunity and make it work. And we knew it wasn't going to be an easy operation to deliver, but I find that with STEAM there's always something around the corner that you didn't expect. That happens sometimes in business: you think it's doom and gloom, and then all of a sudden something happens. It'd be easy to shut the doors and kind of, you know, wait for things to happen, but we've gone out there, made it happen. It's been phenomenal.

*27 April 2021*

We're just prepping now for the election count, which we're hosting as well. This year there's a big push on postal votes, so they've started today, counting postal votes at STEAM. We've also got the vaccination programme going on in tandem, so it's all go. It's a big local election count, and you've got the Police and Crime Commissioner election as well, so quite complicated. Keeps us on our toes! They've had to reduce the number of counters, they've had to implement social distancing; they've had to change a lot of their processes. But sometimes less people are more efficient!

It is interesting to see local democracy and national politics play out in front of your eyes. We were the venue for the election count for the general election. Swindon is one of those towns where it's a barometer, or regarded as a barometer, for the national sway, if you like, of how things are going to perform. So Swindon does have a lot of focus on it, in terms of, if it's happening in Swindon, it's going to happen nationally. We tend to get quite a lot of press coverage. That was the case at the general election, we had all of the media outlets live from STEAM, all these big satellite trucks outside – we had Sky, BBC, the radio channels, local media. Oh, it was great! There won't be the same level of media coverage for the local elections, but it's still exciting none the less.

But, you know, at the moment we're trying to get the museum reopened and get back into the events business. It's like a start-up business now for us; we've got to create a demand again. But I am positive for the future, because we are starting to get enquiries – people wanting to hold weddings and events. So it will take time to build up, but we have a good product.

*Afterword – one year later*

The pandemic has shown that we can adapt quickly, and I'm still amazed how museum staff overnight accepted home working and video conferencing as the new way of working. What was originally proposed as being a twelve to eighteen-month rollout of the technology was implemented in twenty-four hours, and we all learnt together how to get the best out the technology.

And it's been amazing to be part of history. Over 350,000 vaccines have been administered at STEAM to date. Once we became the vaccination centre for Swindon we had a real purpose, and it's united us as a team. The vaccination programme has been extended until March 2023, but due to the slowdown in people coming forward for jabs the frequency of sessions has been reduced to three days per week and will take place in our smaller hall. This move will enable the museum to take larger bookings again in our Great Western Hall. Bookings and new enquiries have been very encouraging since January 2022, and there definitely seems to be an appetite for live events again. Although not at the same frequency just yet, but I can see the museum's events and conferencing business returning to pre-pandemic levels by 2023 or 2024 if growth continues.

# Faith Vaughan

*Everyone always says university is
the best years of your life*

*7 April 2021*

I remember the time Boris Johnson made the very first national lockdown announcement, it was very weighty. I was in the living room with my mum and stepdad. I remember my mum just being like, 'Oh, this is so scary.' But I think, at that point, there was hope that it's going to be a couple of weeks and then it'll be back to normal.

It was very strange, because we didn't have much warning that college was going to end. It was March time, so there were still a few months before it would have been exams. I remember in class, we were all sat on the floor, including the teacher, just like, 'Oh, this is our last day.' It was really surreal because it was so abrupt; there was no official last day. It was just over. We did continue with online lessons, but it was not very serious. And when we knew exams weren't going to happen, everyone was just kind of like, 'Okay, what's the point?' It was anticlimactic – years of work and it just stopped.

I was still working, because I worked at Sainsbury's. My mum used to be the manager, and then my stepdad also worked at Sainsbury's – that's how they met. I was set to do twelve hours every week, which would be the weekends and then Wednesday evenings, but I tended to pick up more because it was very busy. I remember everything flying off the shelves. I'd watch people do these massive panic shops. One time I had to put the new loo rolls out when we had the shipment in, and people were just queuing up and taking it from your hands! And we had one of the carts, and there were loo rolls right at the bottom, with loads of heavy stuff on top of it, and everyone was trying to rip them out, and I'm like, 'That's dangerous, people!'

People are really extreme – some would clean absolutely everything they touched and they wouldn't go anywhere near you, and then you have the complete opposite who would almost go out of their way to make a point that they didn't care, who would get right up in your face. A lot of people were going, 'Ah, this is all just rubbish. I don't care for it at all.'

We had to go on the door quite a bit to control who was coming in the store and if they were wearing masks or not. That could actually be quite scary at times. If you go to these two big men, 'I'm sorry, only one of you can come in,' or 'You need to wear a mask,' some people would absolutely kick off.

Then I went to uni. At first, I hated it. It's especially with my mum, being away from her for the first time was terrifying. I am a mummy's girl, massively; she's also, like, a big support system. I've always struggled with anxiety and depression. Last year, I was diagnosed with ADHD, which was very late into the game, but it was just getting overwhelming. When you're already mentally not feeling too great, and then you've got the stress of A levels, it really blew me off course. Then that's kind of like a snowball effect: when you're not doing as well as you want to in class it affects you even more, and the panic attacks get so strong and so frequent you struggle to ground yourself. I've always described struggling mentally as like you're drowning and no matter how much you try to swim up, you just keep being dragged down and down. And it gets to the point where you don't want to swim any more and try to get to the surface. So suddenly being on my own and in the capital is very terrifying.

At the start of the year, and I mean very briefly, we had a few in-person seminars, now it's just completely on Teams. With no in-person lessons, it's just names on a screen. A lot of people I've got friends with, I've never seen them in person.

You can't meet people outside of your house, so you're stuck with the people you live with. There should be seven people, but two of my flatmates left because Covid was making things too difficult. It's definitely been strange, because any time you think of university you tend to think of a very lively building with lots of people, but due to lockdown it's just been very strict. Security will crack down on absolutely anything, even if it's just speaking to someone in the courtyard.

I remember, for ages, me and my flatmates never directly spoke to each other. We would say 'Hi' if we bumped into each other in the kitchen, but we wouldn't, like, go out of our way. Finally, I think it was just four of us, like late October or early November, we went, 'Do you want to, on Saturday, just have dinner together?' And then, from there, we got to know each other. They're all absolutely lovely, and without them I definitely don't think I would have been able to stay.

I've seen people complaining about their flatmates, who absolutely hate it. And there can be flats where there's only one person in it, because everyone else has left. And I'm incredibly grateful that I got lucky. We're all very different, but at the same time, where it matters, quite similar, so we all balance each other out. No one's got an issue with taking each other's food or using each other's stuff – I've kind of got to the point where I'm like, if you use it, you use it. And that's definitely helpful because it's good to be comfortable in your own home.

*12 May 2021*

This first year is definitely not what I expected. I think I would have rather deferred and just had an actual proper uni experience. Like, I am grateful to get year one out of the way, just to have got through it and at least had that experience of being away from home and having that independence. But there were definitely times where I was like, 'There's no way I can do this. I want to be home.'

I don't know the people I have spent a year with in class, and I've been in central London without actually being able to properly use that to its full advantage. I remember saying to my friends, 'It's crazy because I'm in the capital, like one of the busiest cities in the world, yet I feel completely alone. I'm stuck in this nine-foot-square box and I don't have anyone to really meet or speak to.'

London, it's incredible when everything's going on, but when absolutely nothing's going on it's just kind of like a metal concrete prison. And it's like I am never going to get as central as I am now again – my accommodation is right on South Bank, so it takes me maybe a minute to walk and then I can see the London Eye, Westminster. It's an incredible location. Next year, we've got to find our own accommodation, which will definitely not be as central.

One thing that keeps being brought up is, in our accommodation, we're treated like children. We are paying to live here as any other adult would pay, yet we're restricted and treated as children. And management tries to take advantage and mess around with us. If there's a complaint they won't listen to it. They really used lockdown to their advantage. You can see they're almost on a power trip. Security would be really, really strict, like, 'Let me see your ID, let me see your ID.' Or they'd come into our flats in the middle of the night. I remember one time I was in the flat by myself and someone came in at, like, 2am. They let themselves in, and it was just me, alone. And there was this guy, a random guy, in the flat, and that really made me panic because I was like, no, there should be a warning, and also there was no reason for someone to be in there at 2am. He was maintenance – apparently, they had to check on something in our kitchen. When you're a girl on your own in the middle of the night and there's a random guy just able to come in without warning, it's absolutely terrifying. I did email reception. At first, reception brushed it off and they didn't give me an explanation, and then management finally got back to me and they were like, 'Oh, we're so sorry. He shouldn't have done that. We'll look into it for you.' I didn't hear anything more.

Before, I would sleep with my door unlocked because I trusted everyone in my flat, but after that I've always locked my door. I have anxiety as it is, so that guy coming in, that really unsettled me for a while. I really struggled to sleep because I don't want to be asleep and then there's some random person in the flat.

My personal tutor has been absolutely wonderful and really, really understanding, and a lot of the teachers as well have been like, 'We understand that this is really difficult.' But there have also been times where you can see the disconnect because we haven't met these people, and a lot of them don't really know how to teach when they're not in person – they have been thrown into a world that they aren't used to. A lot of them are academics who have been lecturers for decades and they know what they know – they teach to a group of people in a lecture theatre. Now, they're suddenly online. I think they've been trying their best, but for what we're paying it's not been what we should've got. Anything I've learnt via the pre-recorded lectures I could have easily got on YouTube or googled and had a better-quality teaching experience for completely free. On YouTube, you can have really high-quality videos, and we're paying £9,000 for very grainy, very hard-to-understand videos.

Obviously, hindsight, it's much easier to sit here and be like, they could have done this and this. At the time, it was difficult because it's such unprecedented times, but there is so much more they could have done to make us feel like it was worth coming this year. Like when the lockdown eased up, they could have done one-on-one sessions, or, because they've got massive lecture theatres, everyone can very, very easily sit socially distanced. It's, like, people were in much worse situations, obviously, but for what we were promised and what we got, they definitely could have done so much more.

They knew to help me because I used to attend Child and Adolescent Mental Health Services, but I've had one meeting with the welfare team and that's it. My flatmate – she's all right with me saying this – she struggled pretty badly, and when she was like, 'I need help,' the welfare team emailed her and they got her name wrong. She was like, 'It just shows how much thought they put into it.'

Everyone always says university is the best years of your life, especially your first year, and I've been like, it's kind of something I got on with. It's just been, get through it for the sake of the degree.

*Afterword – one year later*

Currently, our seminars are in person, but our lectures are still pre-recorded, which sucks. But second year has been so much better. We get to go on campus and actually make friends. First year was so awful, and I can only remember how dull it was!

I live with one of my original flatmates, but I'm still friends and meet up with the other two. I'm still central thankfully

– right next to Waterloo Station – which I'm very happy with as I was worried my best chance in central London was when I was in my uni accommodation and it was wasted.

It's certainly been a learning experience – learning that the world can be shaken upside down so quickly is very scary – but I think it's made me more resilient to just go with the flow and make the best of it.

# Louisa Roberts and Sean Stephens

*I've not had a baby out of lockdown,
so I don't know any different*

*15 January 2021*

LOUISA: I love being a mum. I always say to Sean, I just can't remember what we did before we had a baby. What were we talking about and what were we doing all the time?

SEAN: Working in the pub, I used to finish work, I'd have a drink, but now I tend to sort of think, right, I want to get home. I want to get home and see Milo, I want to see Louisa, see what they've been up to. Being a dad, it's been wonderful. It's a very different lifestyle, but it's lovely. Yeah, it's been a big change in both of our lives that we've had to get used to, and trying to figure out, like, obviously, he's not talking at the moment, so like, what's wrong? Why is he crying? Is he tired? Is he hungry? Does his nappy need changing?

LOUISA: I was working in a nursery before I got pregnant, which obviously has helped because I didn't know much about babies before that.

SEAN: My work, it started when I was twelve years old. I wanted a part-time job because I didn't want to keep asking my mum for money, so I went to the local pub and asked if there were any jobs going. On a Tuesday night I'd wash up, and on a Saturday lunchtime I'd prepare vegetables. I always used to watch the chefs, and, yeah, five or six years down the line, I started cooking myself. And that's all I've done ever since.

LOUISA: It was March [2020] that I stopped going to work because I was pregnant – they put out the advice that you were vulnerable to Covid so you should isolate. When I was pregnant, I was a bit more scared of Covid. I think everybody was, just because it was so new.

SEAN: When we went into lockdown, obviously the pub shut, just me and the manager stayed. We decided that we were going to carry on doing takeaways. We did lots of burgers and fish and chips. The busiest Friday night that we had, I think I did 111 fish and chips! So we did the takeaways for about a month and a half or two months, then we opened back up with all the guidelines in place – two-metre rule and everything like that. We were doing, like, lighter snacks; we put a Scotch egg on with a salad and a few other bits.[10]

A lot of the locals in the pub that I work in, like, probably aged between fifty and seventy, they just enjoy coming out for a drink in the evening, meet their mates, and then go home afterwards. They didn't really want a meal. They didn't always eat it, but they had food in front of them and that was what the guideline was.

LOUISA: We were part of a programme when I was pregnant called *Baby Steps*. It's a group for first-time parents and it's like, if you're younger or if they think that you need a bit more support. It was run by somebody from the Children's Centre, and then a midwife as well. It was just talking about pregnancy, preparing you for the birth. We haven't done any face-to-face normal groups, but it was good for us that it

---

10 Is a Scotch egg a substantial meal? Or do you need to add a salad to make it substantial? Under new rules set by the government in December 2020 before the third lockdown, pubs and restaurant in Tier 2 could only serve alcohol to customers if the drinks came with a 'substantial meal', but this policy came without clear guidance, so ministers ended up contradicting each other as they debated whether a single Scotch egg could be classed as a meal. This rule was scrapped when pubs reopened in spring 2021 after the third lockdown.

was virtual because Sean was working. He has a break in the afternoon – he is at home three until six o'clock – so it meant he could just come home from work, join on the video chat.

My first appointment with the midwife when they take down all your details and stuff like that, the really long one, Sean was able to come to that with me because that was in January last year. But everything after the twelve-week scan I had to go to on my own. I had a low hormone reading during my pregnancy. It's called PAPP-A. It can be serious; it can restrict growth. I did have a couple of appointments that were specifically about that, so I would have liked Sean to come to those just to prepare us if, you know, it had caused anything.

When I was in labour, I had to go in on my own then as well. Sean doesn't drive, so my mum drove me and Sean. They waited outside. I'd been in labour all day at home, but it was manageable. I could have stayed at home a little bit longer, but Sean was due to go to work for his evening shift at six, so I said, 'Well, I want you to come with me in case they let you in so that you're not then stuck at work all night.' At the time, the rule was you can have a partner when you're in active labour, so a certain amount dilated, I think five centimetres or something.

When I went in, I wasn't far enough along, I was at two centimetres. I was definitely feeling like I was about to have a baby, but they said, 'Oh no, we don't think you're going to have it,' and they were going to send me home. I said, 'I can't leave the hospital on my own, there's no way I can leave,' because I could literally hardly walk.

If Sean had been with me, I probably would have gone home, he could have helped me. Because I said, 'I can't go home,' they were going to keep me in a bed on the ward overnight. While they got that bed ready, I had to go to the waiting room. And this waiting room was tiny. There were about four other women. I think they were there for some kind of monitoring, so they weren't in labour.

Normally in the hospital waiting rooms at the moment you have a gap between chairs, but because this room was so small it was just all of us facing each other. I did have to wear a mask. Lots of people say, 'Oh, I don't like wearing a mask because it's hot and you feel like you can't breathe and stuff.' And that was the only time where it was really difficult to wear a mask both because I wear glasses and because it was really painful. My glasses were fogging up and I was crying, so I had tears that were making them fog up more. And I was desperately trying not to make any noises because I thought, I'm going to really scare all these people.

I thought I was going to be on the ward, but they moved me to this private room. I had some painkillers and they basically just said, 'Try and get some rest.' I rang Sean and my mum and said, 'Right, I'm definitely staying overnight, and I am going to try and go to sleep.' I did start to feel pretty tired, and I think I probably was just about to drift off to sleep and then my waters broke.

SEAN: I was quite disappointed when Louisa was in labour because, obviously, I wanted to be there, as everyone does. It was very difficult not knowing how she was doing, not knowing what was going on, not being able to get in contact with her. I sat in the car park a few hours, and then Louisa's mum decided to go back home. And I was probably home for about forty-five minutes, and then Louisa texts me saying, 'You need to come back now.'

LOUISA: I just said to Sean, 'You need to come back because I feel like it's going to happen.' So then a midwife and a nurse did come in and check me again – I think I had dilated slightly more, but not a lot. But I just knew that it was going to happen, so they moved me to the delivery room. I was saying, 'Can my boyfriend come now, can my boyfriend come?' And they were saying, 'Oh, we're not sure. We'll just check you again.' When they checked me in the delivery room, they said, 'Oh, yeah, he can come back now.' Lucky I had already rung him, because we live about half an hour from the hospital.

You know, I had been in the hospital for about six or seven hours before Sean came in, and it all just blurs into one, and I wish I had somebody with me so they could have said, 'We were talking about this' or 'Oh, you did go to sleep for a bit' or 'You said you felt like this,' because I feel like a lot of that is missing. Doing it on my own, I just have missed parts of it really.

As soon as Sean got there, the midwife said, 'Well, I'll leave you two, and if you feel like you need to push or you feel like anything's changing, then you can call the assistance button.' It was just the one birth partner you're allowed, because I think in normal circumstances my mum could have come in as well.

SEAN: When I got there, Louisa was quite far into labour, so there wasn't an awful lot I could do to, like, calm her down or anything like that. So, yeah, that was difficult, just walking in and not being able to help her. It wasn't nice at all, I don't think.

LOUISA: I kind of expected that when I gave birth it would be me and Sean and it would all go really slowly and we would have a chat and he'd try and make me laugh and things like that. But when he came back, I didn't even speak to him because it had gone past that point. I was just in so much pain that I couldn't think about anything else. We were together in the room for about half an hour before I needed to push. So Sean called the midwife back in. Then my baby was born. So Sean was only with me for forty-five minutes before Milo was born.

SEAN: It was very overwhelming. It was worrying that we had a little life to look after from now on, and we'd neither of us ever done it.

LOUISA: It was at five past one that Milo was born. I remember saying straight away, 'Can we go home?' And the midwife kind of laughed and was like, 'No, we'll keep you until the morning, just to do the checks on the baby.' I don't know if it was because the hospital was quiet, but they let Sean stay overnight with me. I think I just got lucky because with the Covid regulations it's about four hours that they say your partner can stay, and then they say, 'Right, you, go home.' With Sean there, it meant that I could get up and have a shower and things like that. If I'd been on my own, I wouldn't have wanted to leave the baby that had just been born.

We left by about nine o'clock the next morning. Sean, he did have paternity leave, but it was so last-minute and my baby was born on a Friday, so obviously the weekend is busy for the pub, so he had to go back to work on the Saturday.

We did get to see our family. In August [2020] restrictions had lifted, and they were trying to encourage everybody to go out and things like that, so it meant that people came to visit him. But I felt really nervous about it. My mum and dad are split up, so they came separately. Sean's mum and dad are also split up. So rather than just the grandparents and it was two lots, we had four lots.

It was actually my birthday on the Sunday that weekend. It was my twenty-first. We used to live above the pub where Sean works, so we went and sat outside at the pub. One of my friends came, he's at university and he was back for the summer. I'd invited a few more people, but I'd said to them the day before, 'I'm not really feeling up to it, so maybe don't come.' So it was mainly just family. My brother and my three stepsisters, they all came.

I did feel really, really protective. I mean, obviously I can't say if I would have felt like that anyway, but obviously with that message being everywhere, like, you know, *Stay away from people and stay safe and wash your hands and germs*, I think that just made it ten times worse really. People would come round and they'd say, 'Can I hold him?' And I'd pass Milo over, and I'd just sit there and wait for them to give him back. I mean everybody was being careful and everybody was washing their hands and wearing clean clothes and things like that, but I think that's all the things you do for a newborn baby anyway.

Even just people coming over and looking or touching the pushchair, I was thinking, oh my gosh, go away! Nobody that we didn't know touched him, but people we didn't know came and had a look. I just felt really on edge. I didn't enjoy it at all. I just wanted to take Milo away from everyone.

SEAN: A lot of people haven't seen Milo yet. None of our friends have really come over to see him. I think a lot of people like to see a newborn baby, they're quite, like, squishy and want cuddles and stuff like that. So, by the time they can actually meet him, I don't think it'll be quite as enjoyable for them.

It's been hard Milo not being able to meet any other children. Obviously, he doesn't do an awful lot at the moment anyway, so he doesn't really notice, but I think it would be better if we could have met up with friends that have children, just for Milo to be able to see other kids and know that he's not the only one.

LOUISA: We were due to move around the time that Milo was born. It was a newbuild that we moved to, and we got it through the council, but because of the lockdowns and things like that everything got pushed back, and we actually didn't move until October.

Before we moved in, me and my mum used to come round and just walk past, wondering what was going on and stuff. And one day, one of our neighbours was with her daughter – we had Milo with us – and she said, 'Oh, how old is he?' And I said, 'Two months old today' or whatever it was. And she said, 'Oh my gosh, so's my daughter.' She was born on exactly the same day as Milo! And then we got talking.

But since we've moved in, I mean the restrictions have got a bit tighter again, and, like, obviously, I mean, I guess I could go over and knock on her door, but you don't really, if you've got to stand outside and talk, you don't really want to disturb someone just to make them come outside. If I see her, we wave at each other and stuff like that. I think one time she came over and asked to borrow some paracetamol. We don't really go for that many walks, but maybe once Milo's in the sit-up pushchair where you can look around and stuff like that, then maybe we'll start to see them a bit more often. I would definitely like to, because, obviously, it's literally over the road. And I'd say we got on straight away. I think, given different circumstances, we definitely would have met up or done something by now.

SEAN: The first lockdown, we were going for quite a few walks – having the sunshine was lovely. This one, we haven't really done that an awful lot. I'm not a fan of the winter. You can't do anything. You can't really go out. It's too cold. So that's been quite hard, like, sitting at home doing nothing, really.

LOUISA: Obviously, well, I've not had a baby out of lockdown so I don't know any different. But it's a bit of a shame, not being able to take him anywhere. He's getting to that age now where he is interested in things.

We've done a few groups online. So we've done a baby massage course, and that was arranged by somebody at one of the Children's Centres. The lady had a dolly that she was doing the massage on. I'd just kind of prop the phone up and then copy her. That ran once a week for about six weeks. Then we did a story-time course with the same lady. We just had one session a week again. They were talking about different activities you can do to support reading, so maybe like with props or teddy bears, and then we would sing a couple of nursery rhymes. I mean, normally she would sing and the parents would just be on mute, so the babies would look at the screen and watch her singing. Today, we started one, just about little activities you can do and things. They said bring some pasta and a tube or a bottle, so we made this pasta shaker. I was showing Milo it when I made it, and he was laughing and laughing at the screen.

Milo can recognise people straight away on video calls. He smiles at them, he's so interested. He loves the phone. He also loves the telly. He's always watching the telly. I try and get him to do other things, but if the telly's on in the background, that's what he's looking at.

We've also had a couple of courses arranged by the health visiting team. They're more things that you watch. So it's one lady that's sat there doing a presentation and there's like twenty of us watching, so we don't talk to each other because it's just too many people. So in a way that's been quite nice because some of them have been quite early, like nine o'clock in the morning, and I don't feel like going on video because I've just got up.

When the swimming pools do reopen I will take Milo, probably nearly straight away. I think they say that babies have some kind of a natural ability before they're six months. He's five months old now, so I want to take him as close to six months as I can, just to get him used to it. I don't want him to be, like, scared of it.

*13 March 2021*

SEAN: I've been able to be at home more than I would have been if we weren't in a lockdown, so that's been a massive highlight. I've seen Milo progress and develop, and doing new things each day or every week. But to start off with, obviously, we were still in the pub and I was still working, so it was quite hard to just go to work and not really see him at all.

LOUISA: I think this lockdown's come at quite a good time for us really, because it means that we can all spend time together as a family. And I mean, Milo's a lot more alert and he laughs at things and he's really playing and trying to sit up, and Sean will say, 'Oh, I noticed him doing this earlier.' We've taken this time to get into a routine as well. When Sean was at work, I never even thought I could do that; I didn't know where to start, I didn't think Milo would understand. It just felt like such a big job for me to do on my own. Same with bedtimes – Milo used to just stay up and go to bed when we went to bed, he'd sleep on me and I would wait for Sean to get home from work. Whereas since Sean has been off, we've been taking it in turns to do bedtimes, so Milo generally goes to bed about eight o'clock and we get the evenings together. Being at home, it means we're not busy, we can make sure we stick to the routine and he goes down for naps at the same time. So that's only been since this lockdown started and that's really helped us.

We're not doing anything else for the rest of the week really. It was Sean's birthday yesterday. I did a little treasure hunt in the morning for him so that he would have something to do, so he went round and found his presents. We went for a walk, then we've just been watching telly. We always look forward to the food shop, so we'll probably do that on Sunday or Monday, just for something to do really. I think it's maybe a little bit boring for Milo being at home all the time, but it's just how it's always been for him.

SEAN: Being in hospitality with a child, it's not really the best. I want to be there, I want to see Milo develop, I want to possibly be there when he first speaks. With the pub closed, I've just started going to work for my brother and really enjoying it. He's a carpenter, and he's been on his own for about six years now. He does everything – anything related to wood – from fitting kitchens to doing new roofs. You name it, and he can do it! And he's very, very good at it, so it's a good place to learn. This is my second week that I've done with him. A lot of people say that you shouldn't work with family, but me and my brother, we've always got along quite well. So yeah, it's good to be able to learn off someone that I trust.

I think it'll be a lot better for our lives if I do change to be a carpenter. I go to work with my brother at about 7.30am, I come home at 5pm, and then you've got the rest of the evening and you've got the weekends.

LOUISA: Yeah, ideally, Sean would like to retrain as a carpenter. I think he's just enjoyed having the time with us. And I have started my own business; it only launched today. It's an online shop selling baby clothes, toys, little bits of, like, nursery decor. I've got an Instagram account where I was posting family and baby stuff, so I met a few mums on there that I used to chat to, and that was where I got the idea for it, because one of the mums, she has her own online shop. I've just been doing little bits of it every day. I made a logo, and I've made social media accounts for it, and I got the website sorted. Yeah, so I've had my first order today. I have sent it already. I still can't really believe that it's started now!

I'm planning to go back to work at the nursery. Due to Covid, if I wanted to be in the same room as Milo, then it would be possible. I think what they're doing is they have one adult to a certain group of children, and they just keep them together for as long as possible in that bubble.[11] But they are giving the option to not be with your child, because they say it is detrimental to you as a member of staff, and also to the child. If possible, we do want to be apart because I just think that I want him to be more independent and things like that, so I think it would kind of defeat the point of him going if we were together.

SEAN: I'm on a lot of groups on Facebook and stuff like that, and for the hospitality industry, I think a lot of chefs have actually left. A lot of people have gone to do, like, security or all different jobs. It doesn't surprise me. Hospitality isn't sociable, the hours aren't nice, you're never at home with your family.

I think people were sort of comfortable in their jobs because they were employed full-time and they were getting a pay cheque at the end of the week, or at the end of the month, but now, the uncertainty of what's it going to be like when we go back, and are people going to come out and be able to afford to eat? I think all of that's come

---

11 The term 'bubble' is used in several interviews. Here it refers to a nursery, or educational, bubble, where children were divided into separate groups, with the intention of keeping groups apart to help reduce the spread of Covid-19.

Support bubbles are mentioned in later interviews. These were introduced three months into the first lockdown to help alleviate loneliness. Once in a support bubble, a person could think of themselves as being in one household and could have close contact with others in their bubble. Not everyone could form a support bubble, but those living alone could, as well as households with a child under one, or single adults with one or more children under eighteen.

into the equation, really, and yeah, I think that's changed a lot of people's minds.

I've been doing the pub since, like I said, I was twelve, so how long is that? Seventeen years in pubs! I think if we hadn't gone into lockdown, I don't think I would have probably pursued carpentry; I would have just carried on plodding along and cooking.

*Afterword – one year later*

LOUISA: Sean is working with his brother full-time now, he occasionally works in pub kitchens for various ex-employers when they get really stuck, but this is just one-off weekends and he's able to ask for a lot more money than he would have got as a full-time chef. He much prefers what he's doing now.

When I returned to the nursery, I found it incredibly hard to leave Milo. So did he. I persevered with it until August, but the problem was he had never been without me and it was such a change being around all these new people, especially as we'd not even done any face-to-face baby groups or soft play or anything like that.

The other issue was that being in close proximity to all the other children – both me and him – we often had to isolate for two weeks following a Covid exposure, so as soon as we made the smallest bit of progress with him going into the baby room, he would be at home with me for two weeks, and it would then be even worse than before. The final straw was in August: we unfortunately had to isolate on both Milo's and my birthday due to an exposure in the nursery. This meant that Milo's party had to get postponed – it was such a shame for his first birthday, but luckily he won't remember it!

So then I made the decision to look for a new job, which I found on a Facebook ad. This was the perfect job for me as it's caring for a little boy with additional needs. I walk him to and from school and help his family by caring for him on some evenings and weekends. He is six and has become best friends with Milo; twice a week they have dinner together, share baths and play. This was a brilliant job as it meant I could take Milo with me and wouldn't have to leave him, and also encouraged us to get out of the house every single day for the school runs. I'm much happier doing that than I was at the nursery when I had to leave Milo upset every day.

My online business has taken a backseat. I feel like it was becoming really difficult to drum up the interest on social media and I was having to spend hours a day posting and interreacting to get my content seen.

My neighbour and I have been seeing each other much more and are now each other's best friends. Milo is good friends with her baby too, which is lovely. Funny how things happen like that!

# Steve Murray

*I've always flown – that's just what I do*

*23 February 2021*

I was flying as an airline pilot, flying a Jumbo 747. Gives you a buzz every time you take off with that immense amount of power, gives you this big smile on your face. It gives you a great sense of pride; you're flying this huge piece of machinery and responsible for hundreds of passengers down the back. Sometimes we went to nice places like Singapore or Cape Town or San Francisco. You could get together as a crew and go and have a social time for a night, and a day off doing some touristy-type things. And that was great, great fun. The body clock was continually somewhere mid-Atlantic!

I always wanted to be a pilot, especially a military pilot, that was the thing I really wanted to do. Having gone to war and things like that is very different from routine airline flying, but, I suppose, the natural progression after a long career in the military is to go into the airlines for, you think, longer-term stability. Obviously it's better paid than the military. And, you know, I still enjoyed the flying.

But then, from the lockdown stage in March [2020], everything within the airline industry ground, more or less, to a halt. Then later in the year, probably about June or July, they announced the fact that they were going to retire the Jumbo. They were intending to retire the Jumbo in about four to six years' time, but when this all kicked off there was obviously a massive reduction in worldwide travel, and that's the reason it got brought forwards. There just wasn't the demand, which is very, very sad for everybody involved. You look on social media, there's been such an outpouring about the loss of the Jumbo. Her name held a place in everybody's heart that operated it. And even people that didn't operate it, people just liked flying in it.

So, yeah, in March, for all pilots they said, right, everybody has to take, I think it was, four weeks of unpaid leave over a period of three months. So that was a relatively large financial knock, but manageable. In the initial stages of the lockdown, I think people expected a relatively fast recovery. So, we thought, you know, maybe summer or autumn last year, we'd be back to work as normal.

June or July, they started the redundancy process. It was a pretty gruesome way that the company dealt with the employees, because we had a lot of agreements between the company and the employees about how they would ever manage a redundancy-type situation. Those agreements have never had to be used in the past, because they've never made anyone redundant before. When it came to it, they pretty much tore up the agreements.

The upshot of it is that about 260-odd pilots were made redundant, and a further 600-odd pilots didn't have an aircraft to fly. Those of us that were flying the Jumbo, and a few other people, ended up in what they called a community retention scheme. So, a whole pool of pilots that effectively didn't have an aircraft to fly, and they gave us a very substantial pay cut. Part of the redundancy agreement was that our pay wasn't paid by the company; so we're not being paid by the company at all, we're being paid by our fellow employees, who have taken a pay cut to finance our much reduced wages. So, although on paper we're still employed by the company, they have no financial commitment to us. It was shameful, very shameful.

At first, the company refused to take advantage of the furlough process for pilots, I think because they wanted to maintain short notice flexibility. It wasn't until November that they were persuaded to take advantage of the scheme. Being on furlough has slightly eased the pressure financially – my pay has gone up slightly – but it's still a long way off where it would normally be.

So, since November, and here we are now in February, I've been on furlough with my other colleagues in this hold pool of non-operational pilots. They can make us operational by giving us a course for a new aircraft at short notice, any time. There were some people who were non-operational who were allocated courses on new aircraft types, and they tended to be the more senior, the guys who had been in the company the longest. When it came to us, there were about 320 of us put in a hold pool, effectively with no direction, just sit and wait and see what happens, being financed by our colleagues. Yeah, pretty bad.

So, here we are, a year into the Covid experience, and I know that it will be another, I would think, year and a half before they'll be able to retrain me. If they ever do take us back. I'm hopeful they will because it looks like recovery is on the horizon, but the company has certainly not been very good at filling us full of faith for being looked after.

This is the first stage of my life, since I was about sixteen, that I haven't been regularly flying – I'm fifty now. I've always flown – that's just what I do. Now I'm not able to, and there's no guarantees that I'll be able to for a long time.

I suppose, for the first significant time in my life, there've been a lot of worries. At first, I didn't know if I was going to be made redundant – there was a possibility of that happening. And since then there's been no job security. The 'if' kind of makes you feel a bit lost really, and I think it does get you down. I suppose my identity has been taken away.

Generally, I've always been pretty upbeat, don't look on things as problems – more a solutions than a problems type of person. Definitely. So, yeah, I don't generally get particularly down about things, but I think it's difficult not to during all this fiasco, particularly when your employer has been, well, certainly it comes across, very uncaring.

You know, being an optimist, I'm sure, in time, it'll all work itself out. Somehow. I think so. Who knows. Hopefully things will get better. A lot of my friends are friends from early days, many of whom went into the air force and most of whom are flying for different airlines now. A lot of them are in similar situations and finding it difficult. We have group Zoom calls – it's nice to keep in touch with them, and then you can all have a whinge and a moan and life seems a little bit better when you vent a bit. Or at least not better, but more bearable.

I think I was always in the correct career, and that's why I don't want to rush out of it. But I have had time to think about, you know, what I would do. And the conclusion is, I don't know! But, yeah, I've had lots of time to ponder, mull things over in my mind. I recognise that I'm actually not very good at anything else.

At the moment I'm going through the process of applying for a few cargo flying jobs. Cargo is one thing that seems to be on the improve. Cargo operators are doing well, and particularly with the movement of PPE and vaccinations, so they're expanding. So I do have applications in with a couple of cargo operators, which may come up soon, something to keep me ticking over for a while. Who knows, it may work out that cargo operators are a long-term, more sound place to be.

*13 April 2021*

My wife and I are now both jabbed up. It was really good, really well organised at STEAM, I must say. There were lots of people coming and going, but I ended up only queuing for five, maybe ten minutes maximum. It is well organised. It's nice, you come out thinking, yep, that was worthwhile.

I've been walking the dog twice a day. The puppy was about five months old when the first lockdown kicked off. I've been running a lot, because a few months ago I found out I've got type 2 diabetes. I always was a bit of a sucker for Coke and crisps and sweets, but I think, because I was sitting at home with not much to do, I was probably snacking more than I usually would do. That was an added concern, because I lost my medical for flying. And I knew that in order to get an interview for a cargo job I was going to have to get my licence back up and running. I was keen not to use drugs to control the diabetes because then the spotlight obviously comes on you. So I thought, no, I'll just get this done myself, get my blood sugar back into a normal range. I decided to do a lot of running and change my diet. I'm running six days a week, and I cut a lot of rubbish out of my diet. By doing that over a matter of a few months, I managed to put the diabetes into remission. The pressure was on to get it sorted, so I did.

So, I'm outside walking the dog an hour in the morning, hour in the afternoon. I'm out running an hour and a half each day. What else have I been doing? I've taken up watching *A Place in the Sun* far too regularly – it seems to be on TV every day. Been catching up on admin that I don't usually ever have the time to do, and all sorts of jobs around the house, lots of DIY, again jobs I haven't been able to do for a long time. I now don't know how I ever had time to work, because thinking on what I actually achieve is probably very little, but I still seem to be busy all day!

Hopefully, next year, I'll go back to work, but there's no guarantees. At my work, they don't know themselves what the long-term plans are. How is society going to go? They're just not sure, so they're not planning that far ahead at the moment. I think business customers, and particularly commuters who have families living overseas or they should be living overseas themselves, they must be desperate to travel. But nobody knows what's happening, so I don't anticipate any big news for a long time. I think there will be travel in the summer, but I don't think there'll be much until later in the summer. So yeah, not much happening, really.

I haven't heard anything from the cargo job applications. I did contact them, and they said that something may come up in the next month or two, but there's nothing firm yet. So, yeah, just wait and see, really.

*Afterword – one year later*

Over the last four months I have been working for a cargo company which flies large volumes of cargo worldwide. It took a long time to get any offers or feedback from any of the positions which I applied for, but then it all seemed to happen very quickly in the end. From having never heard of the company before to applying for the job, going through recruitment assessment, starting doing ground school, simulator assessments and flight training to get requalified, took less than a month. It was a bit of a culture shock, going from doing pretty much no academic or commercial work for well over eighteen months to suddenly being flat out day and night for a prolonged period of time. Funnily enough, the day before I started this job, I was also offered a position with the company which had previously interviewed me as far back as January. It seems these jobs were like buses – you wait forever then they all come at once.

The aircraft is essentially the same as the one I previously flew, with a few differences. The main difference being that there are no seats and no passengers, just very large quantities of freight. Freight generally presents fewer problems than passengers and hence things tend to run more smoothly once you get going. However, due to the nature of cargo operations, there tends to be continual delays and programme disruption.

As a job itself, it has been really busy in terms of spending long periods of time away from home and having to cope with constant ongoing disruptions and delays. One of the really nice parts of the job has been that, as it is a much smaller company, you tend to work and fly with the same people on a more regular basis and you get to know each other well. Having spent such a long period of time being forced away from work did make me question my personal value and worth. I am much happier now that I have taken on this alternative job.

# Jessica Thompson

*I almost begged for furlough*

*15 January 2021*

We had a team meeting, we had six of us from the leader team in, which was a lesson learnt: one of them had been to a stag do, had got Covid, didn't know, came into the meeting and we sat together for two hours. I think the next day, he lost his taste and smell, had a test and then most of us ended up having Covid as well. I went to speak to two people to let them know: 'We've had a confirmed case, I've also been told to go home.' And they both got it a few days later. And you know, I just went into a room to speak to them.

Then my husband got it. For us, the initial symptom was complete loss of taste and smell, which was weird but not worrying. We did then both get quite ill. My husband believes it was the illest he's ever been. I'm not so sure. You're told to not see the children, to effectively hide yourselves away. We have a six-year-old daughter and a thirteen-year-old son. Considering how easily it had spread at work, we realised the children were going to get it. We made a decision that we could, you know, make it horrible for them and they would still get it or we could just carry on normal family life.

My only worry, really, was for my daughter because she has a breathing difficulty anyway, and it was whether that would affect that. She was sick and had a very high temperature, but she was fine from the breathing department. My son didn't show symptoms, but there's no way he didn't have it in his system. I tried to carry on working. I mean, god knows why! I don't even enjoy work, I don't care about it. You know, my work is just to pay the bills.

Last year, I had a mini … Oh, I don't know what to call it, but just before Christmas 2019 I decided, you know what, there's so much more I wanted to do with my life. I had meant to join the army as an officer after university, and then went travelling, met someone and that was that. I found out at the end of 2019 that you could still sign up as a Reserve Officer, up until forty-nine, so thought, gosh, I'm going to do that!

I started that process, and I felt like last year was going to be my year to get some of me back now my daughter's six and a little bit older. It would have been a fun, challenging, adventurous time. I'd started to go to the Reserve Centre every Tuesday evening where they kind of do talks and stuff, and I had got my fitness up to the level. I was just getting booked in for the initial two-day assessment, and then I had a bike accident and then Covid hit. So that big plan has gone out the window.

I think the hardest thing for me in the first lockdown was the lack of understanding from the senior management team. I work for a relatively small company, kind of forty or fifty employees. There's six of us on the senior management team. I am the only female, I am the only one with young children, and actually there's only one other with any children at all.

The director is quite young, he's in his twenties, and has relied heavily on me because we kind of get each other, and he does need a figure in his life to be his sounding board and his support. He chose me through that time, which is not what I needed or wanted, for the hard decisions in the company like

'Oh my god, what are we going to do? We're going to need to furlough everyone. What is furlough?' You know, 'Jess, can you work it out?'

I think if you're in an environment where you're all in it as a team, you're all going through the same, you're all supporting each other, then it's a completely different story than feeling you're letting people down when you're not meaning to, but just because they have no concept or understanding of what it's actually like.

Working with the children, in the roles that we have, it was so unnatural. You're in your home, you're on meetings and you're constantly telling your own children, you know, 'Get out!' You're telling them to get out and leave Mummy and Daddy alone. And for them, that's awful. It's horrible. It's unkind. I shouldered more of it because my husband is the main breadwinner, so his job was the one that mattered the most. He definitely did pick up and help where he could, because he knew how incredibly difficult I was finding it.

I almost begged for furlough, without getting down on my knees, and it just wasn't accepted. We did furlough about two-thirds, if not more, of the employees, but my role there is compliance and health and safety.

In a couple of meetings I started to cry. It was just on meetings over Zoom, someone would say, 'Oh, how are you doing, Jess?' And, literally, I would burst into tears. And that's very not me. So they did know, and they did even say, 'Just do what you can.' But they didn't mean that, you know: 'Do what you can, oh, by the way, I've got a deadline for this, get it done,' type of thing.

I know they haven't understood the impact it's actually had on me because I have tried so hard to keep up with my usual standards of work and amount of work. Part of it is the pressure you put on yourself; I'm just not the sort of person who can switch off and say I'm just going to do a half-hearted job here. That's what I need to do.

I have Wednesdays off, usually. That was my day in the house when the children are at school, my husband at work. Just by myself, you know, my music, my whatever. It's not a day off when my husband's upstairs working. It's not a day off anyway because the children have been here the whole time as well. I miss having any time in the house alone to do my own thing.

I turned to emotional eating, and I'm generally fit and healthy, but I've gained two stone over the last several months. I've been eating sweet stuff during lockdown, horrendously so, absolutely disgustingly so. My nibbles are more than what most people eat in a day. I go to the shop and buy several packs of, you know, like, you can get packs of KitKats or Twix with ten in each, and I eat them all. And crisps.

I just, yeah, used that as a coping mechanism. I've done this before, but never for this length of time and this extreme. I'm generally an all-or-nothing person, so I could lose it for a little bit, but I would then get completely back on it and, you know, be back in shape and size. Whereas this time, probably three or four times throughout what's coming up to nearly a year, I have for a month gone absolutely at it and, say, lost a stone and a half again. And then this latest lockdown happened, and I'm just straight back onto eating again.

In the summer, my brother started coming around every second night, and we would do a workout outside. Just before Christmas, I signed up to a personal trainer three times a week – that was really helping and I felt good. And then Christmas happened and I just ate my way through it. So then, when I'm off the bandwagon, I find it hard to jump back on. You know, I'm always like, 'On Monday I'll start, on Monday I start.' So today is Monday, actually, and I've eaten well all day. Whether that lasts more than a few days, we'll see. I will get it sorted, I just need some of the stress to be alleviated.

Near the end of the first lockdown, I read an article from a lady who said how this time teaches you what matters most in your life, and how for her it had taught her what she could or couldn't live without. And she almost decided to bend the rules where she needed to, or even break them where she needed to, to survive from a mental health point of view. So this time round that is what I've done, and I've learnt what I can and can't survive with, and I'm not going to lie: I do break the rules in terms of family. I'm literally just seeing my wider family.

We didn't see my family in the first lockdown. I got very worried about Covid in general; I was much stricter at the beginning. I feel a lot less anxious now I've had it, we've all had it. My dad's ill and I just feel that, you know, that is the priority, spending time as a family. I'm one of five children and we all live within, probably, twenty minutes to half an hour of each other. So weekends now, I pretty much see my family, usually every weekend. We had Christmas together. We hosted here, they all stayed for a good few days.

I feel for my husband that his parents have been very careful, so he's not having anything really to do with them other than phone calls. In the first lockdown, it was hard not seeing my dad. My husband did pop over and try to set them up with Zoom, but they're not very technology minded. Actually, I grew up in a family where we were not allowed technology in any way, shape or form. We didn't have televisions. My mum's a bit barmy, had very strict rules, but, you know, we were allowed to run feral in the hills morning till night and she didn't ever seem to care where we were. Very loving, but she just had her own weird quirks. So technology is not something I like. I don't actually use social media. I signed up to Facebook to join up with the school group, but I don't use it in any other capacity. Technology is not something I think I would choose to have if I had a different husband; my husband is very into technology.

I hate that my son is on it so much. I think he would say he's really enjoyed the last year because he has had so much more time on his Xbox. He's been left to it so much more. But he has got me to watch him a few times, and, actually, I have realised that he is talking to his friends. It is a team, you know, game and teamwork. I kind of thought he was on his own on it all day, but to realise he is engaging with people makes it better. I don't think the amount of time he's on it is healthy. But again, at the moment, it's just a bit of a survival thing.

I still remember my first ever Zoom work's meeting when I was at home. We isolated a little bit before everyone because my son was unwell. I put myself on to the computer, just literally in my pyjama top, no make-up, and they put me on the big screen in the office and someone said, 'Who's that?' And I was like, oh god! I quite enjoyed the more relaxedness of being at home, but when I go back in, I'll have to make the effort of dressing nicely and doing my make-up and hair again. I know I will because that's what they know of me.

The children had very little education. School did send work, but it wasn't in a format that the child could just log on, especially a child like my son who is not going to spend any more time or effort on it than he has to. My daughter, she did fall behind, and she just wandered round the house aimlessly so much of the time. My in-laws did step in – about a month in, maybe later, you lose track – and started doing Zoom lessons with the children, which was brilliant. I think my father-in-law focused on our son and my mother-in-law on our daughter. I think my father-in-law said he was doing something insane, like eighteen hours' planning a week to decipher all the lessons and actually get them into a format that our son could do something with. My in-laws were a godsend. But, of course, there's the constant technical issues or 'Mummy, I've lost my bit of paper,' or whatever it is.

This lockdown is far better than the first lockdown. We tried the first two days with the children at home and realised we were not going to go back to where we got to last time, so we put both children in school. We were originally told there wasn't a space for our daughter, but we pushed and pushed and luckily we did then get a space. My son said, 'None of my friends are going in. I hate it, I'm not going to go in.' But I think, actually, he's quite enjoying getting to know other boys. I think he's realising the people in different groups in your year are normal and are human and are okay to talk to. There's only seven or eight from Year 9; a lot of them are at home because they're able to look after themselves. They're all in the library. It's still: here is the material. They log on through a portal called *Class Charts*, they get on with it and they submit it. I'm not even sure it's a qualified teacher with them; I think it's just a teaching assistant who watches them to make sure they do it. But, according to him, they rush it all in two hours and then they've got the rest of the day on the computers messing around. I don't understand, nationally, how in the first month, when they realised this was going on, they didn't get a group of top teachers together to get all the resources sorted.

I guess, in summary, it's just a learning process. The first few months were horrendous. Then you learn how to cope with it, you come out at the other end and it becomes the new norm. That's where we're at now. It's really made me analyse my life. My husband and I both sat down a couple of months ago and wrote what we want out of life on a daily, weekly, monthly and longer-term basis. And we've given ourselves until the end of next year for me to get out of this job where I don't enjoy the people I work with, which I'm sure must stem partly from how hard I found it in lockdown. As for being a Reserve Officer, well, I got fat and unhealthy, and I'd need to undo that to be able to get in.

*12 April 2021*

I'm absolutely shattered right now, but it's definitely been easier since we last spoke, because we did have the children in school. So, yeah, complete contrast really to the first lockdown. It seems like the world's beginning to get back to normal. It's interesting seeing how some people are reacting post-lockdown. My daughter joined gymnastics last Monday, and today was her second session. She's joined with her older cousin, who's far more confident, but her cousin last week on their first session was just petrified and pale and things, and I think because they'd been at home for longer she found it very, very difficult going into a normal environment again.

My daughter really enjoyed the more intimate group when there were fewer children at school. I mean, I guess it's what it's like in a private school when you have ten children in a classroom rather than thirty. So, for her, when everybody came back, that's been a big struggle.

I did find that first lockdown hugely difficult, surprisingly so for someone who is a problem solver, but I feel like I learnt a bit about myself. I've learnt to enjoy home life a bit more. I guess it's been one of those life experiences where you think, if I could turn back time, would I wish that Covid didn't happen or have I grown as a person from it? It teaches you that you can live in a different way, and afterwards I don't want to go back to being so manic as we were, where every weekend it's busy. I do feel stronger as a person and more able to realise, just because I'm not somewhere, it doesn't mean I'm missing out. It doesn't mean when I'm not with my family or not with some of my best friends they're bonding and thinking, we don't need Jess. I think I've come to the realisation that I can go every second time and still be just as good friends or, you know, get on with everyone just as well. It's kind of showing you there is a different option and we can continue that if we so please. Hopefully, it will be a bit calmer.

I've got two closest friends; one of them's a single mum. When lockdown started, her two children are competitive swimmers and they do an awful lot of clubs. And she said what a relief it was not to be doing that in lockdown, and then the other day we were talking about it and she seemed to have forgotten that feeling and conversation and seems to be raring to put them back into all these things, which I personally find a bit crazy.

Before this, I hardly ever worked from home, I almost didn't feel able, whereas now I certainly would feel able to work from home a couple of days a week. We do want a presence in the office, but there will definitely be more flexibility. I went in today.

When I first started having meetings on Teams and Zoom, I thought they were amazing and we didn't need to be in, but I started to realise the contrast. When I'm at home and everyone else is in, you get left out. Equally, when I'm in and there's someone else on the screen, you naturally leave them out a bit just because you talk to faces who are in front of you; you don't constantly turn around to look at the big screen on the wall.

When you are at home, the only time you chat is in a meeting or something, you know, when it's a serious thing. And, actually, by being back in the office, you get the general chit-chat as well, and it kind of neutralises the serious times. So for me, I found a realisation: actually, it can be fun to work where I work as well. But when you're in, certainly you can get distracted, and I can find that really annoying when some people don't get the hint that you need to crack on with something.

I got given quite a big pay rise; it was long overdue. The director did apologise that he just hadn't got around to it. I still know in my heart I need to leave. I need to work out what I want to do.

The last couple of weeks, I joined a gym and I'm being more healthy. I feel like, with the end in sight, it's a bit easier to be upbeat and go back to some form of normality. My brother goes to a gym, so I joined with him, just because I seem to need more motivation than usual. I got to the gym at six this morning, so I can get it done before the rest of the household is awake. I've just had to adjust my bedtime and go to bed earlier; the only other thing I'd be doing is lying on the sofa watching junk on television anyway.

My daughter did start to wake up when she heard me get up. Initially I wasn't going to the gym, I was going to my brother's, so I would take her. But now, with the gym, I've had to say 'No,' and she's been a bit better at sleeping through me trying to creep down the stairs. There are four creaky stairs and trying to dodge them is near impossible!

I find it quite funny because I was a member at this gym many, many years ago, probably twenty years ago. And it's owned by a different company now, but it's the same building and same set-up and same changing rooms, and on my first day coming down the stairs, I almost had that, oh, I'm twenty and fit and healthy and cool again. Then, I get down and, you know, I'm just an older, larger lady, and there's all these nineteen-year-old boys with big muscles and girls with their crop tops.

Being a Reserve Officer is still something I absolutely want to do. I'm on a group chat of everyone joining, and I suddenly noticed I hadn't seen any notifications. I logged on, and they'd actually booted me out a couple of months ago. I was constantly saying, 'Once I get fit, once I get fit, I'll come back in.' And I've been saying this for a year and I haven't got to that stage, so I understand why they did it. So yeah, I need to actually get fit and then contact them at a point where I'm ready to go.

We're anti-vax, generally, as an entire family. One of my sisters is going to get this one; I think she feels differently about this vaccination because we are in the centre of the pandemic. But my parents decided that they wouldn't get it, so they haven't had it. They are saying they have, which is very unlike my mum – she usually completely holds her ground and her beliefs and things – but I think they realised that a lot of people would disagree with not getting it, so it's easier just to say they've had it.

I'm of the same opinion. My husband is not. I think that will probably, at some point, cause some issues. At school, I didn't opt to get Sebastian tested regularly, and he didn't like that option. I guess my husband's pro-vaccinations, and it's more that's just how he grew up, that's his family. And when my daughter was younger, I said to him, 'I'm happy to have all these conversations, but I want you first to do your own research,' and handed him a big wad of books. And I don't think he ever opened those, so I'm still waiting for the big conversation. I think if the time comes where they want to vaccinate children, that will probably be a big conversation.

I did so much research when my children were younger and looked at both sides of the coin. You can't put something into your body, you know, a foreign object and it not react negatively in some way. And I understand it's a weighing-up of the risks. Actually, you know, as a healthy person in your thirties, the chances of dying from Covid are so, so, so, so slim. The statistics annoy me because I was a mathematician; it just annoys me that there's not enough information out there for you to fully form your own opinion.

I got sent a few bits from a couple of people that I know who are anti-vaxxers trying to make people sign a petition. Me, personally, I don't disagree that we potentially need a vaccine for this and that vaccines have their places. It's just a personal choice not to take it.

My son hurt himself a few months ago at school. It was actually in lockdown. I think they were just allowed to run riot at the school, and he cut his foot open on a piece of metal. I took him into hospital, and they kind of have a clipboard and their pen, they're like, 'Had all his vaccinations?' and go to tick it. And I'm like, 'No.' It's always a shock on their face, and just the questions I get asked, almost as if they assume I forgot. And that's what makes me laugh. You know, he's fourteen years old, of course I didn't forget to get vaccinations for fourteen years! It was an active choice.

I do come against people who strongly disagree with it, but my take on it is there's a lot else you can do, and people who feed their children junk all the time, that's cancer-inducing. I find that crazy. We all have our own ways of keeping ourselves healthy and protecting ourselves and building up our immune systems, and yeah, I just choose to do it differently.

My daughter has something called subglottic stenosis, so it's just narrowing in her airway, so she used to get quite poorly. When she was born, she was only four and a half pounds, very little. There was no reason for it, but they wanted to take her away immediately and pump her full of antibiotics. And again, that's not something I agree with, and I let them just because, you know, I'd been in labour for three days, and it was a mistake on my behalf, that's what I feel. Afterwards, there was a bunch of things they wanted to give her, and I remember asking the statistics of a child getting whatever it was versus the side effects, and this was the senior paediatrician, and he just didn't have a clue. And I found that crazy, you know, to want to pump my tiny child full of something, and you can't tell me statistically the chances of her actually getting it so I can then make an educated decision. If one in two children get whatever it is and she needs protecting, absolutely, but if it's one in a million, then you know, no.

*Afterword – one year later*

I took the plunge and left my job in November. I don't think I realised until I left quite how damaging their toxic attitude and lack of understanding had been. I work with some really lovely people now, so things are much better on that front.

Emotional eating is still a thing, but much better than it was during the lockdowns. I do bootcamp twice a week with a bunch of school mums, which is great. I felt so excited and determined about signing up as a Reserve Officer, but due to fitness and weight gain I have held off and now don't feel it's such a big desire that I need to fill.

My husband got vaccinated, I haven't, and the more I research it, the more I genuinely believe Covid is not detrimental to someone of my size and health. I do not believe I would take the vaccine for travel. It would take an awful lot to make me put it into my body.

Since the pandemic I feel I'm looking at the world differently, and at its leaders with more scepticism. I also find it flabbergasting how most people don't question things. I'm actually envious, in a way, as it makes life easier. I also think it's made me closer to my family and more tolerant too of other opinions, even if I don't agree with them.

# Vadym Gurevych

## *Doorstep portraits*

*24 March 2021*

I was born and raised in Ukraine and I lived there up until I turned twenty-eight, and then I moved to the UK in summer 2005. For me, I guess, I have always been a bit cosmopolitan, sort of, citizen of the world, as they say. From very early childhood in my family, this idea of moving somewhere was always discussed and present in our lives.

My family are Jewish, and being a Jew in the Soviet Union was a very difficult role. Anti-Semitism would be pretty much everywhere, from your next-door neighbour, to your job, to your education. It's about managing groups of people by making them hate each other: the more people hate each other, the easier it is to manage them. If I were to go out and play, I'd be called names and be sometimes beaten up. If I'm at school, same stuff. There were those kitchen conversations constantly, not always open conversations, but growing up in a Jewish family, so a bit oppressed, a bit not happy, you learn to listen and understand between the lines. Adults don't tell you everything because, being a child, you'll go and speak outside perhaps, but I remember conversations about leaving the country. My dad never got to do that,[12] but for me it was quite natural, I suppose.

---

12 In March 2022, after the bombing of his home town, Kharkiv, his father left Ukraine and came to Swindon.

It was fine coming here. It's a new country, so it's interesting. I'm not saying that it was completely without any nostalgia or without any cultural issues, but it wasn't that bad. It's more competitive in Ukraine, I'd say, but maybe because of that, people can achieve more. I don't know. Here we try to, sort of, make everything more subtle, I guess – be nice, be lovely. The society here gives more to an average person of average abilities and average achievements. Here, you go to school, you finish school with something average, what is it? C or D, whatever. And you go and you get a job, and you do that job, and you can afford to buy a little place, and you'll have a little car, and you will have a little holiday and a family, and you'll be fine like that through the whole of life. It is not going to happen over there.

Since I was eleven, I was doing something with computers and programming, and it was a hobby, and then to realise that you get paid for it, okay, fine, cool! So now I do e-commerce websites, and I work with clients from all over the world from this tiny office of mine.

And, since lockdown, I also do photography. I was a teenager when my dad bought me a camera, so we're talking about thirty years ago-ish. And then my second camera was one of those with a battery, a bit more modern. All I was doing was, if I look back, not very impressive at all, to say the least. Like, very disappointing. And it's only the last few years that I really got into wildlife photography, landscape photography, and I started to produce some pictures which I liked.

And so it went, up until last year, when lockdown happened, and I read somewhere that there was a person going round their neighbourhood doing doorstep portraits. They were doing it to raise the morale, I suppose, to give people something. And it sort of clicked in my brain that I could do that too; I have a camera, I like meeting people. This would be something new for me; before then, I'd only done pictures of my family. And then I thought, it needs to be a charity thing, and I said, okay, well, Prospect Hospice can be the beneficiary, because I had a friend here who worked with me and she died of cancer and Prospect were involved. And it all came together: doorstep photography, charity campaign, me affecting some skill. What I do is I go round and take your picture, and they'd be pictures of you, your family, your dogs, parrots, whatever you want, while you are in lockdown.

There is a story behind every family. In the few minutes that you get to meet them, you can sometimes deduce that from how they behave towards each other and towards you, what they're saying and all this. Fifty per cent is about how you, from the first second, smile and talk and how you calm them down if they feel a bit funny. And a lot of them became my Facebook friends because that's how I'd deliver pictures, via email or Facebook, so I got to see them, moving on in their lives. It's fascinating for me. It's a big thing for me.

A lady asked me to take pictures of her parents who were just about to celebrate their fiftieth anniversary in their garden. They were in their pyjamas, because that's how they had spent lockdown, so we wanted to create something which would be real.

There was another couple, they've been together for ten years, they have two kids, but the way they look at each other, it's a love story. There is a lot of body language that suggests it's not just what people declare, right; it's how they behave when they don't talk, so the way they walked together and held hands and stood near each other. I feel privileged to be around trying to capture it.

One young lady booked a session for her family. There are loads of children running around, not looking, and you think, well, what am I doing here? But that young lady, how confident she is! She's amazing.[13]

One of the best pictures I think I've taken was of a young lad and his partner. He comes out with his partner, he comes bare feet, it's raining, so they have an umbrella on them. I myself, I never go bare feet. He's got some funny cropped trousers, and it's a very nice outfit. And his partner, he's in shorts. They embrace and they cuddle and they kiss. You can see some raindrops. It's this wonderful, slightly lit up, but very rainy street behind them. And all this is Swindon.

I would have some very tiny houses, and some very regal houses. There was one particular family where they put on some very smart outfits, I think to add some colour and life into the boredom of lockdown. The baby girl was properly dressed in a little dress and tights and a white thing, what's it called? Maybe a bonnet.

Then, as I was doing the doorstep portraits, I started to move more and more away from the doorsteps. So we'd move to a nearby tree, to a nearby alley, to a green patch here and a green patch there. There was a lady and she said, 'Well, the whole lockdown, I have been doing walks along the canal with my friend, two metres apart, so can you take a picture of us by the canal?'

More and more things like that started to happen. And then more and more of them said, 'Well, do you do events? Do you do family things? Do you do this commercially?' First, I would say, 'No, I don't.' And then I said, well, why not? First of all, I'm

---

13 He is referring to Faith Vaughan, the university student, who says: 'I think it was the first lockdown, I saw Vadym's post on Facebook, and I knew my mum wanted to get some more pictures. It was really interesting because we were all able to go out the house and dress up. He was very, very good at what he did. He's like, "Oh, this area will be really pretty to take a picture," and it's something you've never really looked twice at. It was just something that was a bit out of the norm to be able to get excited about.'

always interested in business as such, even though it's a very small business for me. But second of all, or maybe first of all, it would allow me to somehow consolidate all this experience and skill and process.

Last weekend, I photographed a lady whose husband died quite recently. She and her husband were part of that doorstep campaign, and that's how she knows me. Now she wants a business shot, so I've done that. And there are people who I did maternity pictures for. The lady, she was heavily pregnant, like seriously heavily pregnant, and it was February, and it was really cold. And now they have a baby they want pictures of the baby.

It's very fresh, it's a baby business; it hasn't been a year yet. For me, it's not just work, it's a very nice time; I like meeting people and I like talking to people. I like to get a bit deeper and understand what has brought them here to this day and how they will, you know, evolve in the future. Maybe it's what you do when you write about somebody, you think a lot about them, right? You think a lot about their life path, and where they've been, where are they going to. So, that's what I try to understand about my clients, and, as I say, I use all the clues, how they talk, how they are with each other, how they're dressed, how they smile or not smile, all of this. So, it's a very interesting and positive experience for me, and I see it as something where I get inspiration from. Maybe in several years' time it will be a bit different, you know, having done a hundred weddings or whatever, I'll be like, argh, not again. Maybe not. I hope not. I hope I will never lose that edge, never lose that interest.

*Afterword – one year later*

The photography has become a small business. It brings me a lot of joy, because I don't get to see my clients in my main work, but with photography it's just seeing people.

That time in the lockdown, it was a time of transformation for me, personally. It was time when I had the opportunity to think and feel and, most importantly, or most scarily, time to listen to myself. People very rarely stop and look inside and try to hear themselves, who they are. In lockdown we had to face ourselves, there was nowhere to run away from us.

Whether it was coincidence or not, whether it would happen if there was no lockdown, I don't know, but I can think of a particular time last year when I felt I was ready to meet someone and pretty much soon after that I met Lesia. She is from Ukraine. It was very nice and very meaningful and we knew that there was a lot in common, and us meeting in Swindon, this particular day, this particular place, looking for new love, was quite improbable. If you go the spiritual way, and maybe I tend to do more of that now than before, then I would say the universe sends you people when you are ready to meet them. I proposed on 13 February, and we set a date for mid-June, but that was before the war. That's a new phrase in my lexicon, 'before the war'. What it is now, I've got no idea.

# Robyn King

## Being in lockdown with two very young children is hard

*8 January 2021*

We were quite lucky that we had some savings. We were due to get married in August, which we postponed quite early on in lockdown, so we had some savings for the wedding and we were able to use that. Actually, we saved a lot of money because we weren't doing anything; I realise how much money I spend on going out for food.

At the beginning of lockdown, I thought my fiancé and I are going to want to kill each other by the end of this, because you never spend that much time together. But actually, it was really, really nice and it brought us a lot closer together. When my fiancé's home, he's the best dad I could ever ask for for my kids.

My fiancé is in construction. After six weeks he went back to work.[14] He got a promotion and then he was put on the books, so if he did have time off again now, he would be furloughed. He's really busy at work. They are starting to get very strict with, like, you have to wear masks in the office, have to stay two metres apart. For him, it was quite frustrating that he couldn't

---

14 On 10 May 2020, during the first lockdown, Boris Johnson announced, 'We now need to stress that anyone who can't work from home, for instance those in construction or manufacturing, should be actively encouraged to go to work.'

see his family, yet you can go and see twenty strangers a day at work. It's understandable. It is what it is.

Some nights, my fiancé doesn't get home until the kids are in bed, so that's not very nice. But then some nights, when he is home earlier, he can help with bathing and stuff. Well, we don't have a bath, we've only got a shower cubicle, so that isn't exactly fun. But, yeah, when he's here, he's really helpful. I'm really lucky, I think.

When my fiancé went back to work, that was when I struggled a bit more. My son, he's just very full-on and hard to look after. Anyone that knows him, basically, he just tries to kill himself every day! He climbs everything, he's clumsy. We've had multiple trips to A&E with him. He's got, like, a big mark on his face – he got too excited the other day at seeing his lunch on the table and ran to the table and tripped over and hit his face on the table leg.

My dad gives me lots of advice. He is a foster carer, he often gets kids the same age as mine. We make sure we call each other quite a lot and FaceTime and stuff. My mum, I don't really see my mum, don't really have much of a relationship with her, unfortunately.

My son started walking at the beginning of the first lockdown – it was his birthday, he took his first steps. So I was a bit like, how do I go for a walk with two toddlers on my own? So that in itself was a bit of a struggle. I put out on Facebook, 'Where's good to go?' I needed to find places to go on my own. Not too far because my son, he'd only just learnt to walk. We were able to walk to Coate Water quite a lot, but I would literally walk, feed the ducks at the first bit when you get there, then walk home. Or, like, I would go on walks around my estate.

Most nights, the way I get to sleep is by thinking what to do the next day, whether that be what to do with the kids or what cleaning needs doing. So yeah, I guess that's how I try and be a bit organised, but also not put too much pressure on myself. If it doesn't go that way, then it doesn't go that way. It's fine, it's not the end of the day, end of the world. As long as they're healthy, that's all I care about.

After I had my son, I suffered quite badly with postnatal depression. I felt better when I was out and about. I was very rarely ever at home. I had come off of my antidepressants before the first lockdown. I had to go back on to them because I just was not coping.

I'm so used to being around people. I'm very much a social butterfly. My sister and my sister-in-law are my best friends; I used to see them nearly every day. My sister-in-law has two little boys who are just a couple of months older than my daughter, and they're literally just, like, best friends. It was really hard, every single day, my daughter would say, 'I see Ti-Ti' or 'I see Ro-Ro.' And I would say, 'No, not today.' So we FaceTime a lot; it's helped so much that we've got this technology. But yeah, it was hard to say, 'No we can't go there, we can't do this.'

A few times, I've taken the kids to Tesco with me. I did not take them for a long time because I didn't like it, but then I've had to go. I would have my son in the buggy and I'd put my daughter on her buggy board. It's hard trying to get her to not touch things, because usually she likes to pick things up and put them into the basket for Mummy and try to be helpful. And they both wave at everybody going past. I'm like, 'Don't touch anything, be careful!' I'm quite glad that they're so young, that they don't understand what's going on. They've just got to do what Mummy says, basically.

I had my thirtieth birthday in May and that was when you were allowed to see people in your garden, so we had my fiancé's mum and dad come over to our garden and had a socially distanced barbecue. My daughter remembered them and was like, 'Nanna, Grandad!' But my son wouldn't go near anybody, clung to me. My son, he went from being a baby to a toddler in lockdown, so the first time he saw people, he would cry. It was really strange, horrible to see. My sister, her little girl, she still to this day cries at people she doesn't know, even my mum, because she doesn't see her very often. It's horrible what lockdown has done to babies, I think.

My fiancé had two weeks off at Christmas. For me, it's just nice to not be on my own. We had each other, or more like I had him, he's got used to doing whatever he wants. We were both dreading him going back. So now he's back at work, I'm in lockdown and it feels very different this time because of the weather and not really being able to do a lot. I've taken the kids out for walks around our estate a couple of times, but it's just so cold. But it helps my mental state, a lot, just to get out, even just ten minutes.

From Christmas, we've got a lot of new toys and activities we're doing. We've been making Rice Krispie cakes and playing with Play-Doh. I've got some cookies for us to make today because it's too cold out. Last lockdown, it was a lot easier because my son had naps. He doesn't do that any more.

My daughter is not going to nursery at the moment. She started going when my son was a newborn. I'm a stay-at-home mum, I don't need childcare, but it was more because I think it's good for them. Then obviously they closed for the first lockdown, so I didn't need to pay for it, so that's good. And then I started sending her again when we were able to because I was comfortable with the things that they had in place – they had bubbles, social distancing. Then the week before Christmas, they phoned me and said that they'd had a positive case in her bubble, so she had to isolate. She hasn't been back since. They did reopen this week, but I said I'm not sending her yet, I just don't feel comfortable. I just feel like it's still going to go up and up and up. I just don't feel like it's the right time.

In the first lockdown, it was literally like a religion, having the news on every single day. But then I had to stop myself watching it. And I was getting quite angry at people because I agreed with what Boris was doing. I think, yes, okay, I think he did do it a bit late, but I think they were trying to go for the herd immunity situation, which personally I agreed with. I don't agree with people, like, slating him. It's not his fault. He doesn't make these decisions himself. He has lots of people advising him. It's not like he just wakes up and goes, oh yeah, I'm going to do this today. And I get really quite frustrated when people have all these arguments when they don't know a lot of facts, which is why I don't get involved with things like that. That is my opinion. I think this lockdown could have been earlier, that they should have done it before Christmas.

That's another reason why my anxiety's maybe been a bit higher because I know a lot of people didn't listen to the rules at Christmas. Me and my sister, we're very different, she's a lot more relaxed than I am and she says to me all the time that I'm over the top. I don't care, I'd rather be safe. I've always been quite, like, follow the rules and things like that. However, it's only really since this new strain's come out,[15] and I know a lot more people that have got it, because obviously it's a lot more transmittable, that it's made me more aware and stressed out by it. I think it's going to get a lot worse.

My grandad caught Covid in the first lockdown. He's ninety-three. When he was in hospital, one of the nurses asked him if he wanted to sign a Do Not Resuscitate form, and he said,

---

15 The alpha variant was first detected in the UK in November 2020. It was a 'variant of concern' and began to spread quickly, leading to a surge in infections.

'I don't know, I'll just do what everyone else does.' Considering his age, I don't think he was even very ill, but then he had to go and stay in a care home for two weeks and isolate because of my aunty. My aunty lives with my grandad, and we think he caught it from one of her carers. She is vulnerable, and then actually my aunty had it just before Christmas. It was horrific, horrible. She was in intensive care, and we actually got told she wasn't going to survive the night because all of her organs were failing. Then my dad said, 'They're trying a new mask.' I found out it was a CPAP mask, which, from what I understand, either works really, really well or just doesn't work at all. For her, luckily, it saved her life. She was home a week later.

Now my fiancé's mum and his dad have tested positive. He's got four siblings that live at home and all of them except two of them also tested positive. Two of them are extremely vulnerable: his mum's got MS and his sister's got a heart condition. Luckily, they're ill but they're not super-ill. They're just, you know, bit like the flu and you don't feel very well, but they're still able to phone me and things like that, so it's not too bad.

I've been doing their shopping for them and dropping it at their front door. That's a reason for me to get out and go and do something in the evening when my fiancé gets back from work. When I drop their shopping off, I put my coat over my hand to do the doorbell. Then I run away.

*4 March 2021*

We've literally just got dressed. So, I think when I last spoke to you I was quite, sort of, positive, and we were doing a lot. So I think it probably wasn't long after that that the novelty wore off. We just, sort of, weren't doing as much.

I feel like this has definitely been the hardest lockdown. I feel like I've had literally no mojo. I'll have days where I just don't get off the sofa, unless I need to, like to make the kids' lunch and stuff. And I've felt bad, because all we've been doing is having the telly on, or not really doing much. I do try and make sure I do some things, like my daughter's got these flashcard things that she got for Christmas with letters that she draws over and stuff. So I do try and make sure I do stuff like that with them, but it's nowhere near as much as I used to. I just feel like I have nothing to give. I've no motivation to do anything, not even get dressed most days. The days feel really long. I'm just tired all the time. I think if you're doing nothing, I think that's quite tiring.

I think I said to you before, after I had my son, I had quite bad postnatal depression. Even on my worst days, it was never a case of I didn't want to be at home with them. I will never be able to explain what it is. I don't know. When my son was born, we had quite a traumatic birth. I was five days overdue, I had to go up to the hospital because he wasn't moving, so I was being monitored. They said everything looked fine, but because I was overdue they wanted to induce me. So, I was like, 'Yeah, that's, fine.' And everything seemed okay. And then, as I was in labour, all I remember is hearing the midwife saying to my fiancé, 'Can you pull that red buzzer?' And then the next thing I knew, I opened my eyes and the room was just filled with people. There was a doctor at the end of the bed and he said, 'If you don't push right now, we're going to take you into surgery.' I think it was the cord wrapped around his neck, so he'd stopped breathing. I'm still not quite sure, but basically he told me to push and I didn't feel like I needed to push because of the drugs that they had given me, but I did it anyway. And he just went in and pulled him out.

He wasn't breathing when they brought him out, they put him on me and he was blue. And I said, 'He's not right,' so they had to go and put him on the resus table and luckily he was okay. The next morning when they came and did, like, the newborn checks, they noticed something wasn't quite right about his shoulder. He wasn't crying or in pain; I didn't really notice anything. But we went for an X-ray and then, yeah, they said that his collarbone was broken. You could see on the X-ray, it was completely snapped from being delivered. So I think that started the depression. And then he really struggled with his feeding. He was about four months old when we realised, actually, he had a cow's milk intolerance. He wasn't sleeping, he wasn't feeding properly. It was just, I don't know, everything.

Sorry.

Everything on top of each other and very different from when I had my daughter. So then I said to my doctor, 'I'm not feeling … like, I just cry all day.' I still felt like I loved my children, I would do anything for them, but I was thinking, I don't want to be here. And then I was feeling guilty for feeling like that.

So, yeah, they put me on to sertraline, and then we figured out about my son's milk allergy. Once we'd figured that out, given him prescription milk, that made such a difference. Then he started sleeping through the night, because he wasn't waking up in pain every night. And I eventually came off of my tablets, but then it was in the second lockdown, I started feeling like it again. So yeah, I'm back on them now and they've definitely been helping. I've sort of said I'm not going to try and come off of them until after lockdown. There's just no point. I know that I can come off of them, because I did before, and I was fine. I am such a social person, I am such an outgoing person, and then being in lockdown with two very young children is hard.

I was explaining to my fiancé the other day: so, he goes to work every day, and although, yes, he doesn't have his football and everything at the weekends now, he still gets time on his own or with other adults, right? Sometimes, he'll be like, 'Let's watch a film or something.' And sometimes I just want to be on my own for an hour – I just want to go upstairs, be in our bedroom, just be on my own. It's weird, I never felt like that before, but then before I would have had two evenings a week where he was at football. And although it's brought us a lot closer since being in lockdown and we've definitely benefited, I think it's shown me that I need to have time on my own as well. It's not something that he thinks of, it's only when I say to him, 'I need to have some time to myself,' then he's like, 'Oh okay, yeah, that's fine.' Most of the time, if we do put a film on, he's asleep within ten minutes anyway!

Before I met my fiancé, I always expected that I would be a working mum. It's only when I met him, and, like, his mum and dad, they're quite traditional, they've been together since they were fourteen, they've got seven children; she's always been a stay-at-home mum. As I was introduced to that family, it just made me think, actually, this is what I want. Whereas my mum and dad were divorced when I was about six or seven, my mum always worked, and we had au pairs and things, so I didn't realise that's what I wanted until I saw it. Does that make sense?

My fiancé's so helpful, it's not, 'Oh, you're a stay-at-home mum, you do everything.' I do try and make sure that dinner's ready for when he's home and things, but, at the end of the day, they're my priority. If they need baths at the time that he's coming home from work, tough, his dinner will have to wait, and he'll come and help me. He says to me all the time, 'You've got a harder job than I have.'

On a Saturday, before lockdown, he'd be out all day at football, so he'd only see them on a Sunday, which isn't an insight at all. It's not his fault, it's not any man's fault that they don't understand what stay-at-home mums go through and feel, because they're not doing it. How can I expect him to understand if he doesn't know? But lockdown brought us so much closer together, because he understands a lot more. I know how lucky I am with him. I say to my fiancé all the time,

I feel like I didn't exist until I met him. Like it sounds really corny, but that's what I feel like. Before I met him, I was just really lost. I feel like, when I met him, I actually became me.

*Afterword – one year later*

Our original wedding was August 2020, then rescheduled to August 2021; then we cancelled, due to finances, so that we could move house instead. Then when a friend passed away suddenly, we realised life was just too short, and so booked to get married in October 2021, but on a budget. It was touch and go with restrictions, but we were lucky and had a great day and evening. However, about eighty per cent of our guests actually got Covid after!

# Leon Clements

*School tried to set work, but it didn't really enforce it*

*20 March 2021*

So, I'm Leon Clements. I go to New College and I do music production, photography and English. Music is the big one for me, like listening and writing, and it's a big family interest as well, so it was kind of bound to happen. My grandad, he's been playing guitar since he was a kid, my dad's been playing guitar since he was a kid. It took a little longer for me to get interested in it – guitar was the main instrument, but I've taken more of an interest in piano nowadays. With doing music production, you've got to have a bigger understanding of piano, because it's the main instrument for writing and producing.

I would happily pursue a career in music. It's been the dream for quite a while. And, like my parents do constantly remind me, it's a hard line of work to get into, but I think most big dreams are hard lines of work to get into. My dad obviously gets it, because that was the same dream he had as a kid.

Before I really got into music, I always wanted to be a painter, but I thought that was more of an unreasonable dream to have than music. I feel like the live playing is the most difficult part, because there's no guaranteed line of work out of it, whereas the production side is more of a guaranteed career. But the live playing is the most fun side, which is why so many people want to do it.

When the announcement came that there would be no GCSEs last year, at first it was a relief. School tried to set work, but it didn't really enforce it. During the first week of lockdown, I would try and wake up as if I were still going to school. I got up and sat down to get my work done, and just like an hour would pass and I wouldn't get any work set. Eventually, my science teacher sent over what was said to be work, but it was a video of him talking about his day. I think my English teacher sent over some work to do, my art teacher set work to do. I handed that back and I never got any response. Most work that I sent back didn't get marked, didn't even get mentioned, like 'Well done, you can do this.'

I think it took around a week for me to give up waiting for work. I think my mum was more upset by it than I was. I understood that it would be difficult for them to organise teaching at home – Teams wasn't a big thing at that point. And, obviously, it's a relief not having to do work. It seemed like as soon as they found out that we weren't going to do our GCSEs, they forgot about us.

So once I had free rein, I would, like a lot of my friends, go to bed very late, wake up very late – there wasn't much reason to get up. I think it was after a little while, my dad suggested that I start running, just for some exercise. I kind of started to get into a routine – I would still go to bed very late, but I would try and get up quite early and then go for a short run, and then that was the most productive I was that day.

I found a lot of solace in running. I used to have it in my head that I hated running, like I found no joy in it. But there's quite a lot of countryside near where I live and running through there, it was very peaceful, especially when it's very empty. It's like all your problems don't really matter while you're running. I got out for, like, twenty minutes a day, and I didn't have to think about coronavirus and not going to school and all that.

I did try and set up various routines, like, trying to keep my brain active. I was listening to a lot more music, because that was a nice way to kill the time. I was trying to listen to, like, an album a day. I started off going through the whole discography of the bands I liked, so I started off with Radiohead and then I moved onto artists like Björk. Then I would end up asking my friends about albums they liked, and I got into a lot of music that I listened to as a kid. There's a band LCD Soundsystem, and MGMT, and Nine Inch Nails – they were bands that I relied on a lot of the time. I kept that up for a little while, and then I moved onto watching a film a day. So, I went through various different routines.

With my friends, most of the time we would just talk. It was nearly every day we were speaking to each other, and we still speak quite a lot now. It was very strange at first; it was surprising that we didn't run out of things to talk about. Quite a lot of us are probably closer than we've ever been. Once we could go out and see each other again, it was very strange, it was very different; even then, we would just sit and talk.

After Christmas, it was straight into the next lockdown. That was frustrating because we'd gotten used to being in college. I mean I understand why they had to do it, and I'm behind it all the way if it's going to make England safer for a lot of people, then I completely get it, but it didn't change how irritating it was. That lockdown was definitely different. They'd already brought in online lessons, so we could still do our work from home, so weeks had a structure to them. It didn't feel as dismal, for me at least.

My birthday was in that lockdown. I woke up fairly late, I remember. We did some baking because we were going to have a big homemade Chinese meal for dinner. I think we watched some films in the afternoon, and then I spent the rest of the evening playing some party games online. There's some Pictionary-type game that we like to play, and some wordplay games as well. All of my friends came on to wish me happy birthday, which was nice.

I think everyone had their days in the first lockdown where it just felt, oh well, if nothing's going to get better tomorrow, why do anything? There were times when I felt like that, but I think I got over it fairly quick because there were a lot of times when my mum felt like that, and I had to, kind of, snap her out of it, and say, 'No, there are things you can do, you might as well use this time for the best.' She's a hairdresser. Seeing your mum upset about something is concerning, and I'd never seen my mum like that before. My dad could still go to work, because he does warehouse work, so they were allowed in.

Last year, it seems almost like a wasted year, but, when I think about it, I spent a lot of time on things that I otherwise wouldn't have, so it gave me a nice break, for the most part. I think having so much time with yourself, you're bound to understand yourself a little better, understand how you work and what your interests are. I suppose you're bound to mature a bit. I know my friend said that he saw it as a privilege. He said, 'We're never going to get a break like this again in our lives, most likely.' So I think I somewhat took advantage of it.

# Leslye Russell-Pierce

*It's been a bit of a ride*

*12 March 2021*

My life's been very turbulent for the last two years. I only got married four years ago, and then my daughter became quite ill. She's thirty-one. She lived in London; she's very capable, damn good degree. But last January, she was actually in a secure unit in London, so our life centred around the hospital. Not just the hospital visits; I was there for every consultant visit, which was twice a week. Friends and family helped out with Sam, my twenty-nine-year-old son who's got Down's, because I didn't want to drag him up to London two or three times a week. Debby was hell-bent on committing suicide; it was the only way out for her. She was diagnosed with bipolar with severe suicidal tendencies in November 2018, so we had been going through ups and downs – good times, bad times – but she was in the secure unit when the news of Covid started coming through.

We got her out two weeks before lockdown started. I personally think the hospital knew what was coming and were trying to get people out, so she was with us two weeks prior to lockdown, and then right the way though lockdown. It was difficult to begin with; Debby has always been a very highly strung young lady. If someone had told me she would come and live with me for a year, I'd have given it three or four days before we killed each other. But we have had one argument in a year. I can't believe it myself, and that is the honest truth. We've had one set of cross words, and we both apologised to each other after half an hour of cooling down. In lockdown I felt so sorry for her, I needed to protect her. The world was shit with Covid anyway, but for Debby personally going through an extremely bad series of bipolar crises, it was difficult.

To have to lock my own daughter ... We had to put bolts on the back gates, we had to lock her in the house every night and hide the keys and hide all the medicines. It was what we were told we should do. And once you hit that, and you live through that ...

We have talked about things she never knew about me, I never know about her; there is nothing off the table. We can talk about anything now, and I do mean extremes. Anything. At the beginning, being here was where Deb was and needed to be, but then, because of lockdown, she didn't have a choice, so she had to stay for the full twelve weeks. She would go, 'I'm feeling much better now, Mum, I think I'll go back to my flat in London.' She couldn't do it.

We've only got a two-bedroom bungalow. Luckily, when we got the bungalow, we bought a very good bed sofa. Because of the drugs Debby is on, she needs to be in bed by nine o'clock. So, at nine o'clock, we swap – we make the bed for her, we go to our bedroom, she stays in the lounge. My husband – like I said I've only been married four years – he's incredible with her. I don't know what I'd have done without him, to be honest.

And Debby and Sam were amazing together. I think she learnt to get to know him again. Every morning, they done Wicks out on the patio.[16] She would try yoga with him, which was hilarious. I must admit, that first lockdown, we laughed

---

16 Joe Wicks, fitness coach, TV presenter and social media personality whose 'PE with Joe' became one of the most followed fitness accounts during lockdown.

our way through it. Debby and I talked about our infatuation with Chris Whitty;[17] we both fancied the arse off of him, god knows why! Our friendship grew really close. So by the end of the first lockdown, we were all pretty happy, actually.

Then after lockdown finished at the end of June, Debby went back to London. She lasted three weeks. She was found outside her flats and rushed back into hospital. Me and my husband Jon went up to London and cleared her flat. There was no point spending thousands on rent. We used to call it the most expensive storage unit in London. She always hoped to go back, and then at one point she said, 'Mum, the flat needs to go. I don't want to ever go back in there again.' Luckily we have a garage, so we could store her stuff.

It's been sad. Really sad. I can't say hurtful, because she doesn't mean to hurt, but desperate and sad. And I'm just so glad I can see her coming out of it again. I know in two years' time we could be back in it. With bipolar, you never know. I did get to the point where … To sit up at night planning your daughter's funeral.

This time last year, when she was readmitted – and I mean we do laugh about this now, but it's very dark – they asked her something about her emotions, and she said, 'If my mum died tonight, I wouldn't care. I wouldn't cry.' So that's the thing we now laugh about; I go, 'Great, wouldn't even bloody cry if I died, would you?'

She sat on a work surface in her room with me, my husband and the psychiatrist, and she just rocked and banged her head against the wall. She said to me, 'That's it, Mum, I can't do this any more. If you love me, you'd let me die.' We drove out

---

17 Chief Medical Officer for England who had a high-profile role during the Covid-19 pandemic.

of the London hospital, and I said to Jon, 'I've lost her, she's gone.' And I never thought I'd get her back. I think I must've cried all the way home, because I never, ever thought I'd get her back.

So it's been a bit of a ride, and then we've got Sam. He's been resilient, really resilient. He's very adaptable. He was born in Sweden, we moved around a lot, and he's always the one who fits in, just gets on with it. He's kept us smiling. In Sweden, when I had Sam, the last thing the doctor said was, 'Apart from the obvious, you have a very healthy boy. Now go, live your life.'

Him and Debby's relationship, seeing that blossom – and it really has blossomed – it's been lovely. And when they wind each other up, it's so funny, because he does wind her up, he will tease and tease, she'll shout at him and then she'll chase him down the corridor. It's like a nuthouse in here some nights, to be honest.

Sam's only been upset a couple of times during this, and once was on his iPad to his brother. I've got two other boys as well, two older boys; one is in the Rhondda Valley, and one is in Essex – both ends of the M4. Sam used to go up to his brother's in Wales every weekend, so he was used to seeing a lot of Danny, and then one night he said to Danny, 'Wales, me.' And Danny said, 'No, darling, Wales is closed.' And that was like Sam's whole world fell to pieces.

Sam's in a tennis club, football club. He does drama, a choir. He goes to the gym once a week. He does boxing once a week. And suddenly all of those things, one by one, stopped. He goes past shops, and he'll go, 'Oh, they're closed. Oh, they're closed!'

We told him there's a germ, that he has to be very careful not to touch people or touch things. My husband one day panicked; we'd been somewhere and Sam went to touch his eyes. Jon was, 'No, no, Sam, don't touch your eyes.' So, for a long while, it was, 'Oh no, I can't touch my eyes, can't touch eyes.' So, he knows there's a germ, he knows it makes people poorly because he watches the news with me. That's his level, and that's all he needs.

Sam, he's funny, he makes everyone smile. It's an honour to be Sam's mum. He is such a pleasure to be around. And my husband is very protective of Sam, very protective. I didn't know this at first, obviously, because I didn't know him, but he had a disabled brother, physically disabled. So his childhood, he said, was spent on the floor playing with his big brother, who couldn't walk.

We haven't got a lot of behaviours that can go with Down's syndrome – aggression, stubbornness, anger. The worst thing he does if he really disagrees with us, we used to call it the Sammy shuffle: he'd shuffle back down the hallway and mutter under his breath. Well, we turn that into a joke, so now when we're playing around, we go to him, 'Go on, do a Sammy shuffle for us.'

He is a personality all of his own, he really is. I mean, we were sat here the other week, and he loves *Joseph*, the musical, and he came down dressed in Jon's dressing gown, because it's striped, and a tea towel across his head, singing *Joseph*. Then he'll come back down again wearing a fez doing the Sam dance. We're just sat here looking at each other, as if to go, what the hell is he doing? If he wants to dance to *X Factor* on the telly, I don't care, so long as he is doing no one any harm, he is being appropriate.

And if you want to know more about the sort of character that Sammy is, he was very ill about twelve years ago. He was in intensive care, he was on life support for six weeks, we thought we'd lost him. So they tried to get the tube off a couple of times, and eventually they said, 'No, it needs to come out and we need to see if he can breathe.' And they took the tube out, and they withdrew the drugs. And we were all in there, me, my ex-husband, the specialist, the anaesthetist, and slowly this little one eye opens, and Sam looked around the room, and you know what his first words were? He just said, 'What the fuck?' There was deathly quiet around the room. And then he asked for a bacon sandwich, which is his favourite.

This house, there is a lot of love. And yeah, I try to make life fun. It's got to be fun; I'm not one to sit around being bloody miserable, there's no point. My dad was a mad Irishman, and our house was always full of laughter. I was brought up without a mum. My mum left when I was four. There was four of us. Dad got custody of all of us, he brought us up. We had a crazy life. Not quite normal, but always full of fun, absolutely full of fun.

My sister was telling Debby all about some of the things that happened when we grew up, and Debby said to me afterwards, 'You know, you had a really shit childhood.' From an outsider, okay, my mum left, Dad was in and out of hospital. At one point, he was in hospital in London, and we weren't allowed to tell anyone because social services would have taken us away. My oldest brother was sixteen, and I was eleven, so my dad was gone for four or five months. We had a neighbour about four doors down, amazing woman, she would check on us, make sure we had everything we needed.

It didn't come to a head until, one day, I had cookery on the Monday morning, and I turned up at school without my cookery stuff. The teacher, who I hated anyway, had a go at me, and my best friend turned around and said, 'Do you know what it's like for her with her dad in hospital?' And it all came out. I was marched to the headmaster's office. My brother was brought down to the headmaster.

And I tell you what, the headmaster couldn't have done more for us. He was amazing. He said, 'No one would've known, you're all clean, you're spotless, homework's done, you turn up every day.' He said, 'We will keep this between us.' He ordered the bitch of a cookery teacher to make sure she brought the ingredients for me every week. So you know what? I'm happy. I don't think I've had it rough. I had a dad who adored me, adored my brothers and sisters. I think I had a lovely childhood. I was always loved.

And, like I say, in this house there is a lot of love and a lot of fun – the Irish sense of humour, my dad, that's where it's come from. And when it comes to Sam, if my husband was here, he always says to people, 'We're facilitators, we're facilitating what Sam likes to do. And we've got to give him the best shot at everything.' So during lockdown we helped Sam dress up each week for the Clap for Carers.[18]

It began the first week it started. Sam heard what was going on, because he could hear the people in the street, so I said, 'They're clapping for heroes, and next week, when Jon's better, we can go out.' Jon was really ill with Covid, and we wouldn't even open the doors, you know, because we were so scared of making other people ill. Sam is a bit of a character, so the next week I said to him, 'Do you want to clap for heroes?' 'Wait!' he said. Then he came out in a Superman outfit. He loves being in a onesie, so he's got Superman, Spider-Man and Batman. So that's how it started. And then I said to him, 'Right, why don't we do someone who helps us? What do we see every day?' 'Lorries!' So the next one he dressed up as a lorry driver. And then every week it gave us something to talk about. 'Who else helps us?' 'Oh, doctors.' So he dressed up as a doctor, then a postwoman, because I'm friendly with the postwoman. We had

---

18 The Clap for Heroes, initially called the Clap for Our Carers, first took place on 26 March 2020. It was a weekly round of applause, typically done from someone's front door or window, to show appreciation for workers in the NHS and other key workers during the pandemic.

the doctor's outfit. The postwoman helped us. My husband has a lot of hi-vis because of his work. Then we had to beg, steal and borrow! We got a fire kit because Sam does something called the Salamander course where he's a fireman for a week, so we know the bloke in charge of the fire station.

People used to wave at Sam, and then as time went on you could see people nudging each other: 'What is he this week?' He's done nineteen, and we're going to end it in two weeks, because any medical person will know the other word for Down's syndrome is Trisomy 21, for having an extra copy of the twenty-first chromosome, and so we decided we would do twenty-one tributes.

I'd never say it was a good thing, but lockdown has done us no harm. We've not asked for any help from anyone. We've got on with it. I'm proud that we've done it on our own, and we've all become so close because of it.

I think I had one night where I just got absolutely fed up with the world. I'd just had enough. I was desperate to see my other two sons. I have a granddaughter who's four years old, who I've seen three times in a year. I send her a parcel every two weeks – there's usually an item of clothing, a toy and some sweets – just so she doesn't forget us. I know we talk on Face-Time, but it was the first time at Christmas she hasn't been with us. My other son is in London; I've seen him twice in a year. It hurts, it really does hurt. And I think I'd just had enough one day. I ended up walking out of the house, picking up the car keys. I went to Lydiard Park. It was actually the night of the storm about six weeks ago. Sat in the entrance to the car park, had a cry for half an hour, and came home.

I'm a very sociable person, involved in a lot of charity work and stuff like that, and it's just all stopped. Before lockdown I'd have friends popping over, I'd be out visiting friends. I swim four days a week. The minute I dropped Sam off at UET[19] I was straight down to the gym for a swim. I call it head clearing: I could just get in the water, and everything else disappeared, any problems, anything I had to think about. So that is the one thing I'm desperate to get back to. So now I play a lot of Candy Crush; that's a time I don't think about anything else.

And, of course, all the activities with Sam. So, Tuesday night would be choir. And me and Jon are not the parents who just drop him off. We go and we stay there for two hours while he's having choir practice; we do the drinks at half-time, we make sure there are biscuits. When he goes to the football club on a Wednesday, again, we don't drop him off, we go, and we sit, and we watch. So there was all that social interaction – a lot of it revolved around Sam – and I miss all of that.

I can't wait to get back to normal. I can't wait for Sam's clubs to open up and let him blossom again. Sam's just been held back, he's not been damaged whatsoever. We've made sure of that. We have had competition weekends on the TV – Xbox connect – where all four of us, we would have an avatar and we play golf, we play darts, we do running courses. We've had music nights, putting musicals on that he loves, and we'll get snacks and he'll dress up. So we've tried to give him as much as we can. I don't want him to get bored. I don't want him to be damaged by this, so the more I can do to help him enjoy this time, it'll be better for him.

*Afterword – one year later*

Debby's been poorly again; she spent four months in a unit recently. We only got her out two weeks ago, but we're getting through that again.

---

19 Uplands Enterprise Trust, a Swindon-based charity for young people with special educational needs.

After lockdown started to loosen up, Sam wanted to go back to everything – go back to his football, go back to his sports. And he was owed a lot of presents from brothers and sisters. We've always told our children not to buy him presents; they buy him memories. So they do things with him, or they pay for us to do things with him. So he was owed a speedboat up the Thames, he was owed a zip wire, he was owed all sorts.

It was coming up to Sam's thirtieth birthday, and it was Jon's sixtieth birthday two days later, so we decided to launch Sam's twenty-one challenges to coincide with their birthdays.[20] We had a launch/birthday party and a lot of friends started ringing and saying, 'Well, what shall we do for his birthday?' And I said, 'Buy him experiences.'

One friend said, 'We'll buy him a flight! A flying lesson.' I went, 'No, too expensive.' But there's actually a charity called Aerobility and it isn't that expensive. Then another friend bought him a helicopter flight! Things started snowballing from there, and then Sam would run stalls and make money that way. And then we thought, oh, a Christmas raffle. I contacted some of the firms in Swindon: Tesco's, Asda, places like that; Cold Harbour gave us an incredible hamper. What we were doing was telling a story, and part of this story is to promote positive Down's syndrome awareness: *changing perceptions*, that was the hashtag on everything, getting people to think about people with Down's syndrome, and not just stereotype them. Sam's had over 250,000 likes on Facebook throughout this, and from, I think, twenty-six countries.

Then it led onto other things, which we didn't know about. So a friend nominated Sam to be a baton runner, and he actually

---

20  From flying a helicopter to driving a train, walking over the O₂ Arena and training with Swindon Town, Sam conquered twenty-one challenges during the year to show that people with Down's can achieve their ambitions. Through these challenges, he raised over £6,500 for charity.

is going to be one of the Queen's baton runners![21] Not only that, they chose nine people in the country out of 2,500 to be the face of the baton runners' relay, and so Sam had to go up and do the promotion work. He had his photograph taken by the top sports photographer in the country. That was incredible. And I nominated him for a 'Pride of Swindon', because I was so proud, and yesterday he got that award.

So, yeah, lockdown did happen, and as a family it brought us closer together. My granddaughter I now see on a regular basis, which is fantastic. Debby has been very poorly, but we've got her home and we're piecing her back together again. They've kept her job open; they've refused to take her resignation. And when she gets better, she'll start back. We'll get her a flat nearby; she needs to be near us, she can't be back in London. Sam's kept us going, his twenty-one challenges have given us something to focus on, and we've had so much fun.

---

21 The baton relay is a relay around the world held prior to the beginning of the Commonwealth Games. The baton contains a message from the Head of the Commonwealth, which is then read aloud at the end of the relay to officially open the Games.

# Junab Ali

*You just felt, what's happening?*
*Are we watching a movie or something?*

*24 March 2021*

I've grown up as a brown skin/Asian/Muslim – whatever you want to call it – with prejudice and racism, all my life. I had to break barriers. Going to school, being the only non-white kid, ninety-nine per cent of my friends were white. I clearly remember, in my primary school, first I was called Gandhi, because of Mahatma Gandhi – they all thought I was from India, because of people's ignorance – long as you're brown, you're Gandhi. Then it was Paki, the dirty word. Then you were Asians. And then finally it was the Muslim, and that is still playing its part.

The next generation, I think, they will do a little bit better; like my kids, their white friends don't seem to have an issue with people of other races and religions. So it is slowly happening, but it's taking a long time. And I hope we have that patience and perseverance, and we don't have riots and things to achieve equality in society.

I was the only non-white councillor in 2008 at the council; now both parties have got ethnic minority councillors. When I first got elected, the British Bangladeshis said, 'Oh, you're the Bangladeshi councillor,' and the Muslims said, 'Oh, he's a Muslim councillor.' I said, 'I'm very proud of my cultural heritage – I am a British Bangladeshi and a Muslim – but

I'm not here representing just you or my religion, I'm here to represent every single resident.'

Swindon Borough Council, they've come a long way, but there's a hell of a long way to go to make everybody feel that they will be treated equally and fairly, irrespective of their backgrounds or religion. We try to brush it under the carpet; we shouldn't. We need to talk openly, rather than saying, 'I'm not racist.' I'm sure we are. We all are prejudiced or racist in some form or another. So, the only way is we talk about it. If you don't mingle with somebody, how are you going to know about their way of life or the type of human being they are?

Our families came after the Second World War. Our forefathers didn't come to settle here. They just thought, right, come here, earn some money, go back home. They had that huge connection with the country of their origin. Money was all sent back to the country of origin; so if you're from Bangladesh, India, Pakistan, Sri Lanka, most of your earnings were going there. Nothing was spent here. And now, guess what? This generation, they don't want to even know. All those hundreds of thousands of pounds that was invested in the Indian subcontinent. It's fine, it's the motherland of our heritage, but this is our country, this is our home.

I started my business while I was at college doing my A levels. My family's background is in catering, in Indian restaurants, so I took over one of the family restaurants. From there, by the time I was twenty-one, I had four restaurants, fifty staff working.

You're young and your blood is hot and the world is your oyster. I was running everything. I kind of loved it, until I got married and had children, and then it really hit home because with catering, it is very long hours, and it takes tenacity to stay up there. You know, I booked holidays and I had to cancel because we were short of staff; didn't have a weekend for twenty years with the family.

But before that, I never stopped educating myself, starting from basic computing to understanding how to do Word, PowerPoint, Excel, spreadsheets and all. I just kept going, one thing to another. I came across a one-day electrical course. Never touched electrics before – I wouldn't even take the switch out. From that, there was a course for three years to get into electrical installation. And I thought, why not? It's daytime, I can take one day off a week. So, yeah, did the three years' course, got qualified as an electrician and then set up a business on the side.

By 2011, I no longer needed the income from the restaurants to have a life. So I just decided, right, that's it, I'm done. Wish I did it ten years earlier, but things are how they are. And now looking at it with Covid, glad I changed my career path, because catering and hospitality, they have been hammered.

I run my electrical contracting business, ninety per cent is domestic, ten per cent is commercial. I have got contacts and connections that, if I wanted to, within a year or two, I could have a company with a hundred or two hundred employees, chasing all the contracts. For me now, I'm not into that. For me, it's just to pay my mortgage, pay my bills, look after the family, and, if Covid lets us, go on one holiday a year. I am content with that. Little is enough. I think we need to give back to our community and have a life. So, now, I have a better life; health-wise, I'm mentally and physically much better.

For me, nothing changed until Boris Johnson announced the lockdown on 23 March [2020]. All works were not cancelled, they were postponed. That was fine; in my new house we had lists of work to get on with.

My wife's a teaching assistant, so they closed for a week or so, and then it was for the key workers' children, so they had to volunteer. They weren't doing a rota, it's people who volunteered, so she volunteered to go. They were doing one week or two weeks, then having a week's break. I've got type 2 diabetes, so she had to be careful with that, that she wasn't bringing Covid back to me.

My oldest daughter, she was at university last year, so she had to do her final exams online from home. My son, it's his final year at Reading. And the youngest, she's at work. With the kids at uni, they were coming back every two weeks anyway – because of our cultural and religious background, family is very important.

As a Muslim, one of the articles of faith is five-times prayer, and mosque, especially for the males, is a very essential part of our religion. In my lifetime, and many people's, it's the first time mosque is closed. With lockdown, people find that their whole world has just changed upside down, and at times like that you need places of worships, like mosque, the church, synagogue, the temples and whatever. Those are places where you can reflect and come together. The priest or the imam or the reverends or whoever, they seem to calm people down so they find their way of releasing their worries and tensions, spiritually. When that was taken away as well, people were on their own and it seriously affected a lot of people. When there is no guidance, no men above to tell you, right, stay calm, do this, do that, some people have found it very tough.

A lot of Muslims, I think, suddenly realised, why do they just go to Friday prayer? What is their religion about? A lot of people have got a book of the Quran, some of them don't even read it. But when the lockdown happened, take it from me, they all started reading and understanding. I've got some books behind me that I've had for a few years, haven't touched. I've read quite a lot in the lockdown – every morning, I take ten or fifteen minutes to read something.

With mosque closed, we had to take responsibility. I had to do the prayer for the family here. Actually, it's the first time in my life that we, as a whole family, read together. I was leading them in prayer, and that was, you know, honourable. It is unimaginable. I would follow the imam; now I'm leading my family! It's the first time it dawned on me, you know, I should have been doing that before, because if you read the Quran and the Hadith, you have to lead your family.

When you're reading the prayer, you have to read the Quran text, and I thought I knew it enough for me to pray. When you do it to yourself, you don't know if you're saying it properly or not. When you have to say it out loud with people listening, they pick up on things, so a few times, after I finished, I was told by my daughter or my wife or my son, 'Oh Dad, you know, on that note, you made a mistake.' I thought, right, I have to learn, make sure I don't make that mistake again.

Nowadays, thank God, we've got translations, because when I was growing up, seventies and eighties, we had nothing in English. You had Arabic, or my heritage from Bangladesh, so Bengali. Although my second language is English, I can only read fluently in English. I'm learning to read the Quran in Arabic, but if you asked me a few years ago, I couldn't even tell you a single word, apart from Allah. The more I study, the more deep the understanding, and it just blows away all these myths and all these things people talk about.

In the Quran, when it says do not believe what the imam tells you or the priest tells you or somebody tells you, how do you know what they are telling you is truth or lies? So, go to all four corners of the earth and acquire knowledge, because then you can tell if the imam is saying something from the Quran or the Hadith, or he's just made something up and you're just the sheep, following the flock. If you don't understand a single word of Arabic, how do you know? Take my mother, for example:

she's illiterate; she prays five times a day, and you have to use the Arabic words – doesn't understand a single word. But God wants all of us to acquire knowledge, have intellect, use our intellect to see if it is true or false, right or wrong. And it's very interesting because the more I go deeper, the more I have time for faith and understanding.

I don't know if you've been to Muslim countries, but in this country we're not allowed to broadcast outside the mosque. You have a transmitter at the mosque, so it's broadcast in the mosque, then the majority of the mosque users, they've got a receiver at home; it's sort of like listening to a radio. So whatever is announced at the mosque, they can hear, like the call to prayer. In our mosque, our transmitters were installed nearly twenty-two years ago, so we have updated our transmitters; Covid-19 accelerated that.

Some mosques and imams had gone online even before the pandemic, trying to reach people, because it was getting hard to reach the next generation. It's very difficult for the ones who weren't already prepared for online broadcast and online prayers. But I think what has happened, people who lacked certain things, this Covid-19 has woken them up. I think this has taught us that we need to be ready for any eventuality. So if the mosque or place of worship is shut, or the country is shut, we have a way of communicating to people effectively.

Ramadan was coming about a month after full lockdown started. It's really hard because never in my whole life have we not been able to go to the mosque for the Ramadan prayers, not go to the Friday prayers, not have an Eid prayer. I don't know how to explain it; you can't, because you feel hollow inside, something's missing.

A day before we were meant to celebrate Eid al-Adha, the government announced from midnight, lockdown. All the families had prepared foods for family members coming over, everybody had been preparing for a week or so. Suddenly, at midnight, the night before, we're told, right, no meeting of family, friends, total lockdown. And it got to a minority who think the government was against them because of their faith. They're saying, 'Okay, you're going to have a lockdown, but if the virus has already spread, why couldn't you just wait one day to celebrate Eid, and say, from midnight tomorrow night, we are in total lockdown?' I think that really annoyed and upset and frustrated a lot of people, and it gives that section the excuse to say that the government and other agencies and organisations are against us. And I do understand that. I think Boris was ill-advised and the timing couldn't have been worse.

*6 May 2021*

Since the mosques and places of worship have been allowed to reopen, I think that has given a little bit of confidence back to the people, a bit of relief. But in Islam, when you go to mosque, you do not leave any space – we pray together, shoulder to shoulder. We stand compacted, unified. It makes you feel part of your fellow man and woman in your faith. Shoulder to shoulder at the mosque, we could fit three hundred, sometimes at a squash, four hundred people.

We had to rejig the numbers to only allow ninety-five people, because of the two-metre distance. To all of us, it was just unknown; it felt weird and alien. You just felt, what's happening? Are we watching a movie or something? Are we dreaming this or is this the reality?

In Islam, it's set times, that's the problem. Friday prayer is at the set time – it's called Jumu'ah – so everybody wants to be there at that minute to that prayer, because otherwise, for some of them, the world ends. It's ingrained in our heads and our upbringing that you have to be there at that time. So, what we decided because of Covid, when we opened back, we had to do two sessions of the prayer, rather than one. Both were filled all the time.

For my sins, I'm one of the caretakers. We had to do the risk assessment and measure up. There was an app meant to come out, a booking app – that all failed miserably! So what we did was first come first served. First, people thought, oh yeah, doesn't matter, I can just trot along like usual, I'll get in. But they forgot it's a socially distanced place, so it's gone down from three or four hundred to ninety-five. Soon as ninety-five was filled, we would lock the doors. I'm hated by some because I take a very firm line. I say to all of them, 'Listen, for my son, I won't save him a special place; if he gets there in time, that's it. Otherwise, he misses the first prayer by a minute or so, he has to wait for the next one.' After a couple of weeks, they got it.

As a Muslim, you have to do ablution – you have to wash your hands and your feet. Normally, in our mosque, you come through the back entrance where the ablution area and toilet facilities are, do your ablution; ninety-nine per cent would do it at the mosque. Now, no ablution at the mosque, no toilet facilities – or we did keep one, just for emergencies.

For a lot of Muslims, it's quite offensive to have shoes inside the prayer area. Okay, but listen, this is the time we live in and it is stated in the Quran and the Hadith, you know, when you have times like this, normal regulations don't have to be observed. We said bring a carrier bag, because at least you can feel that your shoes are inside the carrier bag, so it's not putting dirt and whatever unpure on your carpet where you worship.

It was an enormous task for us, because a place of worship, ninety-nine per cent is run by volunteers, and nobody had that set of skills to do so much, from risk assessment to laying things to keep a social distance, getting PPE, getting signage, getting sanitisers and getting masks for people who haven't got them. People had to have a temperature check, people had to register – track and trace wasn't even working properly, so, you know, name, telephone numbers and a postcode.

I say to people now, life's too short, so live your life to the full, and let other people live their lives to the full, because you don't know; like, one of my friends, Covid, he's gone within a few days. And another one, he was a community member with me in the mosque, he used to wear masks and hand gloves in his own house, and he got it. He didn't recover consciousness for six weeks and died in hospital.

I think the last year has been a real time to reflect. People have taken stock of their lives, what it means. I think perception has changed, totally. As I said to you, I don't want to be filthy rich. I think the pendulum had gone materialistic and individualistic. That way, I think, Covid has brought the pendulum back to understanding and being together, rather than chasing worldly things and materialistic things. I think we appreciate everything now, and I hope that lasts a long time.

*Afterword – one year later*

Mosque was chock-a-block today because of the school holiday, upstairs and downstairs. I still wear my mask; some people are still choosing to bring their mat. Ninety-five per cent have done away with everything. Not being able to go for a year, it has made people appreciate the place of worship, and be more respectful as well. It's brought some new people into the mosque, because I think they've woken up to faith, that something was missing.

With the mosque open, I'm not now leading my family in prayer. I might do in Ramadan, because nobody likes to break their fast at the mosque. So, when we break the fast and the first prayer, we'll do it together, and that's a new thing since Covid. Then I'll go to the mosque for two hours each night.

It was a huge responsibility leading my family in prayer – all these years you're reading by yourself and then when you read it out loud in Arabic, you didn't want to be found out that you weren't doing it properly. But actually, that fear probably turned me to go and study, go and read it properly, go and do more digging, more research. So, okay, I've made a mistake, I will double up and make sure I don't do that again. I'll improve and become a better person, rather than take it negatively, like, 'Oh, I'm not going to read it now, go and read it by yourselves individually.' I dust myself down and make sure that next time I do better.

I hope people's appreciation will continue – appreciation of people working in supermarkets, of people working in retail, of people delivering letters and parcels. You know, smile because we appreciate each other, say 'thank you' and 'please'; it doesn't cost anything. So many conflicts could be avoided by courtesies. I'm an optimistic person, I want to see a beautiful world – beautiful human beings being loving to each other.

# Zoe and Kelvin Jones

*Covid – I guess it's been a bit of a blessing for us*

*26 February 2021*

ZOE: Been a lot of sadness, hasn't there? Some people got horrific, sad stories related to Covid. We've had adversity pre-Covid, but I guess it's been a bit of a blessing for us, Covid. It's more like a positive —

KELVIN: — in some ways —

ZOE: — with what happened.

KELVIN: Yeah.

ZOE: Well, positive out of a negative, I guess. So, our youngest son, Nathan, he is now eleven, but when he was eight, he came forward to disclose sexual abuse. The perpetrator was fifteen. Dealing with the challenging behaviours and the trauma has been quite difficult. So, then we go to March 2020, when we first went into lockdown, it was really, really positive, wasn't it?

KELVIN: Yeah.

ZOE: Lockdown, as a result of being at home with him, we then got to the bottom of his triggers, understood his responses, his challenging behaviours. Obviously, we knew he was suffering with flashbacks and things like that, but I could never get him to understand his own PTSD and understand his own triggers. So, having that time with him at home with us —

KELVIN: — was a blessing in disguise.

ZOE: Yeah, it was a blessing in disguise. It helped massively. I mean —

KELVIN: — we spent so much time —

ZOE: — we got a lot closer. I remained working, but working from home. Kelvin was not working at all during lockdown. So yeah, Nathan became closer to you, didn't he?

KELVIN: Yeah. Understanding him is what helps. You know, finally, after all this time, it kind of clicked because we spent so much time with him. We had more time to, you know, adjust and look at things a different way.

ZOE: A lot of the challenging behaviours would be happening at school. So, although we'd hear about them, we weren't with it from beginning to end. So, because he was at home, we were seeing and being able to question him and spend that time with him.

KELVIN: I guess we can relate to things better now, between us.

ZOE: Before lockdown, I think I naively thought the abuse had stopped, he's safe, he'll be okay. And, of course, he is okay, but then I guess you're dealing with the trauma afterwards, aren't you? The abuse lasted for four years. The last two years of it were full-on rape. During that time, I think he just went into survival mode. When it stopped, he had to address the trauma and the feelings, and that's almost harder, you know. And that journey —

KELVIN: We're still discovering how to tackle his anxieties.

ZOE: Yeah, but he's so much stronger. We've got coping mechanisms in place for him. We've got him to the point where he can recognise his own early warning signs so that it doesn't manifest in bad behaviour, you know, recognising that he needs to step away.

Also, like, memory thought interruptions: if he's triggered and it's taking him back, to stop that memory, replace it with a happy memory. School's a massive trigger. There's so many triggers, you know, and it was all about explaining to him we can't ever take certain things away. Like smells – coffee was a trigger for him. And BO.

KELVIN: Soaps.

ZOE: Shampoos.

KELVIN: Foods.

ZOE: Deodorant.

KELVIN: Bleach.

ZOE: So cleaning products at school. The perpetrator used to spray, I think it must have been a bathroom cleaner —

KELVIN: We don't know.

ZOE: He used to spray that to clean up after himself, like the mess on the bed, or whatever. Nathan would be avoidant of, like, showering and getting changed. I guess his coping mechanism is avoidance.

KELVIN: That's how he's survived all this time.

ZOE: How that presents itself is like, 'Nathan, go and shower.' 'Do I have to shower now?' 'Yeah. Can you go and shower please.' 'Why've I got to shower, I showered yesterday?' 'Right, Nathan, we shower every day, can you go and shower please.' 'Oh, it's just stupid, what do I want to go and shower for?' So then you automatically go into parent mode: 'Right, I'm asking you to go and shower, now go and shower, I don't want to argue about it.'

KELVIN: So he would always have a fight before he does what he's told.

ZOE: You get into this battle, and then of course I'm telling him off and actually it's not defiance, it's not naughtiness, it's avoidance of a trauma reminder. I think that's what lockdown taught me. You'd have the same sort of thing for him getting dressed and undressed; he'd constantly want me in the room: 'Can you come and get my clothes for me, can you help me get dressed?' And then of course I guess you're in mum mode again, and you're like, 'You're in Year 7, for goodness' sakes! Right, okay, I'll come and help you get dressed because you're eleven and can't get dressed.' And that's actually quite belittling and would be quite damaging for him. I then said to him, 'Nathan, is this triggering you, does this make you feel prickly?' 'Yes.' 'Why does it make you?' 'Because he used to make me get undressed.' So we put things in place: started him off getting dressed in my bedroom with me being around. Like doing a staggered approach. And now he's at the point where he gets dressed, no problem; he goes in the shower, no problem.

KELVIN: This is only through lockdown. This is recent.

ZOE: Where lockdown's been so helpful. Without lockdown, I don't think we would have —

KELVIN: It would have taken longer. I think it would have taken a lot longer.

ZOE: I don't think it would have —

KELVIN: Not everything.

ZOE: — come out at all. If you think what a day consists of – getting up, getting the children to school, drop them off at school, go to work, get the kids home, fed, homework, things like that. Life's not like that at the moment, is it? You're just at home. It's having the time of lockdown, I think, that's specific to lockdown.

KELVIN: Nathan disclosed in stages through the years. It just brings it back again. You have to find a way of helping him, but you always feel the guilt as well.

ZOE: When he first disclosed to me, what he disclosed was the perpetrator was like, um, you know, like, masturbating in front of him. That was in January 2018 that he told me that. By May 2019, so over fourteen to fifteen months, it came out slowly, slowly – there was oral sexual assaults, there was anal … Full anal penetration. It comes out in dribs and drabs. So by May 2019 I realised that my child was abused over a period of four years, two years of which was full-on penetration. And then it's like, I guess, the massive sense of loss. I think that's what I struggle with. Like his childhood's been lost. And I struggle with guilt. We discipline our children, and that's a normal thing to do, but then, like that example I gave you of me almost belittling him about not being able to get dressed, it's like I sit there and I think, how damaging is that for him? Even like smell, I was using the same bloomin' softener as they were using, wasn't I? So the smell on our clothes —

KELVIN: So that would affect him as well, because he didn't want to change into new clothes, because he remembers.

ZOE: Like, you sit down and you think, that poor child, so many reminders that I didn't even have a clue. I noticed his behaviours very early on, like Nathan would get anxiety and would physically be sick, but there were never any additional learning needs in school, so he had no diagnosis, it was just speech delay.

KELVIN: Nathan always had a speech delay, so he actually didn't even start speaking until he was assisted with a speech therapist through his primary school.

ZOE: When he started school in reception, he probably said about ten words.

KELVIN: Maybe that was an opportunity – a vulnerability – for the perpetrator. Nathan's communication skills were pretty weak, verbally, so you know, how do you communicate that problem you have? So, I mean, it was grooming to start off with, but —

ZOE: Well, from the age of four to six, it was what you'd describe as sexual assault. But then Nathan's very clear that in 2015 the first rape took place. So Nathan would have been six, the perpetrator would have been fifteen. Then eight years old, he disclosed. So, two years of like … It's long and enduring sexual abuse, really, isn't it?

The perpetrator still lives on our street. You see, it's a neighbour. I was friends with his mother. You know, we went on holidays together, we had keys to each other's houses. I used to say, I don't think it's healthy, a fifteen-year-old comes and knocks for a six-year-old. And then, you know, you're busy with work, or doing different things, so you think, oh it's fine, we know him, we know the family. So access was very easy, and then I guess Nathan looked up to him, as I guess you do at that age.

KELVIN: Yeah.

ZOE: He talks of one incident in our shed.

KELVIN: He didn't go there very often.

ZOE: Predominantly it happened at the perpetrator's. The shed came out during lockdown, because the window behind us —

KELVIN: — looks onto the garden.

ZOE: Straight onto the garden, the first thing you see. Then we discovered that he would feel sick looking out, and when we got to the bottom of that, that's when he said, 'It happened in the shed.' So, during lockdown, I got spray paint, I said, 'You can write all your words that you want to get out.' So he wrote, like, 'X's awful, he's a liar,' and he wrote all his angry words out. And then I bought a sledgehammer for him.

KELVIN: The family took part in that.

ZOE: And that, I think, helped him a lot.

KELVIN: The shed's gone now, it doesn't exist.

ZOE: Another thing we got to the bottom of in lockdown, Nathan hated the thought of standing out. I never knew this, but once he told me and I did research about it, it's common for children who are sexually abused to think that, just by looking at them, you know they've been sexually abused. He thought we all just knew and we didn't do anything, which then meant it was okay, because we all know and nobody's stopping it. And then he also assumed his classmates could see, his teachers could see.

ZOE: Lockdown helped with Karl, our oldest son, too. That was also how lockdown was a positive, because Karl became a lot closer to Nathan. He got a lot closer to understanding and supporting him.

KELVIN: Well, yeah, they're constantly together, there's nowhere else to go.

ZOE: And Karl has always been protective of his brother, hasn't he?

KELVIN: He has suffered because of it. He carried guilt.

ZOE: Massively. That's a big issue. We got him registered with Swindon Carers. That was a good support we got him, because he spends a lot of time with Nathan. And that, I guess, was a negative thing about lockdown – he could never escape, could he? He could never have that sort of time to be on his own. They share a bedroom, and a lot of the time when Nathan would disclose things or speak about things, Karl would … You know, you do your best to try and protect him, but then he'd end up sort of being there. So I guess that was part of a negative. I wish I could protect him more.

ZOE: I guess my coping mechanism is drawing on positives out of bad situations, so I speak quite a lot to Nathan to say, like, it would have been so much worse if at eight years old I had police knocking on my door to tell me he'd been in a road traffic accident and hadn't survived. Like, we can't change what's happened in the past, but I still have my son. Some parents don't. Some parents have had to bury a child. We can still make memories, we can still go forwards, and then it's about, also, saying to Nathan, like, realistically, all of my children, they're really safe, because they're probably the hardest children to groom now because they're so aware.

I don't want to transfer my anxieties onto my children, I'm really mindful of that. I don't want them to think the world's not a safe place, but trying to keep normality going for them for school trips and things like that, I couldn't cope. I could always be strong up until the point of them going. When they went, I would end up thinking, what if there's a load of paedophiles there, what if the teacher's a paedophile? I'd be very panicky and everything. Then lockdown came and, of course, there's no school trips, there's no school, there's no going anywhere, there's no doing anything.

KELVIN: So she felt her children were safe, because of lockdown.

ZOE: Yeah I felt —

KELVIN: That was like —

ZOE: — I was happy they were home, because I felt they were here with me. I guess, yeah, lockdown, it's like we're all safe. But we went out once, didn't we, in August, and ended up bumping into him.

KELVIN: Three of us went out for a walk. It didn't turn out very well.

ZOE: I'm constantly anxious; I'm going to teach that to the children. I try not to, but I can't help … It's natural now, I go out the door and the first thing that's on my mind is to look up that way to see if they're out. We looked into moving —

KELVIN: — it wasn't feasible at the time.

ZOE: Their house, they just put it on the market, so hopefully they'll be going.

KELVIN: Hopefully.

ZOE: Another thing with Nathan, it's probably trauma-related; um, I guess because he's had the trauma, he's more aware of potential dangers, so he got quite bad Covid anxiety. In general, we're not, I'm not anxious about Covid.

KELVIN: Not to that extent.

ZOE: From very early on, he wanted a mask. He was quite nervous when he went back to school in September with people touching him. I thought that was contact because of the abuse; it wasn't, it was because he's worried about Covid. Again, it's just that positive reassurance, isn't it? So it was just like reflecting back to him that, actually, we've got the vaccine rolling out, we've got lateral flow tests in schools. And also, talking to him, trying to make it exciting, like we can go on holidays again. Yes, it's nice staying at home like this during lockdown, but do you want to stay like this forever?

KELVIN: He wants the sheltered approach to everything.

ZOE: Nathan feels safe in lockdown because he doesn't have to deal with any triggers.

KELVIN: Home's the safest place for him. Why would he leave it?

ZOE: Yeah.

KELVIN: It's going to take a few years to get to normality for school for him.

ZOE: And now it's difficult, his age, going into adolescence. That's a problem for him. Where his body's changing and he's growing hair and things.

KELVIN: He was uncomfortable.

ZOE: He couldn't cope with looking at his own body because it was, again, the perpetrator. I anticipate we'll have issues —

KELVIN: Yeah.

ZOE: — because of everything that happened. That's what I think I've probably learnt in lockdown is, like, it doesn't end.

# Joy Grotzinger

*I'm not an indoor person*

*13 May 2021*

Everybody knows me in Swindon. I'm not an indoor person. I only come home to sleep, that's all. Before, I was in a jealous relationship; that man was always pulling me back from many things I wanted to do. I was always in the house. I later left him, then I became free in life, and now I like seeing people, making people laugh, making people happy.

Lockdown was terrible. I wasn't able to do the events I host, like the Africa festival. It is always once a year, in June or July; we were planning to host another before the coronavirus problem started. It's a community event, we're a non-profit organisation; we just do it for the public, you know, to come out and to avoid loneliness and isolation. But now, this is what has happened – many of them are lonely and isolated because of the lockdown.

I also do community work as a volunteer in Broadgreen Community Centre. I support the elderly people lunch club – Afro-Americans, Jamaicans, some from Africa, some from the Dominican Republic. I do the free shop as well; we get donations from everywhere – clothes, shoes, handbags, and sometimes electronics. Every last Saturday of the month, people come to Broadgreen to pick up whatever they want for free. Sometimes, if the people are lucky, they get new things. So I was always very busy, from one place to the other. I work as well in Christ Church Community Centre as a volunteer.

Then, with lockdown, it was just as if I was in a cage, you know, just a little bit crazy. It was a very difficult time. But there's something I want to say as well: you know, the lockdown helped as well, do you understand? Because we humans, that was when we realised that we needed each other. Everybody was just calling, asking, 'Oh, how are you today? I hope you're fine. Are you okay?'

People showed kindness, people became more loving than they used to be. I read on Facebook, a lady cooked food and was asking, 'Oh, I made a lot of food, I still have a little left, I don't know if anybody would want some, I could drop it by your door.' I was so touched. My god, people are beginning to love each other! People that had never called me before, they called me to check on me, and then I started checking up on many people as well.

But during this time I was really not feeling fine. I was always in and out of hospital before lockdown. I was very sick, then they found out that I had low brain cortisol – I got that diagnosis in June 2020 during Covid. Cortisol is a special hormone that controls many things in the body, but my brain does not produce enough of this hormone. So then I started taking hydrocortisone.

My eyesight started coming back slowly to normal, especially the right one. The left one is still blurred, but I just read online that once I keep taking the steroids, it might come up to normal again. And then my gall bladder – there were these stones on top of the liver that they removed, and it's quite painful. My son wasn't here, but I've got friends and they were going shopping for me, and sometimes my friend brought me noodle soup.

I used to be a singer when I was younger. I used to sing a lot. In lockdown, in my room, I just put the music on my tablet and start singing. I wasn't feeling well, but that's what keeps me happy.

My son was far away from me, three hours from where I live. When the lockdown started, I became scared, I told him, 'Can you come over here now to stay home, or do you want me to move to you?' Then he said, 'Mum, no, you stay where you are, I stay where I am, because it's safer: if one person got the virus, it will not affect the other one. We all have to protect each other somehow.'

But when my son graduated, he moved back home with me. He's now doing his Master's from home. After his Master's, he's going to do his PhD as well. He's a very good student. He got a scholarship because he got a first class. He's doing computer sciences. I didn't go to university. I stopped at GCSE. I had a lot going on in my life before, when I was younger. I've tried my best. I'm a woman, you know.

My son really took care of me. He did a lot. He was doing the cooking, cleaning. Yeah, I was really happy. We do online shopping, because he didn't want to go to the shop so he could protect me, because my immune system was very low. I remember, one of my son's friends came to Swindon and he wanted to meet up with him, maybe in front of the door. My son said, 'No, I can't. My mum is vulnerable. I can't meet up with you because this virus is also in the air sometimes. We should meet after the lockdown.' I heard him say something like that. We parents are happy the children are with us, but they weren't happy being at home! Staying at home, he did it to protect me. I'm proud of him. He is super.

# Angela Cooper

*We had loads of students that didn't have resources like laptops*

*13 March 2021*

Lockdown, it's not what you sign up for, is it, when you're a head-teacher? In our school, we had loads of students that didn't have resources like laptops, because we serve quite a disadvantaged community. And in the first lockdown, the government weren't very quick at sorting out the laptops. In fact, it was just a complete fiasco. So we were setting work for students to do, rather than doing any online lessons, because obviously you can't do online lessons if your students can't access them. Plus the fact, at that point, we had a few teachers that were really tech-savvy and that immediately were able to pick up how to use Teams and so on, but then, of course, you've got the other teachers that, you know, that's not their thing, they're used to standing up in front of the classroom performing. So we had to put a lot of training into play. Fortunately, the people that were really good at it helped to train other people, and gradually, and a year on, pretty much everybody's really confident now at doing live lessons on Teams. But the thing is, when you're doing a live lesson, however good it is, you can't interact with all of those kids and they could be doing anything. You don't know until you get the work in how much they've actually engaged in the lesson.

When we were setting work in the first lockdown, the take-up wasn't good. The take-up is definitely better when you're doing live lessons. I mean, it probably started off a lot lower, but I think in the end there was probably about seventy per cent of students trying to do the work. It did very much vary on what resources they had, because even when we were setting things on *Show My Homework*, if all you've got at home is a phone, it's not very easy.

During the first lockdown, we were having to print loads of packs for students. We were going round delivering them to their houses, and textbooks. I went round to one house and you kind of thought, how are you managing in lockdown? It was a high-rise set of flats and when I got to the door, the door was smashed in, and you could hear in the house there was a baby screaming. I was there to deliver work for somebody who didn't have a laptop, but when you saw it you just thought, oh my gosh, they're stuck in their little flat all day long with lockdown going on, no laptop, no nothing. It's no wonder they're finding it difficult to engage and do the work. It's an eye-opener: you see those children, you see them in school and you think, well now I've got a little bit more understanding of what's going on with them.

I mean it is true, isn't it, that those who have, get more? Because those that have parents at home that can support, those that have the resources at home, obviously, they've managed. You know, we've had some students that have thrived during lockdown. We've sent out extra online courses and things they can do, and they've lapped everything up. But then, on the other hand, you get those that have got nobody at home to support them or they've not got the resources or they're trying to share a laptop between four of them or something, so inevitably those kids have not done as much.

I remember it being months between when we ordered the laptops and getting them. And, in the beginning, they allocated each school with how many laptops they thought we needed. I think we got allocated about twenty-two or something. We needed about 200, and we are a small school, relatively speaking, for a secondary school, 760 students. They used some formula to work out the number of laptops needed, but it didn't work for a school like ours. The other thing about the laptops is because they've all been done by the government, if something goes wrong with them, you have to go back to the DfE[22] to get them sorted out, which is really stupid. If they'd given the money to the schools, we could have purchased the laptops, then, if something goes wrong with them, we can sort it out.

They're always going on about what to do to help disadvantaged students, like the pupil premium, and they come up with all these newfangled ideas that never work. Why didn't they just give the money for each of those kids to have a laptop? It would have made the world of difference. I said to Robert Buckland, our MP in Swindon, 'Even if you gave the laptop to them and they kept it, actually, that would have been something that the government could have been proud of that they'd done for those disadvantaged kids.' It would have been money well spent. And I don't think it would have cost the earth.

We've got a really good safeguarding team in school, and I would say that they have been inundated, more so in the second lockdown than the first lockdown, but literally that's become a full-time job. Between the first lockdown and the second, the numbers of students that fell into the vulnerable category just increased dramatically. The safeguarding issues went through the roof – domestic violence, all those kind of things. Even students that were, kind of, perfectly fine in the first lockdown, by the second lockdown, they were really suffering.

In the first lockdown, we had about twenty students in all coming into school, so not very many. So we had some vulnerable

---

22 Department for Education.

students, we had a couple of SEN,[23] and we had some key workers' children, and it was very manageable. The second lockdown, I mean, we might as well have just opened the whole school, the list of people that was allowed to go.

In the first lockdown, because we'd only got a few students, we were able to do a much better curriculum. The students that were in school were doing crafts and they had a PE lesson every day. And you know, it was nice for teachers to teach things that weren't necessarily their subject because, each day, we said, 'Right, you've got to spend an hour and a half in the morning and an hour and a half in the afternoon doing the work that's been set by the teachers,' but then we broke it up with creative activities. So you'd find the maths teacher doing a mural with them. The staff really looked forward to coming in, because that was the time when everyone was just stuck in their houses and people were just glad to go out of the house and go to work.

In the second lockdown, the expectation was that everybody was going to be set work for all of their lessons or they were going to have live lessons. So literally, by the second lockdown, the kids were just sitting at their computers all day long, which isn't good for anyone.

The children that were coming into school were your most needy children. So, in the second lockdown, we ended up having twenty-five in the Year 7 group, but twenty-five students you would never put together in a group normally, because they've all got some kind of need or they're vulnerable. There's a reason why they're in school, you know. The key worker aspect of it was minimal. Having a group like that Year 7, they might need to be taken out for a lesson or two and then go back if they're not doing what they should be doing. And, of course, a couple of the kids didn't want to be in school, but if they come under

---

23 Special educational needs.

a social worker or something, they have to come in. They're kicking off, because all of their friends are at home. They play up because they want to be sent home.

We ended up with about eighty-five students in the second lockdown, but literally every single day I could have taken another two or three, because every day I had a parent on the phone, you know, in desperation: 'Please, I need my child in school.' But it was really difficult because there were 114 already on our vulnerable list, so, in theory, all of those could have been eligible to come. There was another load that had SEN needs that in theory could have come; that's not even counting the key workers that were eligible to come.

I had parents crying on the phone saying, well, that they're not coping for a start, that they're not able to get their kids to do anything, that kind of thing. They are finding that they can't get them out of bed in the morning or they're staying on their PlayStation all night or, you know, their mental health is suffering and they want them to come back into school. But the trouble is, you can't just go 'Yes' when they don't meet the government criteria. I have to manage the numbers, I can't just have an open-door policy. I have to say 'No' because, if I have another person in that class, I'm going to have to put another group on: that's going to be another member of staff that we haven't got. It was horrible, really bad, and I lay awake at night worrying about it. You want to be compassionate, but you've also got to be practical about what you can actually do.

In terms of teachers, I think they found it really hard. Teachers were in school doing the key worker group, they were setting work remotely, they were marking work, they were responding to all the emails. It was a really, really long day. The media, I don't think they get it sometimes, I don't think they realise how hard teachers are working. The first lockdown was difficult because you're setting work on *Show My Homework*, and then of course marking it and getting it back. You're doing that individually for each student, it literally takes so long. Staff were working really, really long hours, because they were very conscious of the fact that if someone's doing the work and they're sending it in, they need to have some feedback in order to have the motivation to keep on doing it.

The first lockdown, we had to start doing the enhanced cleaning and making sure all the bubbles were kept separate, and we had to buy two huge marquees for the lunchtimes – for all of those things, my business manager was brilliant. The free school meals fiasco, she dealt with all that. To start with, the canteen were producing food parcels for the students to come in and collect every day, but then you think, well, they're supposed to be staying indoors, so it doesn't really help us if they're all turning up to collect their meal. So in the end we did boxes for the week, so that they could do their own sandwiches and do their own lunches. I put out an email and said, 'I'm going to be delivering some food parcels, is there anybody that can help me?' And, literally, within five minutes, I had about seven or eight members of staff going, 'I'll help, I'll help, I'll help.' So, you know, people were really brilliant like that.

One of my deputies is in charge of curriculum, and he does the timetable. We've had so many different timetables this year. First of all, there was the timetable that he wrote last year, and then that had to be abandoned because we had to go into bubbles and we had to start having staggered breaks and lunches. He had to re-write another one within about a week or so and, because he's so good at it, he could do it. But since then, there've been other timetables: there's the timetable of the key worker group and what they're going to do, and then, during the second lockdown, there's the timetable to make sure that the teachers that are in school are not the people that are also supposed to be delivering the live lessons. So, literally, he hasn't stopped in terms of timetabling this year. If it hadn't been for him, I honestly don't know, I might have resigned by now!

And my other deputy, she's the pastoral one. And I've got someone else who's in charge of teaching and learning. So it's been a team effort. I feel like the only thing that I've really done is appoint people that are really good. Yeah, I think one of the things that I am good at is getting the right people on the bus and getting them in the right seats, if you know what I mean.

One of the things that has made my blood boil this year is that the government have done everything at the last minute, but they never tell headteachers what's going on. The first news you get of what's going on is when it's happening on the telly. Every time Gavin Williamson[24] comes on the telly, I have to tell myself in advance, right, don't be annoyed, whatever he says, just think, okay, take it with a pinch of salt, because half the time it doesn't happen anyway or it changes three weeks later.

It's always best not to do anything straight away, I've decided. If you do something straight away, you end up doing it two or three times. First of all, they'll say something, and anybody that works in the job knows that what they're suggesting is ridiculous. So you've got to say to yourself, well, in two or three weeks' time they'll realise it's ridiculous. And then that's what usually happens. So just hold off, don't do anything straight away. Don't get ahead of yourself!

On the last day of term before Christmas they suddenly said that we were going to have to do this mass testing in

---

24  Secretary of State for Education, 24 July 2019 to 15 September 2021.

January, didn't they?[25] I was so, so cross, and at that point I thought, do you know what? No. I've had enough, because all the way through the year this has been happening: at the last minute they tell you you're going to be doing this, you're going to be doing that, you're going to be doing the other, and you just get your plan in place and then they change it, so you have to come up with something else. And I thought, no, I am not spending my Christmas holiday doing that, because I've got a family. Most of the time school comes first, but at Christmas my family comes first, and I'm never going to have it any different. If you don't like it, hard luck. And I'm not going to be calling any of my colleagues to talk to them about it over Christmas either because they've also got family. So I thought, no, I'm refusing, they've gone too far. I can't magic up people to do mass testing. They've cut our budgets so far that I haven't got spare staff.

Another thing, at that time, I got Covid. It was like having the flu, really, not that I've ever had the flu, but I had a banging headache, sore throat, cold, that kind of thing. I didn't lose my sense of smell or taste or anything, fortunately, because otherwise I wouldn't have enjoyed my Christmas dinner! But yeah, it wasn't very pleasant. I had my mum staying with me as well, because my mum lives on her own, so we were her bubble. She's eighty-two, and so I was really worried. I was literally praying every day for my mum to survive. But she was actually all right; she got similar symptoms to me and was fine. We went on Boxing Day to get tested, all four of us: my husband and me and my mum and my daughter. All of us tested positive apart

---

25 On 15 December 2020, the government announced that teachers and pupils would have access to rapid testing at school from the start of the new term in January. Many secondary schools began organising this, but then the term never began as the third national lockdown closed schools from 6 January 2021. It wasn't until March 2021, when schools reopened, that all staff and children were offered three tests ahead of their return to school.

from my husband. I mean, don't ask me, he was fine; I can't see how he could have been in the same house as us for that long and not got it.

This time makes you think how valuable and important every day is. I used to go into work and think, oh, it's Monday, can't wait until Friday, you know what I mean? But that challenged me, because I thought, well, no, because, actually, how many Mondays have I got left in my life? If I'm just going to spend every Monday thinking I wish it was Friday then I'm just wasting my life away. So I'm never going to get this Monday again, so therefore I'll squeeze every little drop out of Monday and make the most of it.

And I've learnt it's okay to relax. Because I'm a headteacher, I tend to work, work, work all the time. There's always more things you could do. But being in lockdown there has been a little bit more time to myself, so, on my laptop, I started doing some exercise classes. Ordinarily, I would think I wouldn't have time, because I wouldn't make time for myself. Whereas now I feel like, no, I am going to make time for myself because, actually, the world can just come crashing in. I'm not just there to try and get more kids their exam results, I'm here to enjoy my life and to have a healthy life and that doesn't involve spending 24/7 doing school work. So that's been a challenge to me as well.

I wouldn't be doing this job if I wasn't a Christian. I feel like it was a calling. It's not something that I set out to do at the beginning of my career; it's just how I've ended up, really. I wouldn't be able to do it if I didn't think that God was with me in it. I just feel of my own self, I wouldn't have the capability to do it. You would just spend your whole life worrying, that's the thing. Well, maybe some people wouldn't, but I would because I've got that kind of anxious personality.

If something comes to me where you think, oh gosh, what am I going to do, I try and pray straight away before I panic. If I pray, I can get back into an equilibrium. If I'm worried about something then I think, well, I know somebody who can deal with it who's a bit higher than me. So I'll pray about it and leave it. And sometimes I start worrying about it again, but I think, no, God is God, He knows what He's doing. That's how I do it. I don't know how other people manage that are not Christian.

I've got a little notebook by my bed as well, so sometimes, if something's worrying me, I'll write it in the notebook. It's almost my way of saying, you know, not that God's going to forget it because I told Him – I'm sure He'd remember – but it's for me really to know that I've told Him and therefore He's going to remember. And I go back to this little book from time to time, and it's amazing, when I go back to it, I can go: tick, tick, tick, tick, tick. Because, literally, practically everything that I pray for comes good in the end.

It will be nice to go back to church, but it has been fine. I probably shouldn't say it, but it has been quite nice on a Sunday to have the time to do other things, because sometimes church takes up quite a bit of the day.

When you think about all the work that you've done and all of the things that you've put into place to make your school really, really good; all the things that you worked really hard at, and then it all being kiboshed, it's quite depressing. It will take some time to recover, and I don't know how long it will take to recover. In our school, the behaviour was really good. We've got a very, very strict behaviour system. But what we did find when the kids came back to school last time is that we had a lot more incidents of fights and things like that, which were very rare. It was almost like people just lost it, you know, and it got shown in their aggression towards each other. We noticed that the kids are really tired, because they're used to sitting up all night on their PlayStations or whatever, and then the next day they come into school having not put in a good night's sleep, and then obviously that means that they can't concentrate as well, they've got shorter tempers and all those sorts of things. So, although I want the kids back, it's like the anxiousness of what state they're going to come back in. There'll be some of them that won't have had any rules for the last three months, so they'll have been doing what they like at home. We know that, because some of their parents can't control their own kids. So they're coming back and they've got to relearn all your rules. It's like regaining all of those things that you've worked so hard to put into place and having the motivation to do that again when you've done it all once.

But I'm a 'what will be' kind of person. The pandemic, it makes you think, hang on a minute, I think that I'm here to get my school to 'Outstanding', but that's not necessarily God's agenda. Maybe His agenda isn't that my school gets to 'Outstanding' as fast as possible. Maybe His agenda is that we all learn a lot more about what's important in life.

When the exams were cancelled, it makes you realise you're not doing it for the exam results. You don't come to school to get the exam results. That's not the prize; that's just the little piece of paper that you get. The prize is the person that you've become through what you've learnt, and also the learning itself that you've done.

So I think what I thought the journey was going to be isn't now what the journey is going to be, if you know what I mean. I think to myself, what are we going to value in the coming year? And I've thought of two things, really. One is, I'm thinking, the curriculum is really key, because it has to be that what you're teaching is worth teaching whether or not there's an exam at the end of it. The government tries to drive the curriculum, but our job isn't to respond to the latest government crisis. It's about thinking what knowledge is needed and what kids won't learn at home. What knowledge do they need to have that's going to give them the best life that they can possibly have and the best opportunities and the best chances? And then the other thing I was thinking of, which I think is really important for schools to deliver because you can't guarantee that all of our children come from families where they'll deliver it, and that's the character that they come out with. They come to school to develop their character, and when they leave they've got to be somebody that other people are going to want to work with. You want them to be model citizens, really, don't you, when they come out? They should come to school and go out knowing a better way to live.

When in the press, they keep on saying, 'Oh, these poor kids, they've lost out on everything; they've got nothing to look forward to now,' it's so depressing. How is that helpful to anybody? I would never want to say that the lockdowns had done something irreversible to somebody's future, because I feel that that's what our job is, to make sure that it doesn't have irreversible effects on their future. That's the number one thing that we're focusing on, to make sure that what they've gone through can be used as a positive – it's made them more resilient, it's made them more independent. Even if they've gone through a rough patch, how can they use that to then be even stronger in the future? So that's our message, really.

*Afterword – one year later*

The students have settled down now, but what we have been left with is lots of mental health issues. Students that are self-harming has just gone through the roof; we're having to do bag checks in the morning to make sure that people haven't brought something in to harm themselves with. I feel like it's affected Year 11 more than any other year group, and I don't know why that is. The last couple of years their education has been disrupted, and now that year are under pressure to do GCSEs and try and attain in the way that they would have done before the pandemic. I think, for a lot of them, that causes anxiety.

It'll be interesting, this year's results. They're going to publish the results this year, but I feel like it's a bit unfair because it's just been so variable what people have got. You don't know the circumstances that people have been in. How can that be a fair reflection of how well schools are doing?

The curriculum plans have to be modified. That's probably going to go on for a couple of years, but I think our school will recover, for definite, as things get back to normal. And those students that go on, I think they will have developed resilience. Yes, they might not have their exam results as they thought they were going to have them, but I'm sure they'll develop lots of other skills that, perhaps, are even more useful to them in life.

# Elsa González

*I'm a mother all the time*

I met my husband, Chris, through the internet. We came to live here in Swindon, then when my oldest son was born we took him as a baby back to Mexico, and we were living in Mexico twelve years. But then when my little one, Marc, was born, we knew there was something wrong with him, something different. Because of his condition and we want to treat him for it, we came back here in 2017.

In Mexico, we went with different doctors. If they see you worry, they say, 'Do you want me to do this study and this test?' They give you all the attention, but you have to pay. Then sometimes, if I were with one doctor, I get one opinion and then with another I get a different opinion. It was too much information for us to take, you know.

We came here and then it was like, the appointment, just talking, they didn't check him. Here, they don't even stand up to see him, very shocking. I'm like, 'Oh my god, this is supposed to be a first-world country.' It's very different. But at the end of the day, I got results here. In Mexico, some people told us that Marc wasn't going to walk, that his spine was bad or he was, like, low tone, you know, a lot of different things. And right now, thank god, he's walking. He used a walker until he was four and a half, but at the end of the day, he walked here.

Here, people actually know about the autism disability. And, for example, here you have different groups and the blue badge on the cars. Here, people tell us where to go or what to do, you know, like where to get support. Unfortunately, back in Mexico is nothing for disabled people, you know? In Mexico, in autistic children, they say they're badly behaving or that you're bad parenting. People are not as sympathetic as here. For example, my friends are like, 'Let's have a party or a meeting for a coffee.' And then I say, 'I can't, because, you know, with my little one.' They say, 'It's all right, you just give him a bottle,' or 'Tell him off,' or 'Take him for five minutes' time off and then he calms down.' I tell them he's autistic, they say 'What do you mean?'

I had no experience of autism. It was just to learn with Marc. It's hard because you're expecting one thing and it's completely another one. Then again, you know, he didn't ask to be like that, so it's not his fault.

Marc was in a nursery here, the only one who accept him after they knew he was special needs. Because that's another thing, you know, we tried seven nurseries around Swindon and all of them told us, 'Oh, yeah, we have a space, fill the papers and everything.' And then as soon as we mentioned that he was special needs, he didn't walk, he's very picky with his food, it's, 'Oh, I'm sorry, we don't have the ability to have him, perhaps you should try another.' I mean they tell you 'no' but not with that word, you know what I mean? They tell you very sweet that perhaps is better for him to be in another place. Then we found a nursery that would take him two days, then three days, and then, yeah, it was full-time.

Then, in September 2019, Marc began primary school full-time. We were like, 'Yay!' It felt like at last we were reaching out through a hole. Marc was getting used to going in the transport, his routine in the school and everything.

Then suddenly the first lockdown started and schools closed. Suddenly, they push us down the hole again. We were from being a ten, go back to zero. Or below zero, feeling it that way, you know, really down, trapped again in the house, day after day. Bless him, Marc was coming and getting his coat, and then pointing at the window for his school transport. We tried to take his attention from the coat and from the window and keep him busy doing other things. We try to explain to him and say, 'No, that is not possible.' He wanted to go and start crying.

As parents, we try to keep Marc busy, but is not much that we can do because of his autistic things. He doesn't watch television, he doesn't stay still for long, so any activity he spends, like, ten minutes the most, when he really enjoys the activity. Otherwise, he's just running around and jumping. Because we changed Marc's routine, he doesn't sleep – one or two hours' sleep maximum every night. We just close our eyes and then it's, like, wake up again. It's making him a little bit more aggressive with himself, and with us. He has these meltdowns, it's what he does. He shouts or he screams. Sometimes he's noisy and we can't stop him.

The neighbours, well, the houses are too close, so any slight noise, they complain. Sometimes he knocks his head on the wall, and they knock back, like really angry. One time, I have to chat to them, like, 'Believe me, it's not on purpose, the noises he does, and I try to reach him as fast as possible.' I have to reach him fast so he doesn't hurt himself.

The speech and language therapist used to come once a month before lockdown to see how is Marc doing and everything. She just gave us her telephone number and said, 'I'm here for any-thing, like anything you need.' When I say, 'Please help me, give him something to sleep because I'm getting crazy, I just cry and cry all day.' And she says, 'Oh, I'm sorry, we can't do anything about it, but we can talk.' And I say, 'I don't want to talk. I just want to sleep.' You know, I need someone to look after my boy so I can sleep one or two hours because I'm not sleeping really.

All the appointments with doctors and things for Marc, they were cancelled or postponed. We're waiting, for example, for his sight. We wait like half a year for this appointment in the hospital, and then in the first lockdown, it was like, 'Oh, we're sorry, but we have to cancel or postpone until further notice.'

This third lockdown, thank god, it was a little bit different. They offer us two to three days for Marc to go to the special school. But, unfortunately, there was a Covid case in his room, so they stop us. So it's not different really, because we start again with the sleepless nights and with his aggression.

It's hard on our relationship because we don't have a minute for us, we're like 24/7 parents. It's hard because it's not fair for my older boy, Joseph, though we try to pay attention to both of the boys. Joseph's registered as a young carer. He helps us a lot. We don't have any other support; my husband doesn't have any family in Swindon. And it's hard because, well, you don't have a social life. All the time is to be a parent, you know; you forget completely about friends, or your friends are just people that are the same, like you, the same position.

When Marc was at nursery or school, my husband and me have the chance to go to the cinema and, you know, just sit down together and eat at the same time. And there used to be this place that is only for special needs, it was so great: Hop, Skip and Jump. We used to take Marc and you just pay, like, £5 and they look after him. And he can go in the weekends and in the holidays. Our routine was taking him and then go with my oldest son to eat McDonald's in Asda. It was fantastic, you know what I mean? It sounds really very simple, but it was really nice for us. And then they closed that place.

*1 March 2021*

Yesterday, Marc cried and then I was like, what do you need? I check him, I look around him and everything. He was pointing and then I went, 'What do you need?' You know, like, tell me. And sometimes it's frustrating for us, I can't understand him, like, tell me, please help me to understand what he needs or, you know, how can I help him? Some times are really, really upsetting, you know, like thinking, thank god it's another day gone. Last night we have two hours of sleeping on the couch, and then the little one is up.

We just base our life on his.

We had this, it's like a special nursery. There is a little room for parents to stay and have a cup of tea, and it will be like one hour, one hour and a half. So, the ladies were there talking and, for me, it was good because I realised that there's always going to be people in a better situation and in worse situation than me. So when it gets too much into me or I'm depressed, I just think that, you know, like this lady has it worse, like she has to carry her boy, or is two children instead of one, things like that.

And as a mother I have to be positive, you know, and say, oh yeah, he's doing noises, different noises. In a good day, I'm like, 'Yes, yes, he's holding the pen.' I'm working hard just to make him happy, you know, like to enjoy his life. Yesterday, we're tickling, he laughed and he made contact for a few seconds. It's just one moment, one minute, when he finally had eye contact and he laughed. I'm just going to have to be happy for that. You try to do as much as you can, but sometimes it's hard because he's too demanding – all the attention, all the time. I'm so exhausted.

I'm sorry. Sometimes you're wondering, what did you do wrong to pay or —

It gets too much. In Mexico, we're very close to the family, we don't even think about, you know, to put him in a specialist school or leave him to sleep with anybody else or be apart from me. But, after this week, honestly, I was just like wanting so much to be on my own, just to have a shower without listening that he was crying and complaining. Sometimes it's like, well, why God/Buddha/the light – whatever you want to believe in – why allow these, you know, like —

Sorry.

The lack of sleep. The lack of sleep. I don't know. I know it's supposed to be for a reason. I know that I'm blessed, or people keep saying it's a blessing, but sometimes it's a really hard blessing. We leave everything behind in Mexico. We just focus on him, and our life is basically his life and we forget about everything.

Like I say, people say it's a blessing. I think they just want to tell you something positive or they don't know what to tell you. It's hard because I used to be, you know, like a professional. And now, lockdown, I'm just here with him. I'm a mother all the time.

# Daniel Thuysbaert

*When you lose a job, it is a bereavement*

*12 May 2021*

I was working for John Lewis down at Mannington and had been with John Lewis since 2010. Just before lockdown I'd secured a new job with them, and it was training other stores' teams to do what I was doing, to be better at their job, so I was very excited.

I spent the week and a bit before lockdown in one of our partnership hotels, meeting the senior people within the business that were driving those improvements, learning to upskill myself on teaching and coaching and all sorts of things. Got back from that, and then the store closed pretty much straight away afterwards.

Us shutting the shop because of Covid and the move to online shopping then drove the decision of, like, the store closing down for good. We found out on 9 July [2020] that we were going to be made redundant. Then I lost my job in September, officially. It was quite a sad way of ending my career with them. Ten years with them. They've closed more John Lewis shops since.

John Lewis is such a specific brand and it's such a different company structure. You own the business and you are a co-owner of the business and that really resonated with me. It's such a lovely company to work for, the benefits were amazing, the people you work with are brilliant.

So I lost my job, but my partner was still working. He carried on working the whole time. He had quite intense days, to be honest. We didn't have an office or a homeworking environment, because neither of us had to work from home before, so he worked in what we call the den. And then, ultimately, we moved him into one of the guest bedrooms at the top of the house. There's a proper office space up there now with a desk, chair and everything else, so he doesn't get disturbed by me or the cats so much.

It was quite nice in some respects because he'd have a break during lunch, so you'd have those touchpoints during the day. If he had a challenging meeting over the phone, he knew he could come and find me because I wasn't working. He'd be like, 'Can I just talk to you about this? What would you do in that situation?' So that was quite nice.

When you lose a job, it is a bereavement. You go through this sort of anger: why have I lost this job that I loved doing? I didn't want to spend my redundancy on just paying my way, so I pretty much started applying for jobs straight away. I'd been looking before, because I thought something's not right, but I started properly searching that day we heard we were going to be made redundant, going through all the search engines and scrolling through every day to see if there'd been new jobs advertised.

I actually decided that I didn't want to be in retail any more, so I just stopped looking at retail jobs, full stop. I've done retail for over twenty years now and it's like, I need to change. I only applied for twenty-five jobs, because I was quite streamlined with the jobs I applied for. I got five interviews, so I did all right. The interviews were all online. And that was really weird, being sort of smartly dressed from the waist up. This room wasn't decorated, but I purposely put this huge picture behind me, just so there was a bit of a conversation piece that people would remember.

September was the month I ultimately found out that I had the job at Thames Water. Thames Water wasn't really on my radar, but I know I'm going to enjoy the company if I enjoy the interview process, and I enjoyed the interview process. It's just customer service at the moment. When I interviewed, I said, 'Look I'm not going to do that forever, I do very much want to have the opportunity to progress while I'm with you.' I sit better within a sort of productive role, where I feel like I'm supporting people.

Working in customer services, there's been some very upsetting calls, really: people who've suffered real mental health issues during this time with Covid, people who've been bereaved, people who've been going through cancer treatment, people who've got long Covid, people whose other halves have lost their jobs. Sometimes it's heart-wrenching, to be honest.

People have been working from home and that's impacted people's bills, funnily enough, because if they've been at home doing renovation work, like we have, we used more water because we've been doing more, and we've got garden work being done at the minute, so I know that we're using water for that. There's a lot of 'understand your bill' conversations.

Whether Thames Water will be forever, I don't know, because ultimately, actually, my pure passion lies with property developing and with art work, which I've just started doing again during lockdown. I hadn't painted for years. I started a very large canvas in oils and I've never worked in oils before. When I wasn't applying for jobs, I was sketching it out, drawing it. I spent a long time getting the composition right, and then working out how to use the paints. It became a lockdown project. When I get involved in a piece of artwork, you just focus on it and I get lost in it. I carried this picture around in my head for ten years. It's of waxwings. I don't know if you're familiar with them? They're migratory birds that are only seen in the UK in certain periods. But they've got quite large crests and quite large dark eye markings and beautiful wings. I need another chunk of time off to finish the last four pieces of the picture. My mum's an artist, so I think I've inherited the skill from her. I'm not formally taught, but I can pick a pen up and draw a picture or paint it.

As well as painting in lockdown, I spent a lot of time in the garden. We've got an allotment as well. So it was quite nice, actually, because we don't normally get that amount of time to dedicate to the allotment, so it looked amazing last year. When you're working, like this week, it's kind of 'Oh god', because you might go a couple of days without going, whereas last year we were going every day.

I think we've gone through every big major series on Netflix that's out there and rewatched things that we've watched before. So I pretty much watched the whole of *RuPaul's Drag Race* during lockdown, other half came in at about season three or season four, and then it was like, 'Um, let's rewatch season one, two and three again.' So now I'm watching it again, like a year on. We are with Amazon, Netflix and Disney now, so we've got the full gamut of everything that you can stream. I think that's our downtime, really.

We used to go to the Royal Academy of Arts. We had corporate membership through John Lewis, just walk in. I miss that. I miss going with friends and going for a meal afterwards. We started to do Zoom dinner parties. We did a set menu of chosen cocktail, starters and mains, and we did the same meals as each other and then just ate and caught up, which was lovely, but not the same as sitting in front of them and having a good old chinwag.

Not doing those things is hard. It puts pressure on a relationship, which most people would feel. But it definitely made us closer in a lot of respects. We did a walk every day, even if was just half an hour. And then when I started with Thames I was, like, right we need to carry on doing this. And we've maintained that, we'll go for a walk occasionally. But sometimes we need to do it separately. I think there were points where I was like, 'We spend too much time together!' I think everybody would understand that; lots of people were just going mad.

Christmas [2020] was challenging because you'd normally see family, and then we got close to the anniversary of the first lockdown. February time, I had an absolute low. I remember sitting at work going, what am I doing? You were having conversations every day with customers who were impacted by it, you had your own impact from it. Everything had kicked off in March the year before and I hadn't seen my parents since September at this point. There was no prospect of when you were going to get your Covid jab, when things were going to start to ease. And I remember sitting there at that point and just going, I feel lost. And it took me a whole weekend of sitting there going, why do I feel like that? And then going, right, what is this? I was like, right, I've got to be careful now because my mental health is where it is. And then I just went, right, I'm not going to hide it. So I told people at work, put a post on Facebook saying, 'I feel really low and really lost.' And posted that I don't normally feel like this, but it's really important to recognise it, and I'm sure I'm not the only one. And then I posted a load of photographs from the most recent family holiday that we had in America, and going, this is just to remind me of the good times. And I was surprised by the response I got. Loads of people I hadn't spoken to for years just going, god, I feel like that as well, and until you put that post on there, I hadn't even talked to anybody about it. And then every time I went to Waitrose, I had friends that I worked with going, oh my god, you just put words to how I've felt for the last two weeks. And I just said, 'Well, look, I'm here, talk to me.' And I was blown away for two weeks afterwards. It was just like this weird connection all of a sudden of other people feeling the same way.

This last year, the big thing, it makes you know what's important to you. It made me touch on making sure that I was focusing on what I could control, and not worrying about stuff I couldn't. Family and being able to see them and telling them that you love them – those simple things became very important. I certainly have missed my parents. That kind of impacted me and made me think a bit more about making sure that is something that features regularly, not just Christmas, Easter and birthdays.

# Anna Dudley

*Safeguard from abuse and Covid,
they don't sit well together*

*22 March 2021*

I was told a lot that I wouldn't achieve much, by my family and schools and welfare officers; that I would end up on the dole, I wouldn't have work, I'd only be good for having kids, this, that and the other. I went to a high school that was very well known in the area for pumping out high achievers. I tried going to a different school, a less prestigious school, but they didn't want me. I was fourteen and I was sat there with my mum, and the headmaster said to me, 'If I allowed you into this school, I would be importing failure.' I went to a centre for teens who were truants.

At twenty-one, well, I was in my own experience of abuse. At that time I was working in retail. After some time I decided to go back into education, and I thought I'll give counselling a go. I had to understand what had happened, and how and why, and how do I stop it? Never sat an exam in my life, I don't have any GCSEs, but counselling, I carried on until I qualified. Counselling really does draw on your empathy, your ability to sit with people in incredibly difficult situations, not try and fix it, just be with them. I developed those skills very quickly as I really felt how important they were to help people heal. So, academically, don't even know my times tables, but ask me to sit with somebody when they're at their lowest, I'll be able. That's where I belong, that's my strength.

I wanted to work in domestic abuse, so I applied for roles all over the country and ended up in Swindon. Now, I'm Refuge Team Leader with SWA.[26] Our Refuge is an amazing facility; there's not many like ours. Our facility is purpose-built: we have two emergency rooms, and then we have twenty self-contained flats, varying from one-bed to three-bed, depending on the size of the family. Everybody's got their own front door. From the outside, it just looks like flats with some gates around it and CCTV. But actually it's far more than that. It's a block of flats with panic alarms, CCTV and bulletproof glass on the bottom floor. There's a marker on the address – basically you press the panic alarm and the marker means that the police will respond within, well, it's meant to be two minutes. The police are always very supportive of us.

We're trying to keep this address as safe as possible, but if a woman comes in and her ex-partner is what we call a domestic abuse serial perpetrator, or a DASP, then he may already know where we are. Often that perpetrator might also be involved in criminal activity, and unfortunately some of those individuals know where we are as well, so the information can get around. We have had multiple alleged perpetrators show up outside. Fortunately, I think one of the deterrents is the fact that if you come to the building and cause trouble, you will be arrested because there's CCTV everywhere. I'm hoping that's enough of a deterrent, but I don't want to tempt fate at this point. On the one occasion we've had somebody come in, it was because the ex-partner let them into the building.

Nobody really knew what the situation was in March [2020]; we were all confused. It all felt a bit Doomsday-ish, actually. It was incredibly intense and the amount of referrals we had

---

26  Swindon Women's Aid.

escalated. Four to six weeks after lockdown started, that's when the floodgates opened.

I help assess the referrals. We're only accepting high-risk victims of domestic abuse. I remember on one day assessing six referrals, making all those calls, assessing the risk on those: who is at highest risk, who do we need to support immediately, what can we do in the meantime? And making sure that while I was making these decisions, they were safe. It was, give me half an hour, I'll look at this; give me half an hour, I'll look at that, times six. Plus the helpline calls, plus about fifteen other women at the time needing support.

The Refuge staff had to split up into two teams. All the domestic independent advisors worked from home, so there was just two of us holding Refuge. Before, it would have been at least three of us holding Refuge together, and we would have also had admin staff, so they would have helped take your calls, take your referrals.

We've had women in here who have been self-employed and very successful, as well as those who are in low-income families. During lockdown, people would come through, such as teachers, social workers, even policewomen, even very involved professionals in domestic abuse who needed support. Things had just escalated so much in the home that they needed to get out. I think what probably happened is relationships that were stressed had then become abusive due to lockdown. So maybe if they weren't, well, necessarily abusive before, they had escalated to that point because of tension and stress, and the difficulty especially around home-schooling and homeworking and not being able to go out and see your friends. So everything had just condensed, bit like a pressure cooker for some people, I think.

In lockdown, we found people didn't stay long. We'll welcome anyone in who wants respite from their abuse, that's not an issue at all, but it definitely increased in volume, people doing that.

Individuals seemed to feel as though, I can't take this any more, I've got to get out. But then the cycle would quickly return back to honeymoon phase, and, 'Oh, he's said he'll change, they've said everything will be all right, so I'm going to go back.' They would be here for maybe one or two days. Usually, they'd be back. If not, sometimes the violence, otherwise emotional abuse, had escalated so much that they would need to go out of area, because it was just too intense and it wouldn't have been safe for them to remain in Swindon.

Some people who call our helpline won't give us their full name; they won't tell us the information that we might need to be able to properly safeguard them if they were at immediate risk. We never put any pressure on them to give us that information, and usually that means they'll call us back again, because we've built that trust. A massive thing for us is autonomy, so if you want something to happen we'll support you to make that change. But if somebody doesn't want to make that change now, it's not about us trying to convince them of that, because that's just an added pressure and it can cause an element of judgement, of, oh well, I should be doing this/they don't understand. So it's very much like, nope, you're in complete control; whatever you want and when you want, we will help you do that.

In terms of Covid, it wouldn't be a barrier to a woman coming in. We check temperatures, and we ask a woman if they've any symptoms before we accept them in. If they did, if they had a temperature and they had a cough, we would work out a way for them to go through another entrance into their flat without seeing anyone and isolate for ten days. This person needs safety; if her health is bad, it's only going to get worse – well, she could potentially be killed, because those are the women we accept in, those at risk of homicide. So I know what I would prefer to do: get her in, get her safe, get her fed and watered upstairs, leave her for two weeks, but she's safe from violence and abuse.

Something we have seen, especially with individuals who have high physical health needs and their partner should be, what do they call it? Shielding. So they should be staying in as well, they shouldn't be mixing with groups of people. But we've found that they're showing complete disregard towards shielding and then going home and intimidating by being in their personal space, or coughing, or whatever it might be. It's dreadful. As if we needed another way to intimidate people. It's really horrible, but, unfortunately, power and control mean that some people are going to use whatever tactic they have. Very unfortunate.

This is our lounge. Usually, before Covid, the door would be open and residents could come in and sit down, watch TV, make a cup of tea all together. Children could come in, they could watch a film, they could do whatever they wanted. We would run pizza nights, curry nights, karaoke, film nights. We can't do any of that now; this is always closed. It's very isolating for every individual family, and it's not helping them realise that, actually, life doesn't have to be the way that it was; it can be different and you can make friends and you can be with people who understand you.

Every flat is an individual household, and the guidelines were that that's the way that it should be treated, so the residents weren't allowed to meet with another household. We would normally allow female visitors, so residents could have their friends or their mum or their sister, whoever, come and visit them and stay in their flat until 8pm that day. During the first lockdown, that stopped. Nobody had anybody to visit.

We have put guidelines in place now that you can only have one support bubble family, that can either be in Refuge or outside; it can't be both. You can't have two. But there's not always the respect for guidelines we might hope for in Refuge.

We have had multiple families mixing in one flat. There's a balance to be found between 'Look, you really can't do this, we really need to keep everybody safe' and residents rebelling and seeing us as authority, or as 'they', so to speak. It was – well, it is still – very complex. It did raise a lot of tension in Refuge between staff and residents. Residents would all mix together, we would challenge that, and then we would get an onslaught as though we were monitoring them or surveilling them, which is uncomfortable for us. But on top of not seeing our families, making all the sacrifices we are making to be here, that then does – I don't know how everybody else would speak about it – but it does bring on a feeling of resentment. It's like, I'm being here for you, I want to be here for you, I want to stay well, I want to stay healthy, but I want to make sure that you are safe from violence and abuse, but you're actually having a go at me for trying to do these two things, which are complex, together. Safeguard from abuse and Covid, they don't sit well together.

One of the massive things that I noticed for individuals who have experienced domestic abuse is how triggering the restrictions are. When they were coming out and somebody asks, 'Oh, have you been out today already, where are you going?' then all of a sudden they're back to when their perpetrator used to try and keep them inside and used to ask them where they were going, what were they doing, how long were they going to be. We appeared to be like the perpetrator, but actually we were trying to safeguard, especially around this new disease. And to be stuck indoors all the time, to not be able to see their friends and family, they already came from that. So it almost extended the experience that they were having. Residents, in their minds, feel they're trapped in Refuge. I've heard some residents calling it a prison because of how it feels during lockdown. We would then get the brunt of that. Horrible.

There's a lot of trauma in this building. There's a lot to hold at any one time. Often when our women are triggered they might appear aggressive, argumentative; they may even be verbally abusive at times. It depends on your experience, and how you feel that day, how you cope with that. It's incredibly difficult to stand opposite somebody who is blaming you for what is going on; one side of your brain is upset and hurt because you're doing all you can to help that person, but then the other side is trauma-informed and knows this is not meant for you. Part of our job is to hear that anger, because, although it's not meant for us, that's part of their expression and they wouldn't have been able to do that to the perpetrator, because they could have been killed if they expressed themselves. So they feel safe to tell me how angry they are or how much I've annoyed them. I don't stop them; I'm just like, you do yourself, you express. Very complex, very complex. You will always have your human response and then this educated part of you, and they don't always sit together well, they conflict often, don't they? But in this type of work you need to have that awareness.

When schools closed, it was incredibly stressful. We didn't even have a Children and Young People Worker at that point. There were mums who were trying to entertain the children and trying to get them to wear off their energy, but they were only allowed out once a day. We've got a car park and then a smoking area, a cycle store, a bit of a grassy area and a play area on the other side, but we had to close the play area due to transmission. We've got a playroom as well, but children weren't allowed to go in it. Now, we've got a Children and Young People Worker who supports activities and can help children with homework, and who can help speak to the schools if there's any added difficulties at home, so that's been a massive change and support for mums here. But the children, they just wanted to let off some steam.

They didn't understand, they just wanted to run around and get into shenanigans, as children do.

It was hard to help the children understand that they couldn't get close to us. And that was another difficulty; like, in this room, children would usually come and play with my hair while I'm talking to mum, or they would, I don't know, want to play with my watch or something. Or a baby would sit on my lap. But we can't do any of that any more. And trying to tell that to children when they've been potentially so deprived of attention and care and kindness, to have to say, 'Oh no, you'd better go and sit back down with Mummy,' it's devastating. It is.

Normally we would walk around, we'd chat for a little while, we would see three families together, we'd have a natter; we would abandon our work for a little bit and go and have a laugh with the kids, play with trucks or whatever. We just can't now, so the atmosphere is very different.

We run a programme, Recovery Toolkit, but we're doing it online at the moment. It's just not the same, not the same at all. The participants can't connect with each other as well. Usually, after maybe about three or four, they've built such strong bonds with each other, they're so supportive and healthy towards one another, but that doesn't develop online. Last year, when we did face-to-face, they were going swimming together, they were going to the gym together, they were going for walks. They had a WhatsApp group. They'd have a bad day, they would give each other a call. They would have all of this support. I suppose the ones who were doing the online have nothing to compare it to, but as facilitators we do see that change. Once you trust people, you're more willing to engage and share, aren't you? But it's hard to build trust online. And I think online it's very easy for it just to be something you watch, instead of engage with. And there will be that caution of, I'm not going to share this way; somebody could be on their phone, somebody might not be interested, somebody could be distracted.

A change for myself: I've always managed depressive episodes, but as of September 2020 it was no longer containable and I ended up on antidepressants. I think a lot of people are just on autopilot at the moment. We've just got to get through. We're wishing our time away and not really being present. For me, I think it's incredibly difficult to replenish that part of yourself that needs it when you don't have your usual support network. So, haven't seen my parents, haven't seen my brothers or my nieces. Usually those things would all replenish and make you feel a little bit better, wouldn't they? But it's just not possible.

In the summer [2020], I went to see all my college friends from counselling, and I saw my very best friends, and it just makes the world of difference. Just spending that time and remembering who you are a little bit, because, being in this environment, you're giving so much of yourself, it is almost like forgetting what is my personality like? Am I funny, am I calm, what am I actually like?

I think when things settle down and we all have some space, the reflection and the things we're going to realise that we've actually observed, I think that it's going to blow our minds. When we really look back and think about what this has been like. But I wouldn't want to do anything else. I couldn't. I count myself fortunate to still have a job, and to be able to get up in the morning and go to work, because that's not something a lot of people have been able to do.

# Wojciech Orczyk

*Be elastic and be sure of nothing*

*19 April 2021*

Unfortunately, my grandmother died a few weeks ago because of Covid, my mother's mother. I went to Poland for her funeral. We were exempt from the restrictions of no travelling due to the funeral. Because of the whole costs of all the tests and travelling, it was just me and my mother. Her funeral ended up being on the day of my twenty-first birthday on 15 March [2021]. We couldn't view the body because she had Covid. She had to be cremated straight away. She got Covid during her treatment for cancer in the hospital; the whole hospital floor had Covid because someone came in with it.

The beginning of 2020, I was just finishing my second year at Bournemouth University, business studies, and I had to do exams and hand in assignments, and that's when Covid started. Uni was cancelled; well, it was moved online. I also got ill, because I had a hernia, so that was quite a journey to get an operation at the beginning of Covid. Because of the operation I couldn't walk for roughly a month, so I had to come back to Southampton, to my parents' house. My family is close with each other, I visit quite often, so it wasn't really a big change.

So now this is my uni placement year. I was planning to go into a big corporation and have the experience of working for a massive company. That was my goal, but then when Covid started they started shutting down opportunities. Me ending up in Swindon is actually quite connected to my mum. At the end of summer 2020, my mum was looking for an office and she came to the Polish Community Centre in Swindon. Basically, the person that showed her round, she joked about you can rent a restaurant as well. So the opportunity to open a restaurant came up and I was like, why not? So, from a joke, it became a reality, actually. Doing business studies and opening a business is like the ultimate placement you can have.

There had been a Polish restaurant in the Community Centre, but the lady left the place. She took all of her stuff, so it wasn't actually purchasing a restaurant, it was making a new one. It was September [2020], we had a look at the restaurant and we decided we wanted to rent it. I was always saving up for something, and I figured that's it. We moved to Swindon to take care of the premises. My dad moved with me; he helps me a lot.

I mean, if I knew what it was going to be before I started, I'm not sure if I would have started. The restaurant itself was really old-fashioned, and it didn't look nice and people didn't really come over to eat there before. So I had to design the restaurant, not knowing anything about interior design. The whole of October was a lot of planning, a lot of work, a lot of hours spent on painting and redecorating, getting the stuff for the kitchen, cleaning the kitchen, making it all up to date. We ended up going to London – there was a business shutting down because of Covid where we bought most of the fridges and microwaves and other necessary things. Chairs and tables were already at the restaurant, and because all of the expenses were massive, we have to cut the costs and do the best we can with the things we have.

The biggest challenge of starting was catering for a big celebration. It was the beginning of October [2020], just before 31 October lockdown, it was the opening of the Polish church.

So next to the Polish club there's a Polish church now, and they had just finished building, and there was an opening ceremony. We had to cater for them and that was our first event, before we even started doing takeaways. We catered for, I think it was seventy-five people or something like that. That was quite a big deal for me, because obviously I had nothing to do with cooking before, not professionally. I was just a uni kid that's opened a restaurant! We had to start preparing two days before. Polish food is a lot of work; we have a lot of food that requires prepping a lot. Doing pierogis themselves, doing the stuffing inside, putting them together, it really takes a long time. Polish restaurants are very focused on using raw materials to make everything, because Polish families are trying to keep their children away from fast foods and anything that's not healthy. My family had to help; I wouldn't have made it without them. My sister made the desserts. Everything just came together; it was perfect.

The people were so impressed with the food, they made us come out to the hall where they were all sitting and we had a standing applause. It meant a big deal to me, because the guests were, like, really posh. They were from London, from the Polish embassy. High-end guests, I would say.

The Polish church really acts as a social structure more than anything else, because that's where all the Polish people get to meet each other and speak Polish with each other. I think it's very important to have a structure that actually supports each other, because there are still people coming over to England that maybe don't know the language or anything. So Polish church is somewhat a way of meeting other people.

So we had the opening of the church, then once the second lockdown came we opened for takeaways. We didn't actually have a lot of contact with our customers; it was all by phone or online. It was really sad to have two or three people in the building cooking, and it was dark during the winter and rainy, and we had to do deliveries, so we've seen people for, like, three seconds.

We ended up having to compete with companies that do takeaways, but they cook from home. It's like you sign up for, let's say, a week of catering, and every day they deliver food for you. Their prices are much lower, so we had to reduce our prices. We did a lockdown offer. I think it helps a lot of people when, obviously, because of lockdown, they had less money. I think we also helped people like builders; they came back from work and they had fresh food delivered to the door. It was Polish customers mainly, because they heard about us from Polish community groups on Facebook and stuff. We're trying to open up to English people and everyone else now.

It was really hard to make a profit with the takeaway prices. Basically, each month we have to put in money. I had to, literally, go on the border of bankruptcy. We still haven't made a profit from the restaurant.

We have a cook now; she has a lot of experience in the kitchen, so she really helped us a lot. She was actually my nanny; she used to take care of me when my parents were at work in Poland. The food she cooks in the restaurant is really what I was raised to eat. She left Poland a few months after we did, but she didn't come to England, she went to Spain. After she lived in Spain, her husband and her decided to move to England, to Southampton. We didn't know we were both in England, and we had no idea we were both in Southampton. But a few years ago my dad came out to our driveway in front of our house, and her husband was taking a picture of a church nearby and they saw each other. She worked in a few Polish restaurants in Southampton, and we even have customers recognising her pierogi; they said that they ate the same-tasting pierogi in Southampton.

You go to a restaurant, you sit down, you have food and go away, and you never think about all the things that go on behind the scenes. It's really made me appreciate all the hard work that goes on. When you open your own business, you're not only the manager, you're also your finance management team, you're also marketing, you're also, as it turned out, the interior designer. I had to do a lot of things from different areas that I wouldn't expect myself to do. I'm glad I did it, because I could have been working in an office, picking up phones for the last year. I'm quite open-minded to new experiences, and last year has proven that I have to be elastic and be sure of nothing. Everything changed from day to day, week to week. Boris Johnson had his new speeches, new regulations came out; we didn't know what to expect.

I'm a calm person, but I got stressed a lot. I kind of took out my stress on doing physical things. I had a lot of physical work with the restaurant, renovating the inside seating spaces and all of that. And I often have a coffee and play the guitar, and it helps me with the stress of the restaurant and everything. I'm a self-taught guitarist; all of the things I learnt were from YouTube and free online lessons. I play in a band. My journey with the band started when my sister was getting married, and she wanted me to play something at her wedding. So I met the vocalist and we started playing with each other, getting ready for the wedding. It's a Polish vocalist, but he sings English songs as well, it's actually mostly English. We played at the wedding together, and then we started playing at bars and restaurants. Basically, because of Covid, we had to stop practising, stop any gigs from happening. So that was quite sad.

This year, I learnt that, if you keep your mind open, there's many opportunities you can take. Setting your mind on one thing limits every opportunity you get; you just turn it down because you think you want to do something else, but it might turn out it's the better option to take. I'm still waiting to actually see how it goes. We don't have the experience of opening the business when there is no lockdown, we only know the reality of Covid, so we still have no idea what to expect when everything comes back to normal. For now, the seating area outside, it helps a lot.[27] For the last two weeks I've been doing the garden. It was full of bushes and stuff; we had to take all of that out. We put in some marbles, like little rocks, and put some benches out to have more seating area. It was really nice to see people actually coming over, having fun, enjoying the food.

*Afterword – one year later*

It's been difficult lately trying to balance running the restaurant and uni, especially as it's my last year at uni and I need to do a lot of writing for my dissertation. I am planning to finish uni and go back full-time to the restaurant at the beginning of the summer. We have managed to attract several English customers, as well as Bulgarian and even German ones. As it turned out, Polish food is respected among many other countries with similar cuisines. To support this transition, we have developed a more English-friendly menu with better dish descriptions. I'm hoping to gradually increase the amount of customers we have per day, and maybe finally see some stable profits during 2022. I guess it's nice to have your own business, but also very tough and challenging.

---

27 Hospitality venues could serve guests if they were seated outdoors from 12 April 2021.

# Sophie Hughes
*We adapt, don't we?*

*24 March 2021*

I'm fifty-three this year and I've got a daughter who's twelve. Hairdressers aren't actually supposed to colour anybody's hair under sixteen, but, you know, we break the rules. I said to Maddy, 'I'm bored, I want to practise something.' So, nothing dramatic. She's got beautiful hair but she doesn't let me cut it. It's really long. When she was little, we'd go to parties and someone would say, 'I bet that's your daughter, isn't it?' And there'd be this cute little girl with these lovely braids, and Maddy would be the one with wild, curly, crazy hair because she wouldn't let me touch it!

It was myself and three employed staff: two stylists, one of ten years, one of five, and an assistant. Things changed quite a lot through lockdown. It's been a very stressful year. I remember getting the news that last week of March [2020], and suddenly having to move all the clients, and then I was doing the maths and thinking, okay, I can afford to pay the girls. And this was before anything like grants or furloughs were mentioned. I mean, nobody even knew what that word meant, did they? I remember talking to my mum and she said, 'Wow, that's a really old word, furlough. I've not heard that word for a very long time.'

I'm a director, so how it works, I'm employed by the business. You become a limited company; I'm no longer a sole trader. A lot of that's been in the news, how as director you tend to pay yourself a small wage and then you pay yourself in dividends, but the furlough scheme only works on the PAYE amount. So, I was only getting eighty per cent of my PAYE. I was getting about £500 a month.

I recently bought the building, so we've got a mortgage on the building, so it's the equivalent of having two mortgages. And then my husband was furloughed and he's on half his money, because although they say it's eighty per cent, obviously there's a cap on that, and because he's a high earner, eighty per cent of his money is, like, half his income. So it all got a little bit scary, but I'm an optimist, you know, so I kept saying it'll be okay.

We're very lucky, luckier than a lot. We've got a nice house and room and space. We bought this house about six years ago and did a lot of work, so we've got a big, open-plan kitchen. We did laugh because my husband, we thought he'd carry on working, so we ordered a desk like thousands of other people from Ikea. And then he was furloughed. Even my daughter went, 'Oh, Dad, that's ironic, isn't it? You've just made an office, and now you can't work!'

Maddy tried working in her bedroom for a little while, but we just felt she was, like, locked away a bit. So she then was doing it in the kitchen. At the start, she was still at junior school, she was really happy because, of course, there were no SATs. But they missed out on that final, farewell bit.

The junior school were not quite so on it as the senior, but then it was so new then, I don't think they really thought it was going to last that long. Maddy's dyslexic so it wasn't great for her at first. It was just, 'Look at this work,' and we were looking at it, and, you know, I thought it was boring. So, I said, look, let's do something else, and BBC Bitesize was our saviour. It was brilliant for Maddy. Her reading's not bad, you know, but she just doesn't like it because it's hard for her. But there's videos teaching it on Bitesize, so there's that feeling of interaction, and then questions at the end to see what she's learnt.

I couldn't work, so I was really lucky, I wasn't one of those poor mums that's trying to work and teach their children. You fear, don't you, for their learning? But I went from thinking, school starts here and then we finish here, to thinking, do you know what, school starts at 10am, we will do a few Bitesize, we'll have lunch, and then we'll do other things.

We cooked a lot. We were teaching her how to use the washing machine and other skills. My husband was getting her to knock walls down in the garden. Once I'd chilled out, I just enjoyed the extra time with Maddy. We had some good fun: rainbows in the glass windows, you know, lots of things. We'll sit and play cards with Maddy after dinner and stuff. It's none of that rushing from work and feeding each other and then flat out in front of the TV. We've made use of that time together.

We were always worried for Maddy, you know, with the struggle with the dyslexia. But we realised what a bright little girl she is, and just to see how determined she was, and how strong she'd been through the whole thing. So yeah, without lockdown I'd have missed so much, and she's just turned twelve, so she's getting to that stage where she wants to be in her room on her own a little bit more.

So we have had times of just brilliant things, and then we've had other times where it's been tense and emotional, you know; there's shouting and crying. A lot of it is fear-led because of the worry. And my husband particularly, I think, is, yeah, he's quite stressed with it all. But I feel we come together quite well under pressure. It's the everyday, when it's just normal, that we probably irritate each other, but when it's serious we're a bit like, nobody can break us. So, we're quite lucky, I think.

On 4 July [2020] hairdressers could go back. The run-up to that was extremely stressful. As an industry, we knew as soon as you knew, when it was on the news. Our industry is so disappointed with the government and the lack of worth that they feel about our industry. I mean there's lots of jokes going on about Boris's hair, and that's why he doesn't really care about our industry.

Luckily, I am a member of the National Hair and Beauty Federation, who have been absolutely amazing. They were communicating to us all the time. They're on social media, and when you're a member you get legal advice. I've always employed under five people; there are a lot less regulations that you have to follow, but all of a sudden I'm looking at social distancing rules, health and safety checks. And do we wear masks? Visors, no visors? Do clients wear masks? Because one minute the clients didn't have to wear masks, and then it was changed and the clients did wear masks. It was changing all the time. And then communicating that to my staff, and they were scared and worried and misunderstood that, actually, I knew as little as they did.

I'm very small; I've only got four chairs. There was another girl due to join us, renting a chair. So suddenly we were going to have to change our timetable from four or five of us can all work in the room together to only being able to have one side each, because of social distancing. So that was tough for everyone. We had to dictate shift work; we said, right, only two of us can work at the same time. And then we had to have fifteen minutes' clean down between each client. And then we couldn't double-book. Double-book is if I had to put your colour on and then you're sat there for thirty or forty minutes, then I would do a gent's cut in between. So that would cover that cost, that gap. But you couldn't do any of that. So we were already losing, sort of, two or three hours a day of possible income.

In the past, before lockdown, we had talked about the two stylists buying into the business, because they get to a stage where they want to make more money. They're both twenty-five. But then they didn't really want the responsibility of that.

So, went through lockdown, kept in touch all the way through, and then there was a lot of confusion with regards to having to alter our hours and coming back on part-furlough. And I think it gets to the stage that it's time to leave. They'd already felt they wanted to move on; they'd got to that stage before lockdown. It was already a seed, you know.

Anyway, they handed their notice in the first day back. It was sad; you build a relationship. I mean, they'd stayed at my house overnight and come for dinners. And they knew my daughter. I mean Maddy cried when she found out they were leaving.

When you work in a small business, there are some massive advantages to that because you have this lovely family element. But my experience is, the employed, they're happy to take that family and all the extras of that, but when it comes to you suddenly having to put your boss hat on, it's hard. It's hard for them to understand that all the responsibility and the debt and risk is on my shoulders, not on theirs.

So now it's myself, my friend who rents a chair for three days a week, and my assistant. Then I've got another friend who's joining the team later in the year, a stylist. So, yeah, gradually building the team back. It's a lot of change and quite a lot of stress. But we adapt, don't we?

When we reopened in July, I wanted it to still feel lovely for the clients. I did lots of research, lots of training online about returning to work and Covid. What's been lovely, actually, a lot of our industry have come together now, and not that whole competition thing. Other hairdressers, they were like, don't go crazy investing loads and loads of money on stuff, because you might not need it or it might not be the right stuff.

I'm going to have to put the prices up, slightly, not just because of Covid but because everything else has gone up, you know, electric, cost of stock. I'm L'Oréal, so that's French, so it's gone up. And the loss of money between clients now in the fifteen minutes' clean down either side, and not double-booking clients. It's a lot of lost time. I talked to my clients about it and said, look, either you can pay for that thirty or forty minutes and you get me throughout your whole time, or I can double-book again when we go back to normal. And they were like, do you know what, I like it, I like the fact it's quiet. And we've got used to it, I think, a little bit, haven't we? Less busy and less proximity to other people.

Sometimes clients come in with these beautiful white masks and then have their hair dyed dark. So we supply them with a disposable. I don't like disposable things. You know, we'd just got so far becoming as eco as possible, recycling everything we can. And then suddenly there's all this disposable stuff. And I've always bought Ecover or Method products, trying to be as natural as possible. I think we all went into a bit of a panic, and so I bought into the whole Dettol and stuff. I tried lots of different hand anti-bac, because people are like, oh, it's too sticky or it's too wet. Who'd know that we would be experts in hand anti-bac? It seems like a massive step back, doesn't it? We were getting so far one way with environmentally friendly things, and then suddenly, you know, you see masks floating around, which is sort of double whammy disgusting, isn't it?

My clients, I have been doing the majority of them over thirty years, so they know we're slightly obsessive anyway, clean-wise.

A lot of the stuff that we were told to do, we did, but you just wouldn't have seen, like all our equipment is in something called Barbicide, which is like an antibacterial. We always did that, but it was behind the scenes. So now we have it out so people can see. And we're very, look, we are spraying down. We would have done it, but it wouldn't have been with bleach, it would have been with polish.

Any clients that were nervous, I would book them in really early; I'd come in at 8am for them. They would be my first client, so they wouldn't see anybody else. And then I found I gained more clients, actually, because of, well, they said because of the look of the salon, because it was small and they could see it was clean. That was very comforting because you feel like you're doing the right thing.

Then, of course, we got locked down again. Then when we were allowed to open again at Christmas, the rent-a-chair stylist and I just worked ridiculous hours. We just went crazy, and then rightly so, because I think we both thought, what if we go into lockdown after Christmas because people just relaxed a bit, didn't they? So we just thought, right, let's just earn as much money as we can, do as many people as we can. I was doing, probably, sixty or seventy hours a week.

Now this lockdown has gone on a lot longer than I expected. I found this one really tough at the beginning, because it was cold and wet and grey. We ate too much and watched too much Netflix and had a bit of a wallow. Bit tired of Zoom by now, you know, like Zooming your friends. The whole novelty of that has sort of gone off really compared to last summer. I've emptied every cupboard and emptied the loft and gone through old photographs.

I've done a lot of online training; I bought some courses and there's lots of free ones. I've taken on an online booking system. Before, I was old school, writing it in my paper diary, so I've been concentrating on that, seeing how that works. It's given me the time to do that because before it always put me off, the thought of uploading 170 people's details on a system. I'm enjoying it, actually, I'm like this crazy convert now to online booking.

I think any of the parties would have made some mistakes. I mean, they're not my sort of government, they're not somebody I've ever voted for. Some of the things I just couldn't get my head around. The whole, you know, Eat Out to Help out,[28] I just thought it was unbelievably stupid. I feel for the pubs, but I thought, rather than Eat Out to Help Out, maybe just give them the money and let them stay shut. It seemed incredible to encourage people to go out in groups, especially when there's alcohol involved.

You know, a lot of people just didn't comprehend actually how serious it was, and still don't. I mean, I've got a couple of clients that think it's been made up and exaggerated. I had one between the lockdowns, a new client, she was very, 'Oh, it's all made up, do you know anybody?' And I do. So you politely sort of say, 'Well, yeah, I do.' And she said, 'Well, I think it's all made up, it's a conspiracy.' And so I just played the 'Oh, that's really interesting, why do you think that?' But it boiled down to nothing; she had nothing to say. I said, 'A worldwide economy, what, the whole world wants to wreck their economy, for what, what reason?' There was nothing; she had nothing to say. I mean, that would be one hell of a trick, wouldn't it, if the whole world had got together.

Racism, bigotry, or if anyone's, you know, offensive, then we're fully booked to that person. I just don't book them in

---

28 Eat Out to Help Out was a government policy to support cafés, pubs and restaurants when they reopened after lockdown. Under the scheme, which ran Mondays to Wednesdays from 3 to 31 August 2020, people could get a fifty per cent discount when eating at any participating business.

again. It's not nice for other people to listen to either, you know, the client on the opposite side. Anybody who makes anyone feel uncomfortable, we don't have to listen to it. I think, when you're younger, you want as much business as possible, but then when you get older, you learn you're better off saying no. But this conspiracy lady wasn't offensive, she just had a bizarre point of view. I think the flip side is, it is important that we question things. We shouldn't just go, yeah, yeah, that's fine, we're just going to do that. You don't want to stop questioning things, do you? That would be equally as wrong.

*Afterword – one year later*

I think we three are still adjusting. My husband working from home has its benefits: no travel, around for family life. But he sometimes feels isolated. As for myself, after going back to work last April doing fifty or sixty-hour weeks to make up for being closed, I made the decision to close the salon every other Saturday and not work late evenings, so that I and my staff can have more quality time with our families. Lockdown definitely made me and many other salons have the confidence to close. Also, clients' free time has shifted; for example working from home means they can be more flexible.

# Maddy Hughes

(Sophie Hughes' daughter)

*I did something called virtual sleepover*

*24 March 2021*

When we were at primary school, we had to leave because of Covid. There are some people that I never properly got to say goodbye to, and I'll probably never see again. I was a little bit annoyed because we would have got to go to a theme park once we had completed our SATs, so we didn't get to do that. I've never been to a theme park.

The days felt a lot, lot longer. I think because they weren't separated as school, friends and home, it all more merged together. My mum was really strict at the start, but then, nearer the end, just gradually, it softened and it started just to become summer holiday.

We made a lot of banana breads in lockdown, and then poured a load of honey and stuff on it. And on TikTok, I saw loads of people, because it was summer, they were all doing tie-dye, and I was like, 'Mum, we need to get tie-dye.' So we bought some tie-dyes. I thought all the colours were just going to mush into one, but it actually turned out quite nice. I don't think any of the things fit me any more. I got some money for my birthday, and I'm going to buy some white masks, and I'm going to tie-dye them.

I got a new bed in lockdown; I got a double bed. Mum put new wallpaper up in my room. Then, with the extra wallpaper, I found these really nice frames, and I love my dad's handwriting because it's really like swirly-whirly, and I got him to write on the leftover wallpaper some comments like 'Don't Give Up, You're Amazing' or 'Keep Going', stuff like that. And then I put them in the frames, and then he put some screws into the wall and I hung them up.

I did something called virtual sleepover. So I'd call my friends, and we do everything we do at a sleepover, but on the call. That was quite fun. We did stuff like facemasks, we watched movies, but on our own devices. And my birthday just went in January [2021], and I did a Zoom call with my friends. I got this really nice cake my parents bought for me, and it was made by a specialist and it had roses on and stuff. It was really, really big. We were never going to finish it all, so I chopped it up and I put a piece for each of the people that I was inviting and then I delivered them. So then on Zoom, when we would normally eat cake, they could eat the cake that I'd taken round.

And I did Guides. I don't do Guides any more, but I did do Guides. We did stuff on Zoom, like games and stuff, like picture drawing. You start drawing and people have to guess what it was, or you'd get to draw one line and then someone else would have to follow on with a shape or a line. We did camping badges where we had to either put a tent up or make a tent in our house somewhere. And my friend Lottie, really, really clumsy, she decided to do it under the table. She slept under her table; amount of times she hit her head! I slept upstairs in the office, and we put a sheet attached to the window, and then we turned the sofa bed round, and then attached it to that. I don't really like sleeping bags, so I brought my quilt upstairs and just slept with my quilt. Some people had put up tents outside, but we didn't have the room because our garden's still being done. They gave us two hours to go off and watch a movie if we wanted, or just do what we wanted, and then we ate tea. Then the next day, we came back at ten o'clock, I think, and did some yoga, stuff like that.

In the summer we went out and did a few more picnics and met up with a few more friends than we had before, because we were allowed to. This newspaper person, they came up to me and my friends and they were like, 'Can we take some pictures for the newspaper because it's all about summer in lockdown?' So he came up to us and just started taking loads of pictures. That was quite cool. But the way he had got us facing, you could see my friend Lottie, but then me and my other friend, you could just see the backs of us. That was quite funny.

I was supposed to go on holiday with Lottie and her family to Greece. We were supposed to go last summer, but that's been pushed back, so we're now going to go in 2022. The villa we're going to stay in, it was booked all the way to 2022, so that's why we had to book it then. It's got a hot tub, its own pool, and me and Lottie will share a room.

I knew a lot of the people that were going to secondary, so that was okay. But – I think this is really rude – they were like, put three people down that are your best friends, so me and my friends, we all put each other down, and then they split us up into three different tutor groups! I think they don't really like chatting, and they want you to make new friends.

At first, my tutor group was a bit scary, but once you get to know them I think a lot of them are really nice people. A lot of the teachers say that our tutor group is the best because we interact. The other tutors, it's hands up and answer questions. Well, our tutor group gets involved; we make conversation and stuff like that. And the teachers have even said to our tutor they don't want to tell us to be quiet because they love that we're talking and interacting so much. We have had some of the funniest moments in our class. So our tutor, she loves

David Attenborough, because she's a geography teacher. So for her birthday I organised everyone to put a pound or two in to buy her a life-sized David Attenborough cutout. So now, in the corner of the classroom, we've got a life-sized David Attenborough. Our tutor loves it because she loves David Attenborough, but she also loves it because it freaks all the other teachers out; they come in and they think there's a man standing in the corner!

When school closed in January [2021] we did it on Zoom. The timetable was still the same, with times and stuff like that. Enrichment and PE and dance would just be, get out and do some exercise, get away from the screen. I think my concentration is a lot better at school, because it's separated from home, and it's like in its separate environment. Whereas, when you're at home on the screen all day long it's harder. You'd have to register at the normal time, and if you weren't there you were marked as absent.

I must admit, a lot of people didn't even turn up or they would say 'Here' and then they would leave the group. There's one boy, hilarious, he'd leave his camera on all the time; he'd say 'Here', he'd then, we could see him, put his shoes on and walk out his front door to go on a walk with his family halfway through maths. He had the camera on and the teacher didn't even notice. What I found odd was that the parents were actually letting him go out on a walk halfway through maths.

Some people had really, really bad internet connection, because either their parents were working from home or they have a lot of siblings or they couldn't actually access a computer. One person's mic just wouldn't work; it was really glitching, you couldn't hear them properly. Near the end, actually, my connection just got really bad; it would kick me out of Zoom. I was like, I don't think Zoom likes me! Sometimes the teachers' internet is really laggy as well and the teachers can't access Zoom, so they put stuff up on Teams for us to do.

The teachers said, 'If you can have your camera on, please do,' but not a lot of people did. If, like, two people had their camera on, then I would turn mine on. But I didn't want to be the only person with my camera on, because that feeling when you're the only person with your camera on is just really awkward. But then I was like, that's probably how the teachers feel. Some people were on their beds doing their Zoom in their pyjamas. And the teachers said, 'Is there any way you can go to a desk or a table because sitting on your bed, arching your back, by a screen, trying to write all day long, it's not good for you.'

I tried to get outside, because my parents were like, 'You need fresh air because otherwise you're just going to get really stressed sat next to the screen all day long.' Our garden's really nice and our next-door neighbour's dog, she comes round, and she's like adopted us as her second family. So that's nice.

I think in lockdown I've learnt some people aren't as close to me as I thought, because they've just not contacted me at all. Like I messaged someone, and they've still not even read the message. I think you have to accept that maybe they're not as good a friend as you thought. You need to try and keep in contact with the people that are and you are closer with.

Going back to school, it's quite a relief, because I get to see my friends. I felt really lazy; I was out in the playground and I was just running around and I got really tired out! And I was like, if this is tiring me out, what's going to happen when I do PE later?

We have to wear masks all the time. If people are not wearing them over their nose and everything, they get told off. And the teachers are only allowed to take them off if they're two metres away from the kids, and two metres away from everyone. I think they had a lot of backlash with the teachers wearing visors when the kids had to be wearing masks; they're all wearing masks now. The only time we can take them off is in physical activity and when we're outside in the playground. I think you get used to it after a while and it's almost like they're not there.

We test regularly, so they say you need to do a Covid test every three days. I do mine on Sunday and Wednesday. They try to rely on the kids and the parents, and they have sent emails home saying your kids should be bringing home Covid tests to do, can you make sure they're doing them. To be honest, I find it quite fun. If you hold your breath, it doesn't hurt as much. My friends are all like coughing and gagging, but I don't have any gag reflex.

I tried to stay safe, and I took a lot more precautions. Like, if I saw someone, I would back up for them and let them go past me, whereas before you'd, like, shimmy past each other. Now you don't want to do that, you want to keep as much distance as possible. Some things will never be the same, like you'll never blow the candles out on your cake, because otherwise no one will eat from it, will they?

I clean everything. As soon as I get in from school I take my blazer off, wash my hands and then put my mask in the wash. Then I anti-bac my phone. My friends make fun of me because I like doing chores, and I clean my table down and stuff. Before we spoke, I was cleaning out all the drawers and hoovering and anti-bacing the kitchen, so I'm going to carry on doing that now. Then I'm going to move on to the utility. Yeah, I think, since Covid, I've turned into quite a clean freak.

# Ed Dyer

*Our pub had to close*

*2 March 2021*

You know what the lockdowns are like; it's a bit purgatory-like and everything's very similar.

This last year, you know, you were lurching – it was one disaster to the next one, one huge stress bomb to another huge stress bomb. Constantly. And not feeling in control. I mean, I cried in public in March last year when we were told our pub had to close. You were watching your entire life just crumble before you, everything that you'd worked for. You felt like you were stood on the edge of a cliff, and there was somebody trying to push you off.

I have two hats, as it were, when it comes to work. There's The Tuppenny, which is a pub that I co-own. Two couples involved, it's myself and my partner, Linda, and some friends of ours, who are a married couple. We opened November 2016, but prior to that, and concurrently to it, I also work for a local brewery, which is very handy when you have got your own pub. So yeah, pre-Covid, life was all about selling beer to pubs and to off-licences, and then, of an evening, I was doing the other thing, so getting involved in the bar.

When we started the bar, we always wanted to have an element of live music. So part of my duties, as it were, was programming live music. I've spent a long time working in local venues as a music promoter, putting on grassroots shows. We did some comedy, we had some poetry booked in, we did talks. We see ourselves as a social and cultural hub, as much as somewhere that sells drinks.

We wanted to have a very particular type of business – we wanted to have the kind of place that we would hang out in and hope that other people would join us. Call it prejudice or something, but there were people we didn't want to come in. We didn't want to have to deal with the sort of person that only drinks to get drunk, the sort of person that doesn't care what they're drinking, they've just come out to have a good time and if that ends in a fight and them being ill in the gutter, so be it. We wanted this arty, social space that attracted people who would want to experiment with the drinks and try something different, something new. They wanted to have a conversation. They wanted to meet new people or hang around with their good friends, you know, play games. We were quite happy for people to come in and linger and just generally relax.

It's a crap business plan when you think of it! You know, if you think of a business plan in terms of making money, we're never going to make as much money as a lot of places are because we're not catering to that mass market. We're specialist, but we are happy that way. It's always a point of pride that in the four and a half, coming up to five years in November, since we opened, we can still count the number of people we've ejected from the premises on one hand, which is silly. We beam with pride when single women come in and say, 'Yeah, this is about the only place that I've come in on my own and waited for my friends ahead of time.' We've had people come in and they've struck up great, long-lasting friendships.

When we first opened, the floodgates opened to all of the trolls out there who are going, 'What, you're not doing Fosters or Carling, pff, you'll never survive!' 'What, how much is that?

You'll never survive.' People thought we were crazy when we opened, because we were the first to do what we do. The Hop over the road had started the whole micro pub thing, but their focus was very much on traditional cask ales, so their clientele base was older, whereas we focused on more contemporary craft beer, so kegged beers, cocktails. The similarities between us and them were the lack of big brand names and this independent, free-spirited nature.

We have beers that we would retail out at the equivalent of £15 a pint. Now no one's going to pay £15 a pint, even in London. But of course this is a beer that's ten, twelve or thirteen per cent ABV. You don't want to drink it in a pint because you'll black out; it'd be like drinking a bottle of wine. So, we were the first place in Swindon to start doing one-third of a pint and two-thirds of a pint measures. There were some beers that we would restrict – you can only buy it by a third. Seriously, and I've seen this with people, 'No, no, I want a pint.' 'Honestly, try a third, see how you get on.' And, you know, halfway through the third, 'You're right.'

So our model was totally different to everything that had come before in Swindon. It's something that we've seen elsewhere that we wanted to bring here, but everybody thought, Swindon, chav town, it's fairly lowest common denominator, it's fairly mainstream, you're mad. But we had recognised that, particularly in Old Town, there are a lot of people who weren't getting catered for. You think, Swindon supports a Maserati dealer, a Ferrari dealer, a Porsche dealer, BMW dealer, Jaguar dealer etc. etc. There's money in Swindon and around Swindon, there's a lot of corporate high-flyers, there's a lot of people with decent jobs and decent salaries. For entertainment, they were going to Oxford, Bath, Reading, London, Bristol, anywhere except where they lived, which has been one of the curses of Swindon. So I think we recognised that there was an opportunity to keep these people. We've created a home for people that didn't have one.

Come February [2020], you could already sense that something was heading our way. Then, come March, things really did start to quieten down as people started pulling back from being out and about and socialising. Normally, March is when we really start to ramp up and build into the summer season, through Easter and spring. And it was getting quieter and quieter because all the news reports were coming out – you need to be careful with what you're doing, and who you're hanging around with, and washing hands and singing 'Happy Birthday' to yourself as you do it.[29]

And then up pops our esteemed leader in mid-March [2020] and says, 'Right, people, you need to stop going to the pub.' And that's what he said, basically: don't go to the pub; going to the pub could kill you; it could kill everybody; don't do it; it's the worst thing you could possibly do at the moment. End of conversation. And you're sitting there in your pub thinking, well, what does that mean for us? Have we just been made illegal, essentially? All of a sudden, our entire business has been forcibly closed by the government, but without actually forcibly being closed. He hasn't said to the pubs, 'Close, we'll look after you.' He said to the pubs, nothing. It was how the government had decided they were going to do things – say one thing and not tell you how they're going to deal with it. And I think that was the point that I started blubbing in the bar. You know, we were still open at that point, but there were only the hardcore regulars who wanted to support us. I was just sitting there, crying at the bar going, 'What we going to do?'

---

29 In March 2020, health professionals advised that to get rid of germs people should wash their hands for at least twenty seconds, which is as long as it takes to sing 'Happy Birthday' twice.

So we sat there, ashen-faced, panicking, thinking, okay, right, well, we need to check our insurance because basically we've been closed down because of this pandemic, but we haven't been closed down and the insurance won't cover us. So, where are we? How long is this going to go on for, where's the money coming from? You know, there are two households reliant on this business. My other job is tied into this one. So we had headless chickens at the brewery, headless chickens at the bar. We'd put, at this point, four years of our lives into this business; every penny of our spare money was tied up in it. If it went under, we'd exit with nothing. Eventually the government came and said, 'Yeah, pubs now officially have to close.' So everybody's looking at their insurance documents going, well at least we've been told to close, so this might be valid.

Then eventually Rishi Sunak[30] comes out and, like some little diminutive, well-coiffured superhero, says, 'Yeah, there's going to be some support.' That did for a little while. But the whole thing was so complicated. There was no idea of how long it was going to go on for and whether the funding was going to continue or what was going to be the next step. We were just finding out titbits from those afternoon briefings they used to do. There were no industry conversations. The government weren't talking to anyone within the hospitality industry. We were as in the dark as anybody was, despite being an industry that employed millions of people, that put billions into the country's coffers through tax. I mean, we're the most heavily taxed industry in the country when you think of beer duty and VAT and business rates and all of that kind of stuff.

Some of what they were doing was great. The business rates moratorium is fantastic; that makes a difference. We were lucky: we just crept over a threshold in terms of our business rates

---

30  Chancellor of the Exchequer, 13 February 2020 to 5 July 2022.

valuation to get a slightly higher level of support. So those first three months we had a reasonable amount of money behind us, but we're not the sort of people that are going to just shut the door, lock it, make sure the lights are off and come back to it when it's all blown over. We're like, we need to do something, this money isn't going to last forever, it doesn't cover our fixed costs on a monthly basis, it doesn't pay us. So we had to sit down and think, what can we do to keep this horse running?

I was thinking, I'm going to come up with a way out of this. I look at a problem and I have to tackle it; I have to make myself see it as a challenge. I can be quite a miserable, depressed kind of person. I have to avoid that. When I was married, I had some mental health problems, I had a breakdown, and I've learnt that you have to fight, you can't give up, you can't retreat. Or I can't. This is why I keep busy. I don't want to think too much about things or take steps backwards. So, for me, it was a case of, I've got nothing to do, I'm going to do something. I can't sit around and watch Netflix. I've had to train myself to be like that and not wallow or retreat into myself.

Typical of a pub, a lot of the money sits in the cellar. You buy a cask of beer for £70 to £90; some of our kegs of beer are over £100. You've got a fridge full of cans of expensive craft beer. You've got shelves full of spirits. So yeah, you've got hundreds and hundreds of pounds of stock tied up and, in the case of the cask beer in particular, going off – it's got a very short shelf life.

And we lost nothing. Absolutely nothing! We lost nothing because we very, very quickly decided we needed to do something (a) to get rid of this stuff, but (b) to keep money coming in. So what could we do? Well, we do a product range that isn't the same as other places, so there was probably still a demand for it. You can't go down to Tesco's and buy a lot of the stuff that we do at a fraction of the price, because they don't stock it. And we hoped we had a loyal enough customer base that they still wanted something like that. So we thought, well, we're allowed to do deliveries, so we'll set up a retail operation. How do we do that? Right, the easiest way is online. So I spent a very, very, very busy two days building, stocking, launching and promoting a web shop. I did that on a Friday and a Saturday, had a lie-in on the Sunday, and on the Monday, launched it. Four hundred products! And it was bizarre. It was very strange moving from running a bar to running a warehouse with delivery drivers.

My contacts at the brewery helped immeasurably. I could source empty bottles and crown caps and empty nine-pint, mini kegs. So we started selling that way. Our core beers were going into the nine-pint mini kegs, because they're the sort of easy, all-day-drinking-type things. And then, for all of the other guest taps, we were selling them in bottles. So we bought bottles, bought a capper, and started filling and capping bottles ourselves and selling that way. Then obviously selling the cans and stock and that kind of thing. And it's just grown.

So yeah, we set up as a retail business doing deliveries, and then, when we were allowed to, sort of click and collect. And the response was great. Amongst all of this despair and depression and horribleness, there've been these little shoots of wonderful things happening for us. It got us a lot closer to our customers because we had time to communicate with them. We took to social media and I was writing blogs. We moved things like our quizzes online, and we became this little beacon on a Sunday evening of silliness doing these music quizzes. Then we started doing general knowledge quizzes, and they're all a bit bonkers, but people were loving it. We were getting twenty teams logging on to do these quizzes. People were messaging us saying, I look forward to this for days, it's great, it's just a little bit of light relief in all the doom and gloom. And this was before people got fed up of doing everything on Zoom. We wanted to try and help people get through this.

That is something that we can look back on and be very proud of, and that online shop has kept us going financially, in the sense that we're here. It's kept me going. I've really enjoyed doing it. We've made it grow, and we now do coffee, sort of third-wave gourmet coffee, and our cocktails are up on there; we do those in little medicine bottles, so you can buy our classic cocktail mixes in medicine bottles and just finish them off at home. This retail thing isn't bad and we can grow something from it – the possibility is that the shop, even when things return to normal, will stay open, so it's given us a slightly different future plan.

We have a very key part to play in the community, and this has been one of the biggest gripes for me, in particular, with the way that the licensing and hospitality trade has been treated by the authorities. I can understand people's fear that we're super-spreaders, but if they actually came and saw most hospitality venues when we were allowed to reopen, they'd realise that we went above and beyond anything that you've seen anywhere else – anything in retail, anything anywhere other than maybe healthcare – in terms of track and trace and hygiene practices and sticking to the letter of the law.

Opening under social distancing regulations as a publican is not fun; when we were able to reopen in June [2020] we had social distancing, table service, one-way systems, masks. We had bloody notices everywhere. We had to implement nobody standing at the bar, but table service suits us. Linda was walking around, she'd see an empty glass, she'd say, 'Oh, do you want another one?' We liked that whole continental service style, where you sit down at the table and we take your order and bring your drinks, and before you know it, you're three sheets to the wind and you haven't got up out of your chair!

We were the whipping boys, even though we were the goody two shoes that did everything properly. You look at the figures and there's still no scientific evidence, in my mind that I've seen, that proved there were outbreaks courtesy of hospitality. We did track and trace; we never had anybody contact us from track and trace and say, someone's been traced back to you guys as the centre of an outbreak. But then you go down the shops, they weren't doing track and trace and you were picking up a bottle of drink that had been handled by fifty people that day. So we found the way that we were being treated was wrong, rude, dismissive.

We wanted to try and paint a picture that it's not like the way the media and the government are portraying our industry; actually, we're the answer. If you do things properly in a regulated way, it's a lot safer than going down Tesco's and buying a couple of bottles of vodka and having your mates home for a bit of a party. We've been licensed and regulated for a long time as an industry, the track record is generally good, and where the track record isn't good, in my mind, you can point the finger at enforcement because if these people with bad practices had their licences enforced properly, the problem would go away. So we wanted to try and advocate that the trade was a solution. And you cannot escape the fact that the pub trade in particular is a key component in the mortar that holds the brick wall of society together. It's somewhere you can socialise, and we're social creatures, we're not designed to be on our own all the time.

In the summer, it wasn't too bad because it was the rule of six – mixed households.[31] As long as you were organised with your friends, you could come out and have a few drinks. It became more problematic for us as a business when that changed after

31 The rule of six meant the police could disperse gatherings of over six people and issue fines, but gatherings of up to six people from different households were allowed.

the second lockdown. December [2020] was horrendous. That was when the rule of six changed to single household. You've just had six months of being stuck indoors with your other half and your kids, and the only people you are now allowed to go to the pub with are your other half and your kids. That ain't happening! And then add to that the food thing.[32] We don't have a kitchen, so we don't do food. We either had to find a way to do food or stay closed after the November lockdown. We're not the sort of people who are going to take the idea of staying closed lightly, you know; we're battlers. So we had to work out a way that we could produce food ourselves without having a kitchen. Luckily a good friend of ours, he runs a hotel, and his place during lockdown has been hired by the council to house the homeless, so he wasn't using any of his kitchen facilities for that. He just turned around to us and said, 'Well, you can use my kitchen. I've got loads of gear for banqueting and all of this kind of stuff.' We started doing chili nachos with a vegetarian/vegan version. We then moved on to doing other things, just to keep it going. But it was a massive ball-ache, because we were starting early, prepping up in a kitchen the other side of town, having to transport it halfway across town, having to keep it to temperature, having to constantly monitor these things. We had nowhere to wash anything up, so we were stacking stuff up and washing by hand in the sink, and then putting it through the glass wash to sterilise it. It was just horrendous. We have said, if they were coming out of this lockdown with the same, 'You must have a substantial meal,' we're not doing it this time. It just wasn't worth it.

You got very quickly tired of all of the toing and froing, all of the, for want of a better phrase, fannying around, that the

---

32 The requirement to have a substantial meal with your drink, as previously mentioned in the interview with the chef, Sean Stephens.

government were doing. It appears to us they were making things up as they went along; they were leaking things ahead of time to test popularity. We're used to working to a list of rules and regulations, but you're used to them making sense and being understandable and knowing about them in advance and being able to plan for things. But, throughout this year, Boris will make an announcement, and then you'll find out the following week from the Treasury how they're going to support that, so you've got an entire week of waiting to find out. Then the rules will actually be published five or six days after that, so you don't know the nitty-gritty details, you're just making it up as you go along, hoping you're right.

And, you know, you find you're working for days and days on a problem, and then the government change their mind. You just get to grips with one thing and then it changes, and you have to then totally switch how you do things. And it's physically and mentally exhausting, and it has been all year. They're such a populist government, that's how they are governing, not governing on any basis other than does this make us look good or not?

One of the things that we thought would have been better would have been to put a lot of the decision-making back down to local authorities. So the local authorities could work out who was safe to open, who wasn't safe to open in terms of local businesses. They already do that through monitoring our licensing conditions; it was just a very small extension of that, checking you're following the guidelines, saying, 'You're fine, you can stay open, but that pub down the road, well, we've just had to send the police in to break up a mass brawl, they can't open any more.' The mechanism's there, but they were doing everything centrally. And the people at the local government, they're like, we just have to wait for notification, we have to wait for funding, we have to wait for this piece of information.

I think this time will change people's attitudes. I know that there are people that, for a long time, are going to be too scared to go out to places like pubs because the government told them that pubs were inherently evil and the ninth level of hell. So there's a chunk of people who aren't going to have the joy of that communal experience. And we're not going to have the joy of counting their money at the end of the night. And then there are going to be people who do the opposite and they go nuts for it.

There are regular customers of ours who live on their own, and you start worrying about these people because the majority of their social contact takes place within your pub. We have a little early-evening crowd of older gentlemen, the widowers. They come in, and they have a natter with my other half and a couple of pints of cask bitter, and that's their social interaction for the day or for the week or whatever. Every pub has those. I know of situations where one or two of them aren't coming back, and it's sad that they spent their last days trapped at home, lonely.

# Lydia Smith

*I was getting paid for not going to work*

*6 February 2021*

At first, lockdown was quite nice, because I didn't have to go to work, and I was getting paid for not going to work. It was all right, I was just catching up on TV. Didn't binge watch *Tiger King* like everyone else, but I tried to cook every recipe from one cookbook and just, yeah, tried to keep myself busy.

We don't have a garden or anything at our flat, but there's a nice green around the corner, but obviously we weren't allowed to go and sit there and read or anything like that. But I made use of my hour-a-day exercise, just walking around. And I discovered loads of places. I've explored the railway path, the Town Gardens. In the thirty-three years I've lived in Swindon, I don't think I'd ever properly been to the Town Gardens until last year.

It's just trying to stick to a routine which is the hardest thing. I've been up since 5.50am, so it's just like, what now? It's also hard to be motivated when you're not in a routine and you don't need to get up and do stuff. You have to have a lot of discipline, and I don't really have that.

So, before lockdown, I was working for Better Leisure. I work on a project delivering chair-based exercises to older adults in Swindon. I did it in two care homes, then the leisure centres as well. I used to teach an exercise class a day, five days a week, so that's a lot of different people. You build good friendships with people, and I absolutely love older people and talking to them. Some of them tell me some really interesting stuff about Swindon and what Swindon was like.

Then, at the end of March 2020, I got put on furlough. I used to do quite a lot of other stuff, like I used to go to the Coffee#1 café in town for an event called We're Open, which used to run every Thursday, and it's for refugees in Swindon. Obviously, because of lockdown, that stopped. Basically my life has been brought to a halt. Me and my partner had to postpone our wedding as well, so obviously that's quite a big change because we were getting really hyped up for that. My partner worked throughout. He works in manufacturing, and they kept the factory open, which is good really, because two of us in our tiny flat would have just been a nightmare, really.

I have started my Master's in nutrition, physical activity and public health. I was quite unsure about that as well because it's a lot of money to do it, like, wholly online, but the uni said that it would be blended learning, but actually it's ended up basically being online. It's kind of a blessing in disguise because it means I don't have to travel to Bristol and stuff like that.

I'm quite open about my mental health. End of May/June [2020], I ended up having a bit of a mental health crisis. I've had mental health problems since I was, probably, about ten years old. Then I got diagnosed with bipolar in 2010 and put on medication, and so I was quite stable from about 2013 until last year. Then in September 2019, I decided to try and come off medication under the doctor's supervision, and then, I think because of lockdown, it just wasn't the right time and things got very difficult. I think I just got very stressed out with the uncertainty of life. Also, when I'm not at work, I feel like a bit of a drain on society, I just feel like I'm not contributing. I think I found that very hard with not keeping active and not keeping busy.

I'm a carer for my partner; he's paraplegic, so he can't feel from the chest down, but he's got full use of his arms. He was ill one night and so I didn't sleep, and I ended up going to the beach in Bognor. I remember I was thinking about my relationship and how I thought that I wasn't cut out to be a carer and look after someone that's sick, but I didn't want to break up with my partner because I loved him. I just thought it's better to not be here. I texted my mother-in-law to say, can you look after him because I'm not coming home.

I think the way depression works is it kind of tells you you're worthless or that people are going to be disappointed if you tell them that you're not well. I thought my mum would be so upset if I broke up with my partner, and also because I'd been so well, like I didn't want her to be disappointed. I just thought it's better to disappear and not be alive.

Yeah, so I ended up on the beach, had all my tablets in the car. My nan was scattered at Bognor beach, her ashes, and I kind of thought, if anyone knows the answer, then it will be her. While I'm driving I'm obviously calming down, like my head's arguing, do it/don't do it. I'm giving myself that chance. And by the time I got there, I was able to ask for help. I think it was my sister that phoned the police, and they found my number plate on their number plate detection cameras. They thought I'd be more local but, yeah, I don't know, my brain just does weird things.

My parents came up to Bognor to pick me up and take my car back to Swindon. In a way it was a blessing in disguise, because my family and friends were able to realise what was really going on, because I'm very good at hiding how I'm feeling. I'm quite high-functioning, so people sometimes don't think that it's such a big thing. So at least it became a way to, like, open the story again.

So, yeah, I was under Swindon intensive team for a while, and then I managed to get some counselling. I got a different diagnosis of EUPD, which is emotionally unstable personality disorder. Basically they've just added EUPD on, so it still says on my notes bipolar as well, but I don't actually think you can have both. I've got put back on some of my medication, but not to the same level. Hopefully it won't have to go up to that dose, because the reason why I was coming off it was so that hopefully, once we got married, we could start trying for a baby. You can't be on this stuff when you're trying for a baby. So, obviously, they didn't want to put me at the same high dose because in the future, after we get married, I'll have to try and come off it again.

After my mental health crisis in June last year, I was going to my parents' house because things got a bit more relaxed about who you could see. So I was going to my parents and just spending the day there, and then my partner was picking me up after work. But then, in the December lockdown and this lockdown, I'm just on my own in the day. My mum always says, 'Oh, you're in our bubble.' But we're not. It's hard because, if I was on my own, I would be in their bubble, but because I've got a partner, then I'm not technically allowed to be a bubble, but then because of my mental health and because I'm a carer as well, it's kind of like, I think, he doesn't count. So I am allowed in their bubble. I don't know. They don't really make it very clear.

I think my partner wished he'd been at home with me. I think he's quite worried. I don't think he's really had any experience of somebody with mental health before, so it's quite new for him. And, obviously, when I got with him I was really well, although I did tell him pretty near the beginning, like, these are my tablets and this is what I have to take and this is why. He accepted that, but I don't think he really truly understood because he's not experienced it before. I love him to bits, but it's hard.

Now at least I have uni work to do, so I can structure that into my day. I have to implement self-care and exercising. I worked in a gym, so I was always in the gym after work or before work. I'm lucky that I enjoy exercise, and last lockdown I managed to borrow some equipment from the gym. This lockdown, I didn't get in quick enough before they locked the doors. But I try to at least go out, like, ten minutes a day, even if it's just walking to the little shop round the corner to get milk or something like that.

I can't wait to get back to work, but I think it's given everyone an opportunity to appreciate the small things, like just going to the Town Gardens for a cup of coffee. I remember that first takeaway coffee after the first lockdown; I was craving a real coffee for so long, and then I got it, and I just remember really appreciating that, and even now it's making me smile just thinking how good that was. So, I do think you appreciate the small things.

I think that I've slowed down, and although slowing down has affected me in ways that I didn't think it would – like, a lot of past memories and traumas came back up because I'm not so busy – it's also good because it's given me the opportunity to deal with it. And also, I'm looking after me a bit more and just taking things at a slower pace. It's not all finish work, to the gym, to this or to that.

I think, eventually, I'll be glad of this time, but I think at the moment it still feels quite raw. I think I'll be glad that it's allowed me to be a bit more real, because I think when I was working and holding everything together, maybe people didn't see that depressed, mess side of me. I hid it so well. Like, my work, they wouldn't have a clue; if I if I told them about what happened, they'd probably be like, 'Nah, you're talking about someone else.' I'm glad I managed to have that time to work on myself and have counselling. Eventually, I'll look back on it and think, oh, it's a good thing, but it doesn't completely feel like that right now.

*Afterword – one year later*

We finally managed to get married in September 2021, which was fantastic. Thankfully, life seems to be getting back to normal – I'm studying on campus and back at work. And the most exciting thing is we are expecting a baby, due in October, so hopefully things continue to go well and remain stable.

# Claire Vega

## *Work's been a godsend*

*13 January 2021*

I'm a very compliant person. I think that's probably why I'm in the police. And work's been a godsend, just going in, with the banter amongst colleagues and sounding off against each other. With Covid regulations round the station now, every team is remaining quite insular in order to avoid any spread. I think that's probably why our team has become so strong, because we've all been working in our little bubble for quite a long time now and without much interaction with the rest of the police.

I work with offenders in the community. It's people that have been in prison, released on licence or no longer have a licence, also people that have received community orders, and also there are some people who, because of the nature of their crimes, are forever monitored by the police. As a general rule, maybe ten per cent of your nominals (the offenders that are allocated to you) would be high risk or very high risk, where there's an imminent risk of reoffending or an imminent risk of harm to somebody.

Obviously, within our role, we go into people's homes; that's what we do. And we have to do that in order to manage their risk and see if anything they're doing or having in their home environment is breaching any conditions of any orders they might have; you know, additional computers, contact with children, stuff like that. That cannot be done on the telephone because they could give you any old load of baloney. So we had to go into people's homes. But actually, even right from the beginning before all the lockdowns started, within the office, we decided that we weren't going to visit any of the vulnerable people that we had, because we've got quite a few offenders that we manage that are over, sort of, seventy or eighty. So we started doorstepping them – I assume that makes sense – we just had on-the-doorstep meetings with them, check they're in their home. So we'd doorstep them for the first lockdown and did phone conversations with them, but if anybody was high risk and we felt there was a need to go into the home then we would. What's been very good is they've been in when we've been going to visit them, because normally they can be out in all sorts of places!

We wear facemasks when we're double crewed in a car and stuff like that, then we just crack on. I don't know if that's fair on the offenders, actually. I don't know if it's fair on us, making us go into people's homes. However, that's our job. If we didn't do it, then the teachers would have every right to say that they're not going to school and the shop floor workers would have every right to say they're not going to go and stack shelves. So, you know, that's what we do. However, if any offender said to me, 'No, you're not coming in because of Covid,' and all the rest of it, then I would accept that, because I think that's acceptable on their behalf not to have me in their home environment. Hasn't happened. Not a single one yet. Not a single one.

I take a mask for them, and a lot of them do wear it. Some don't. The chap I went to see today didn't. I always wear a mask. I always document that I wear a mask, so if there were any comeback it could be seen that I was wearing a mask throughout.

My boyfriend bubbled up with me and my children. He was working from home and hasn't been back since. So we were travelling between where he lives and here, so I suppose we were quite fortunate in that aspect in that it gave my children another environment to be in, which was completely safe because my boyfriend's such a hermit – he doesn't get out and see anybody.

I could be speaking out, but I think everybody around here, you were sort of caught up with the excitement of, 'Oh my golly, what is going on? This is completely bonkers.' It was almost like a war mentality; everybody was actually really excited about something out of the ordinary, something community-spirited and all the rest of it. So there was definitely a buzz, I think, going around, bizarrely, as opposed to anything sort of fatalistic or bemoaning or, you know, woe is us, about all the things that we couldn't do.

Being a single mum, I waited with bated breath trying to figure out what this key worker thing was for the children going to school because, you know, I think there were a few days before that was all announced as to who was going to be eligible. It was very debatable as to whether they were going to let children in at all. It was all very last-minute, which is quite stressful when you're trying to organise childcare around having to go into work. I was going into the office and seeing all the other mums in there; they were like, oh my golly, our school's doing this and our school's doing that. Thankfully, my sergeant was very good. She's a single mum herself, so she completely understood and was incredibly flexible for all of us that needed help.

At that point, my children were at two different schools. My son's school were a little bit more painful about it. My daughter's school had a very can-do attitude: 'Yup, nothing's a problem, we can take in all key workers' children, we'll be open every day.' None of this 'you come in on Wednesday, Thursday, Friday' and all that business. And they said, 'You know what, your son is living with his sister; if she's got something, he's got it, so if the other school are being a pain just send him to us.' And so my son actually spent some days up at my daughter's school as well. Yeah, they were so kind. I mean the most kind-spirited people. The headmistress, really unbelievable, they had just such a great attitude to it. Straight away, they were not mucking about, they were making sure all the children on pupil premium were going in. In the holidays, while my daughter's school was open, my son's school was closed. My son's school would close last minute, and the thing is they'd send you an email, like, three o'clock on a Friday, so you couldn't even get hold of anybody. You just had to muddle your way through and, luckily for us, the sergeant was incredibly accommodating.

What I found slightly panicking was, going to school was disadvantaging the children because they weren't doing any work. They were having the most wonderful, magical time going out for walks, creating amazing things and loads of art, but they weren't actually doing any maths or English at all, or any sort of education. And subsequently now, my daughter has the spelling age of a six-and-a-half-year-old, and she's nearly nine. I think because everybody had this world war attitude, they were thinking how can we give everybody a lovely, wonderful time when we're having this crazy situation. They're very holistic up at that school, so they were worried about the children's well-being. I spoke to a primary teacher at another school and she said, 'We're just meant to be like a childcare facility because it's not fair to the children at home if the children in school are being schooled.' And I remember thinking, I'm not sure I agree with that because the children at home have got parents who could school them if they wanted to. You know, if little Elsie May, heaven forbid whoever Elsie May may be, has cancer and can't go to school, you don't stop schooling the entire class just because Elsie May can't be in school. You've got to keep going. I was unhappy about that to the extent that when I had a working-from-home day, I actually kept the children home and schooled them. So that was concerning, and I think it is still taking its toll now to be honest with you. I know people that have children in private schools, and the private schools in that first lockdown, because people are paying so they have to provide something, well, they had Zoom lessons all day long; loads of work.

It's different now in this third lockdown. What my daughter is experiencing in primary school now is excellent. Everything is clearly laid out, it's supported by additional documents. They've got an excellent online platform that they use; they respond to the children's work over this platform, literally within ten minutes. Obviously, we're very lucky that my children have their own iPads. We've got a laptop at home. My son's now at secondary, and they have Teams lessons all day. They just follow their normal timetable, and he is busy all day long. I don't see him from 9am until 3pm, bar half an hour for lunch. So I think either I'm very fortunate or people have got their act together now and realise it's not quite as difficult as they thought it was going to be educating the children, you know, on a home-learning package. They've just got to embrace technology, haven't they?

I did feel sad when the third lockdown was announced. Not for me – I'm sufficient with everything I've got and have a very full life just doing what I'm doing – but for the children. They love seeing their friends, and they love going to school and interacting with everybody. Just even playing out in the fields outside the front of the house with all of their friends; for my son, that's just him in his element. For him, that is really tough not being able to do that. I think how exciting it must be starting secondary school, but now suddenly he's not even going into school. And even when he was at school, they all had to stay within their class and they weren't moving around the school, and that's a real shame because they're not getting to feel that difference between secondary school and primary school.

At the start of the first lockdown, I think there were about two days or so where we weren't quite sure whether the children would be allowed to go to their dad, David. And then I think it was the senior lawyer for family law in the country, he released a press release saying that if you're from separated families the children can still continue to go between the two parents.

This whole single parent thing – the children moving between parents – is a tricky one because obviously you've got court orders in place and you don't want to breach the terms of those court orders. At the same time, it's also complete lunacy in the fact that I'm a key worker, so the children go to school, then you've got David travelling on public transport in Birmingham, his wife doing the same thing, and their baby daughter going to nursery. Nurseries are hotbeds of germs; there's no way the nursery nurses can distance themselves from the children. And then them all mixing with the children, then the children coming back to me. And, you know, it did cause some tension because David was still letting them play out the front with other children and calling me absurd for not letting them play out the front here. I said to him, 'You know, this isn't your risk to increase, because ultimately if the children get unwell it will be on my head. I'll be the one who's not going to work for two weeks, four weeks. Who knows how long we'll have to be self-isolated because you've decided to be slightly reckless.' It did make me very nervous sending them to an environment where there seemed to be more risk taking going on than back here. I wouldn't want the children not to see David just for the sake of it, but I do think we've got a responsibility as key workers, and key workers' children going into school, to keep those children as sanitised as possible outside of the school environment. And I don't feel by sending them to Birmingham and mixing with another three pools of germs that that's fair, really, on the school.

The very first week they were due to go, about ten days before, David said that he thought he had Covid, because he was in bed for a couple of days and was feeling awful and quite a few people in his office had felt like that. So I said to him, 'Look, I would like to extend the period before the children come to you.' It was going into the Easter holidays, so I could push it out by a few days and add the lost days onto the end. David was so incensed that I thought it wasn't right for the children to go when his ten-day period was up, but I thought, you're ill, you're not self-isolating from the other people in your household, so I don't know if you're passing that on to them. If their baby were asymptomatic, then mixing with my children, then that's just not acceptable in my eyes.

That pushing it out by a few days, which I thought was just being sensible, well, that started a whole storm of events, which culminated in having to go to court in the middle of the summer.

The telephone stuff worked quite well in the court: we did it all over the phone, and it all seemed to be quite efficient. It's quite hard because obviously you can't see people, you can't read body language. I decided to be a litigant in person because it was just so expensive; I couldn't afford any more solicitors' bills. I had a McKenzie friend.[33] We took on the might of David's legal team. I think David must have been communicating with his legal team by having Teams open or something like that and typing each other messages.

---

33 A McKenzie friend assists a litigant in person in a court of law by taking notes and giving advice. They don't need to be legally trained or have any professional legal qualifications.

Family law is very interesting in that matrimonial law and all the financial stuff very much recognises what women bring to a relationship and to the economics of the family, even just by being a mum staying at home and keeping the fires stoked, as such. But when it comes to contact, family law is very much on the father's side. They've probably got a very unconscious bias over the fact that you often think that mums are trying to be difficult about contact with dads, so they seem to have that stuck in their minds when they go into it. It didn't seem to make any impression at all on the magistrates that I had single-handedly managed all the Covid problems with the children, all the extra responsibilities, all the schooling and home-schooling. All I was asking was not to have to drive the children to Birmingham, because David was the one that moved there after all. I didn't ask him to go and he didn't need to go. He moved there and now he was not happy driving back and forth and wanted me to do the journeys on a Friday. I was just trying to point out to them that I've got so much on me already, and I really can't afford to lose a Friday evening to drive them to Birmingham when normally I would just stay on at work on the weekends the children went to him.

It fell on deaf ears. It didn't help that there was not an ounce of compromise within David. So they had to create an order that was going to be sustainable, I suppose. What the judge decided to do was just split it down the middle, so now I have to do half the driving.

Because the children go off to their dad every other weekend, it makes you value the time that you have with them a bit more. As a family, we've all discovered lovely things that we can do together, and now spending time with the children and my boyfriend is more important to me than looking outside my home. We've done more cooking and arty stuff. We got a turbo trainer, so we all jump on the bike and do some cycling in the house. My daughter has become passionate about it. I've seen such benefits to family life by just being a tiny bit more insular, rather than spreading yourself so thinly amongst so many things. It didn't feel that much of a loss not rushing around here, there and everywhere to go and see that friend and this friend. Actually, you realise when you remove that stress, life's very nice!

I think what I'd love to come out of this time, not only that people just remember that we don't have to rush around like lunatics trying to be everywhere, but I would love things to become a little bit more like the olden days, like your area becomes more of a community and is able to provide you with the things that you need. I mean they've got the farm shop now, haven't they, which does a bit of bakery stuff, and they've got the butchery stuff in there as well. How lovely it would be if we all sort of close down into little communities a little bit more. That would be really nice.

I've got to go and make a cake for my team now. Shall I tell you, we arrested somebody today, and it was my offender. But I had to leave early afternoon because I had to collect the children. And so that left them with a house search, some lock-up searches, search of a car and the remand file to do. The guy's been recalled to prison and I'm like, 'Sorry guys. I've got to go.' So I owe them cake.

# Paul Mitchell

*Without Covid I would still be there in marketing*

*31 March 2021*

I'm working on a really big design project at the moment. It's for somebody in Swindon; they've got a huge garden. It's a blank canvas. I go and survey, take note of what's there, ask questions, get a mood board together. I put a design together, client loved it, so now we're in execution mode. This is very different to what I was doing before. It's been really good, but it's a huge learning curve.

I was an art director in marketing. I'd been in the marketing business for thirty years, worked my way up from a junior all the way to senior within various companies. In January 2019, I wanted to be a freelance art director. Never gone freelance before, little bit scary, off you go into the big world on your own and fend for yourself. But within no time I picked up freelance work, and that was great. Then in March the company where I first started had just won a huge banking account and were on the call for creatives. I went to see them and basically they said, 'Look, we'd like to offer you a full-time job.' I was quite enjoying freelance work and I seemed to be getting a lot of work, but then at the same time I kind of fell into that security trap a little bit and just thought, okay, I'll go for it. It seemed an exciting proposition. That was all great up until the start of 2020. On 16 March I was at a double funeral, and in the evening I had a phone call from my boss saying you're not to go in the office.

We were all told to stay at home. Then I think it was April when the furlough option came available to a lot of companies. They selected a whole bunch of people and I was furloughed. It was just the most bizarre time; it felt really difficult knowing that I was at home being paid and my colleagues were half staffed and really, really under the cosh. Anyway, they called me back in in July when they took me off furlough to work on several big projects for the banking organisation.

Then I was on holiday. We've got a caravan, but as soon as I got to the destination I found out that, purely because revenue was so bad – the work had just completely dropped off in the marketing world – they had no choice but to make redundancies. The two weeks I was away, I kept having to do video calls and emails back and forth, being consulted for redundancy.

I was interviewed three times and, yeah, they had to let me go. I was sitting in the awning of the caravan in Cornwall of an evening when they told me; it was the start of the second week. I was really upset, really upset. Proper kick in the guts. I thought I'd done really well. I mean, it was just that there were too many people with my job title, and I'd only been at that company a year. There were three of us, and the two other people had been there at least five years longer, so I kind of thought, well, it's a no-brainer because those guys know the other clients inside out and they'll be more valuable to the company. But I think you can never not take it personally. You get haunted. You keep having, not flashbacks, but you keep reliving moments and you think, was it something that I did? Or did I not present that properly? Were the ideas not good enough? I don't know. The whole process seemed really awful, the way they went about it.

Obviously the holiday, I mean, it wasn't a holiday for me. My children were great, they tried to take my mind off it and said, 'You're in Cornwall, your favourite place, just try and forget about it.' I didn't want to bring everyone down and be upset and have them, you know, worrying. Luckily the weather was incredible, made a massive difference, best weather we've ever had.

I've never liked to be in a situation where I don't know what I'm doing. I thought, well, they don't want me, so I need to move on. I've got the responsibility of a family and what have you. We're not in the situation where I can sit around and think about what to do; we've got bills and a mortgage to pay, and I had to do something fast.

With my wife, we talked about it, you know, what could I do using design skills? I love gardening. So we put two and two together, you know: wouldn't it be great to have my own garden business? Garden care/garden design. Just started floating some ideas around, ideas for names. My parents had a farm, and we always did everything ourselves where we couldn't afford to get people in, so I learnt everything from gardening, painting, decorating, making things out of wood. I always loved plants, loved shrubs, loved growing stuff. So then, being a designer, combining the two together just seemed a natural thing for me. I designed my own branding, because that's what I've always done. I did my website. I got Instagram together.

First, my sister got me to do a couple of jobs for her. She was very pleased. She then told people at work, so then I did bits and bobs for those guys. It kind of snowballed really; before I knew it, people were just contacting me. It's just like friends of friends of friends. Going back, it was just garden maintenance, so hedge cutting, lawn cutting, weeding, pruning, all that sort of stuff. And then people said, 'Oh, I see on the website you do a bit of design.' So I'd say, 'Well, yeah, that's kind of what I do, and I'll do some ideas for you.' I've always been able to draw stuff to try and get an idea across. I've got my own unique style of just boshing it all together, like I would do if I were doing a job for Volvo or for whatever. As I say, the project I'm working on at the moment, it's a big design project, stemming from 'Well, I've got this blank canvas, what would you do with that?' And I seem to be doing more of that designing now, rather than just garden maintenance.

Right now, touch wood, it's proving pretty successful, so much so that I'm fully booked out until past June. I've had to turn work down. I'm finding that there's a lack of design out there. There's a lot of people that just want to cut a hedge, cut the grass, or, you know, prune, but there's definitely a market out there for more design. And I think, because of the lockdowns, a lot of people haven't been away on holiday, they have the money and they're spending it on their surroundings. They want their garden to feel nice, to be inviting. They want to take five from the screen and walk around their garden, or even to sit somewhere with a laptop. A lot of people are very much into their nature. A lot of the designs, I say, 'Well look, do you want something formal, do you want something modern?' No, they really want something very natural to attract bees, butterflies, what have you. Because they can't go anywhere, at least they've got somewhere to sit and they can watch things. They want it buzzing with wildlife.

I've been sat in an office for all those years, so nothing has prepared me for this! All my kit is at my parents'; I go there and lift heavy stuff into the trailer, get everything ready, go to the job, unload, do it all, put it back on the trailer. And I have to get rid of the stuff: green waste or heavy bricks or slabs. It's absolutely exhausting; it's an absolute killer. If I was ten years younger it would have been great. No, I mean, it's the fittest I've felt for years; I'm just tired. Generally I'm asleep by half past nine: bang. Probably lost about two stone. I think I need a bit of help. I've had my brother working with me today, but mostly it's just me because I can't afford to pay for somebody else unless I get a big design job come in.

I'm also doing something else as well, so maybe it's a little bit too much. I love woodwork, so part of the business – it's all a bit mad very quickly – I make rustic furniture, so tables and benches and also shelving to put pots on. It's part of the design. I'm trying to learn to do it really quick, where before I was spending a week making a table; actually, I've got to bosh that out in, like, two days.

I'm also doing a course, which is an RHS Level 2; this is the horticultural correspondence college. That's everything to do with what I'm doing: taking the survey, design, execution, and, of course, learning about plants and shrubs and all the right conditions. I've got two years to get this done, and I'm finding no time to do it.

Then, on top of that, just to say, I've got another business; I design websites and do email campaigns. So I'm doing that kind of thing for people as well. I do that in the evenings; well, when I'm not feeling so tired. This garden business is so physically demanding; if there is a rainy day – and I'm not saying I'm a fair-weather gardener – but it's really quite nice just to be sat here and not lifting. I can sit and design websites.

I'm working out how the garden care is going to work for us as a family. What is this business? When I first started off it really was maintenance, so I have a handful of clients and one morning I'll be here, the afternoon I'll be there. But I found that, with these design projects, it block books me out. All those clients are saying, 'Can you not just pop over for an hour?' I've lost one or two because all they want is maintenance, somebody that just quickly comes in, cuts the grass, does the hedge, does some pruning, does some weeding, whatever. So yeah, it's a difficult one; do I decide that I eventually employ somebody that can go and do those bits? I'm certainly getting a big buzz from coming up with ideas; it's a much more attractive proposition than just cutting the grass. And it's more profitable, so I think that's the leaning of the business now.

There is a client who's got a huge property and a massive garden; it's almost like a field. And he just mows this field, and he wants ideas, something dramatic. So, you know, it is getting bigger and bigger, the projects. There is a sense of nervousness about it because someone's giving you a big chunk of money. It keeps you on your toes. When I'm spending their money, I think, what would I expect? You can easily slip up, get it wrong. You have to check with the client: you know, 'Are you happy with this stone? Are you happy with this colour?' I've had two very nice clients, they love everything I've done, but I imagine not all clients will be like that.

It's a big learning curve, you know, these big design projects; you've got to account for man hours, you've got to account for materials. You've got the lead time on the plants. I'm learning that big garden designs are designed a year in advance. You've got to let the nursery know; you have a deal with a wholesaler, who will then be, 'Right, what's your planting schedule?' And suddenly you're thinking, planting schedule, what the hell is that? They want to see your design, they want to see your planting plan, and then they grow this stuff for you, so when you come to execute that design, the plants are ready to put in there.

When I worked in marketing, it was Monday to Friday; weekends, we could do what we wanted. Now, having my own business, I am working on a Saturday and Sunday, and also my wife is involved as well. She's been an unbelievable part of the business. She has helped with invoicing, dealing with HMRC, doing the quotes, scheduling. It possibly would have been a car crash without her; she's just been such a fundamental part of the success.

Way back – my parents – I was asked to join the farm, but at that point I wanted to be an artist. I wanted to paint; I wanted to be an illustrator. Then I found myself in the marketing world; that was where the opportunity was. I've been very lucky, I've had a fantastic career in marketing, I've worked on everything and, you know, I've had a lot of successes, and have enjoyed it. But, to be really honest, I was getting bored. When a good project came in, great. But there wasn't many of those, not exciting projects, not anything really new. It seemed to be the same old thing, same old thing. But without Covid I would still be there in marketing.

Now I feel like a different person, completely different. I feel really happy, like really happy. I feel happier than I ever have done, and I don't miss my old life for the world. I do not want to go back to that, although it is a bit scary. It's scary because it's good at the moment, and work is there, but I'll just have to see how it goes. It's way off what I was earning, and we've invested a lot of money in kit. However, since August we haven't done too bad.

*Afterword – one year later*

Basically, I've not stopped since we last spoke. The business has evolved to more of a design landscape offering, rather than just general maintenance. This ranges from making things from planters, pergolas and gates to outdoor kitchens, patios, paths, small walls and planting, which has resulted in enough work for the years to come.

At the same time, the company that made me redundant has been asking me back on a freelance project-by-project basis, which has felt a bit surreal but been very handy financially. I still do some freelance work too for my client in London, so it's been quite a task scheduling. I've been way too busy to do the RHS course!

I'm tired, but in a good way. Being outside in all weathers has its ups and downs: too hot, too cold. When I started, I was like a steam train, didn't stop, just kept going whatever it took to get the job done, but over Christmas I definitely felt I overdid it physically and realised I needed to look after myself if I want to make this work going forward.

I don't miss my previous life. I have freedom to do my own thing, to make it work, and it seems to be working. Losing my job, and knowing that there were no other opportunities, I was forced to do something I always wanted to do, but was nervous about not having a regular income. But, after the success I know now, I wish I had done it sooner.

# Lancia Estrocio

*We didn't even have a proper leavers' prom*

*24 March 2021*

I'm in college every other week – it's a week in, a week out. It's because of Covid, because there's a lot of people in college, so they just want to lower the risk. I'm just chilling at home, doing all the work online. I'm in my bed eating and barely paying attention.

I moved to Swindon four years ago. I used to live in Wembley for five years, and before that I was born in Goa. It was a big change because in Goa, like, I didn't know what the internet was. We had a little old box type of TV and sometimes the cable would go out, and when it used to rain the lights would turn off and we'd have to generate the power. We used to play with tyres on the road, and like, cricket, badminton; then any time a car would come, someone would shout 'Car!' and we would just all scatter to the side of the road.

My family back in Goa, since the pandemic, everyone has got internet now. So my uncle who still lives with my grandma, he had to buy internet because my cousins, they needed it to access school. It's strange, because now we just call all the time. We started a WhatsApp group chat, and they're like, 'Everyone's in one room!' It was so loud the first day because everyone was talking, and my grandma was like, 'Where is everyone?' And we're like, 'We're all in different houses.' Before we would phone call my grandma every weekend, but now I can see her. Obviously the internet is so bad, but it's still insane.

It was a massive jump coming here; like I thought I knew how to speak English, and then there were words I'd never heard of, and I was like, oh my god, are they swearing at me? What's happening? Are they calling me ugly? British people have this tendency to talk really quickly, and I'm, like, slow down, I don't know what you're saying, my brain's trying to process this.

All the moving, I think it's helped me grow. I just know how to communicate with people easily now, because I can be like, 'Hi, I'm Lancia.' I always try projecting happiness and just being happy, even though some days I might not feel like that.

Lockdown's had an impact on a lot of things. So, March [2020], we had the day we found out lockdown was happening. Everyone was really panicked because we were like, how are we going to get the GCSE grades? I think, at the same time, people were just glad to leave school. They were like, oh my god, we're leaving school, we're out of prison, we don't have to worry about detentions, we don't have to worry about this and that. So everyone was happy, but at the same time sad, because we wouldn't see each other; everyone was going to different sixth-form colleges, or just doing an apprenticeship straight up. We didn't even have a proper leavers' prom, no leavers' assemblies or any of that. I was looking forward to the prom. My dress, it's just sitting in my closet.

I uninstalled all my school apps. I was like, I'm going to take a full break, I don't want to work, we're definitely not doing any tests. If there were any important things, they would message us. From what I've heard, I don't think they set work; I think they just sent quizzes and stuff for us to do, so we're occupied, I guess.

Me and my friends had plans this summer, like we were going to go to carnival in Notting Hill, we were going to go to Thorpe Park, we were going to have so many picnics. Obviously, we have like 2p in our bank accounts, so I don't know how we were going to fund all of that! But we made all these plans to go places and do things, which didn't happen, and we were just all gutted.

From March until June, when the lockdown was hard, I didn't leave my house. Literally indoors because my mum was like, 'We're not going out.' I think I went on one shopping trip. We would be very safe. My mum was, like, anytime anyone would go out, we come home, we drink a glass of hot water, we have a shower, we wipe everything down. I was sitting at home, doing nothing, like, FaceTiming people, just to make sure everyone's okay and no one's taking it too hard.

Then my friend's mum died, and it was because of Covid, an overdose. My friend was so traumatised. I was just like, I want to be there for you. I just wanted to hug her, but Covid was like, 'Nope! You can't do that.' Of course I called her every day.

I like being with people; I find it much easier than being by myself, because I feel like it's a good escape. Being with myself, then I think a lot. I'm just thinking, thinking constantly, my mind is racing through sixty scenarios. When I'm with people, I don't have to think about things.

I started working out a little bit, because before, I used to love going to the gym. And me and my mum would try new recipes; she would teach me how to cook Goan dishes. It was like being back in Goa; she was a housewife in Goa, so it was kind of the same thing, so it was bringing back a memory. We would make so many barbecues. Every year we try beating the amount of barbecues we had the previous year, and I think this year it was definitely above thirty.

We're Christian, Roman Catholics. We would go every Saturday or Sunday to church, and then we pray every day as a family. With the lockdowns, oh my god, it's literally been a year since I've been to church. I think you have to book a place to get into church now, so I haven't really attended. We've just been praying more than usual at home. It's definitely strange not going to church. I love the singing part. Even though church is an hour long, for some reason the fifteen-minute prayers at home seem longer. Church is just fun.

For college we had an online induction, and then there was one day where you had to go into college to look around. It was just all weird, because I was like, oh my god, why's everyone taller than me? Why does everyone look different? It was the first time I saw some people I knew since before lockdown. I was just like, everyone's changed and I still look like a weird potato. They're all so perfect. I'm just there, arggh, like terrified.

But college has been going good. I joined the student rep programme so I could make some friends. And I got promoted to a senior rep. I don't know what I did, but apparently I was good at it, and then I got promoted again to an executive rep. So it's like you get to make all the big decisions. We had a meeting and the teacher started talking about how they're still going to continue with doing the first-year exams. I was like, 'Sorry, can I just butt in, I don't think it's right to do the first-year exams because of Covid, no one's really been paying attention, some people don't even know half of the spec.' I was definitely stressed out about it, because if I don't pass my business exams I would have to do the whole year again. And I feel like, if I'm feeling like that, there will be so many more people feeling like that, but they just don't want to say it. Because of me, there was no first-year exams any more, so everyone's passing their first year. And no one knows it was me, so I'm like a secret Samaritan! It was actually very good, because in school teachers usually don't listen to you, but in college they definitely listen to you more and give you more freedom. It's strange; I was like, ah, my opinions are being listened to.

My dad never stopped work. He works on the buses, like a bus driver. My sister got a job there as well, because there was literally no jobs, so my dad was like, you might as well work for the buses with me until you find something. She has to stay there for three years or something.

Oh my god, my dad; I hope everyone has a dad like mine! He is the sweetest little person, he honestly doesn't belong on this earth. He's just the nicest. I study photography and I had an Android phone, and I was like, 'I need a camera.' And he's like, 'Well then, what are we going to do about that?' So then he was like, 'Wait a few months, let me save up money,' and then he bought me a Canon camera. And I was just like, 'Thank you so much, I'm not going to make you regret this, I promise I will use it to my fullest.' We never grew up spoilt; like me and my sister were always taught to work for what we needed, but I was so grateful. He was like, 'Now you better do what you need to do, you better be making money now.'

I've started a YouTube channel. I was like, everyone does a Q and A, I'm just going to post a Q and A, and I'm going to see how it goes. I put on my Instagram, 'Ask me questions, I might film a video,' and then I got so many questions. It was mainly weird people who answered – weird men asking for feet pics and nudes and 'make me food'. And I was like, okay, you're getting blocked. My friends asked me the questions, like are you single? What is your favourite food? What college do you go to? What do you think about this, what do you think about that? I tried answering in a funny, not so serious type of way. I want to make people happy when they watch my videos, even like two seconds of their day. Like I want to just distract them from their normal, mundane life. Lockdown just made the world seem so grey, so boring and dull, which it shouldn't be, especially at our age, it really shouldn't be.

My first video got three hundred and something views. Everyone was really excited, and everyone was like, you're doing so good, you should do more videos. And they were giving me video ideas to do. They were saying how I could improve, which was so helpful. Some people disliked the video, but I think that was people that didn't like me or something like that. Someone was like, how do you feel about the dislikes in your videos? And I was like, it's still engagement, you're just telling me you don't want to see that type of video. If someone doesn't like it, then that's their opinion and they're allowed to have that opinion, it's fine. My dad was like, people who write hate comments, there might be something going on in their lives that they want to just vent out on you. And I was like, that makes sense. I feel people just don't understand how to deal with hate and criticism. I've learnt not to feel hurt by other people's words. How are you going to hate on me or cancel me, if I don't care about your opinion?

I just don't feel emotions that much and I just don't react that much. You could say my dad would be my biggest supporter, yet my biggest hater. So he would be like, 'This is good, but you could improve.' He'd criticise me so much. I'm so grateful for it, because now I've created a shell where it's like no one else can hurt me.

My dad would always tell me, whatever you do, don't get scared. If you fall off the bike, get on it again! What's the worst that can happen? Once, I went on my sister's big bike; I couldn't even reach the pedals, I fell in the ditch and I was like,

'Oh, help me.' My dad was like, you can do it, you can get up by yourself, come on now! He was always there for me when I needed him, but he would always make me do it first. And he was like, 'I will always be here for you, it's just it's a hard road, you need to do it yourself.'

I'm always seen as the strong friend. I'm always seen as the one everyone comes to with their problems, and I feel like I'd rather be that than me going and crying to someone else. Also, I have so much support in my own family, so if I'm ever down or anything I can just talk to my dad or my mum or my sister and it should all be fine.

When I look back on this time, I don't know, definitely a lot of sadness for everyone that's passed away; also a relief that it's over. Me and my friends were talking about it the other day, how my parents would be like, 'I used to walk six miles to get to school, barefoot, without any clothes on,' and obviously they were lying, but we can be to our kids, over-exaggerating, 'We had to wear masks every second of the day, and we weren't allowed to see people.' We were making fun of it like that. We will just look back and it's kind of crazy that in my life I can say that I've been in a pandemic, a full global pandemic.

# Sarah Townsend

*We had a massive increase in demand for funerals*

*1 March 2021*

I went to Bath College and did beauty therapy and wanted to work on a cruise ship doing beauty. I did a couple of weeks' work experience with the funeral directors, because I also wanted to do stage make-up, and my tutor jokingly said, 'Why don't you go in?' I wasn't squeamish or anything, and I thought, okay, that could be interesting.

My first day, they were all men, and they kind of just said, 'This is a picture of the person; could you do make-up because we don't know how to do it? We've just been bumbling along.' You just got on with it, whereas now, I mean, obviously, you get all kinds of warnings and risk assessments. So yeah, I came in and did these things and did hair, and curled, and straightened, and did whatever the families wanted. And I just thought, wow, this is really a worthwhile job – not that anything else isn't, but I just felt like it was something that I could do. And you know, the families say, 'Oh, you did that. And you did this. It was good.' I had one, she said, 'Did you do my sister's hair?' I said, 'Yeah,' and she went, 'She looked beautiful. She would've loved that.'

I came in the mortuary way, and then I've learnt the other side as well. I felt very comfortable straight away working with deceased. It was just one of those things. It wasn't how you imagine it to be in the films or anything; it wasn't spooky or creepy or anything like that. You know, it was very peaceful, respectful, and light and airy.

It was unusual to have a woman. Even the manager said to me, 'It's a risk. I'm taking a risk on you.' It's not really very PC, but you know what it was like back then. He sort of said, 'I hope families take it okay, having you on funerals.' Now you quite often see women out the front, leading funerals, which is great.

I'm married to a funeral director, doesn't work at the same company, so that's interesting because we were both hit with similar situations with Covid. Never, obviously, seen anything like the last year. We have two small children. Luckily, we were recognised as key workers from the start, so we were able to have our children in school. So that took a lot of pressure off, because it's no secret, is it, that we had a massive increase in demand for funerals, So yeah, it was just a bit of a juggling act, but everyone's been trying to juggle, haven't they?

We generally do, on average, between the seven branches, four or five funerals a day, maybe more, maybe less, and we saw that massively increase because of Covid. We doubled on some weeks. And obviously, along with all funeral directors, we were worried about how we were going to care for those deceased. All councils set up local death management committees for Covid; they would make sure people were able to be stored correctly, you know, respectfully. I've just done it, actually, sent off how many spaces we have in our fridges, how many spaces we have in our other storage. If we need help, they will find space for us.

When someone dies of Covid in the hospital, the family needs to let the bereavement office know who they want to use as a funeral director. So, say they've chosen the company I work for, we would then get a call from the family and the hospital office. Two members of our team go to the hospital. The whole year, since Covid started, every time we enter the hospital, we have to fully PPE up, which is gloves, mask, visor, overshoes. If someone's died of Covid they are sealed, so that there's no risk of infection to us or the mortuary workers. We would check ID, fully masked up, and then we would transfer them, sealed as they are, into our private ambulance. We bring them back to our chapel of rest, where they are put into the temperature-controlled area.

We would then ring the family to arrange a funeral. Usually, that was always done face-to-face, so either we go to their house or they come into our offices. Unfortunately, due to Covid, we have a locked-door policy. The only time they can come in is to the chapel or to drop some paperwork in. All arrangements have gone to Zoom or Teams or on the telephone, which obviously has its own challenges because sometimes some of the people we deal with, they don't have the internet, they don't like doing things like this. It doesn't feel personal for people when they're talking about something so precious to them. You don't have that connection, like you would if they were sat there. Usually you have a cup of tea; sometimes we have families sat with us for two hours, which is not a problem at all.

At the moment, we're allowing two people only at a time in the chapel together. So, you know, a couple can come in and sit in the chapel of rest or, you know, a spouse and someone else to support them. They'll sit with a special piece of music playing in there, or they'll sit with their own thoughts. Because of the risk of infection to our team, and also to the family that wanted to come in, they would have to view with a closed coffin. I mean, some people have that anyway; even before Covid, we were doing closed coffin in the chapel of rest, but it feels very different for that to be the only option for someone, rather than their choice. It's uncomfortable, especially after all these years of looking after deceased, and especially as that's how I came into it, because I know how important that is for people.

Pre-Covid, we weren't having to do these restrictions with the family, so it felt a lot more natural; we could offer what families wanted. So, if a family came to us and said, 'Can we have the coffin at home?'; 'Can we have all these different things – all these different ways of getting to the crematorium or cemetery, so different transports?'; or 'We want to come in and help dress our loved one.' Straight away, with Covid, that control was taken off them because of all the restrictions. I think the hardest thing for me and the rest of the team to deal with was not being able to give the families what they wanted. You know, it felt very unfair: Covid is not something that you can nurse someone through; there's all kinds of infection controls. You can't do the things you would normally want to do; you feel robbed. And for me and the team trying to navigate through that, we were feeling that pressure quite early on. Churches weren't open for some of it. All kinds of things that make a difference to people when they grieve, we weren't able to provide. That was down to national restrictions, it wasn't down to us, but we were the ones translating that to families, so it was really quite tough. You know, families were angry with us, and I totally understand, and afterwards they'd come back and say, 'Okay, we understand, that wasn't your fault.' But at that time we were someone else telling them 'No.' They probably already had that from nurses who were not able to let them go into the wards. So, yeah, it was definitely the toughest time I've ever worked.

Near the beginning last year, we had one family that asked us to hold on to their loved one until the restrictions eased. The father was very well known, and they knew they would have had a big funeral. They asked for us to wait until things were back to normal. So we waited and waited; four weeks went by. We waited and waited, and it was six weeks. We had to phone the family and say, 'There is no end in sight. We don't know when it's going to end, and unfortunately we can no longer hold someone indefinitely.' We can't keep someone for months and months, you know; it's just not the thing we can do. You've got public health and all that involved; you have to dispose of the deceased within a decent amount of time. And obviously we need to make sure we've got room for other people that are coming into our care. We had to put in that rule, because people were asking for it, so they made a ruling that you had to have your funeral within six weeks, as long as the dates could be got.

We can have thirty people at the moment at a funeral, and we have been at thirty since the start. Some areas went to no mourners – Gloucester did – but we didn't in Swindon, which was good because I think that would have been impossible to have tried to explain to someone. What we've advised people not able to go to the funeral to do is to go and stand where the cortège is going to go past. We can go slow if we know there's going to be people waiting on a route; the conductor can get out and walk in front of the hearse. That's quite an old, traditional thing.

When we're out on the road on a funeral, we're seeing a lot more people pausing, people that didn't know the person. I think, because of the effects of Covid, we've seen masses more respect shown to the hearse. We've had cars stopping, where we used to get cut up through lack of respect, or people not realising – they are in their own world and they're driving around thinking about what they've got to do, and then they suddenly realise they've just cut up a hearse.

Crematoriums around the country had been recording services before Covid. It was usually 'I've got an uncle in Australia' or something. Now, sometimes, you can have up to a hundred people or more logging on to watch a service. There are two different systems, and they used to crash, and though people can watch it later on it's quite hard because they've probably psyched themselves up to be part of a service.

You are in that moment, aren't you? And then you can't take part. So we were getting lots and lots of phone calls from people saying, 'It's not working.' So it was a new challenge, and it's getting a lot better. Well, it had to really, because it was something people needed.

I've done it. Unfortunately, one of our colleagues passed away. His funeral was last Saturday, and we watched it online, so that was quite interesting to be on the other side of the Covid watching service. The system crashed because so many people were trying to log on to watch his funeral. So we were in that mindset watching it, and then we couldn't. He was only forty-seven.

We have seen a massive uptake of funerals with no one, so a lot of people doing these cremations without ceremony services. Because restrictions were very tight and people were scared to leave home, especially in the first lockdown, people were saying to us they didn't feel they could go to a funeral. They said, 'Oh these people wouldn't come and these people wouldn't come, so actually we're going to do a cremation without ceremony, and we will have a memorial service when we can, when the restrictions open up.' No one is there, except for our services; there's no minister, there's no family, nothing. They call it the Bowie effect, because that's what David Bowie had, and it became more mainstream. It was always seen as a pauper's funeral. Obviously it's not, because David Bowie did it. It did take some getting used to, walking into the crematorium without having anyone there and putting someone on a catafalque and then leaving. We bow and then leave. It's really quite odd.

My nan passed away, about two months ago, and I feel like she was robbed as well. I don't mean of years, because she was eighty-six; I mean she didn't get the service and the wake afterwards. Wakes are restricted to six people. You can't share the memories with all your family. I think it lengthens grieving because you're not able to share those happy memories; there's nowhere for that outlet. Obviously, some funerals are just desperately sad, there isn't really a lighter moment, but on a lot of funerals you can have a bit of a, 'Oh, I remember when they did that.' And you do that afterwards, don't you? You have the funeral and it's very heavy, and then you come away and you go somewhere, and you might talk about funny memories. The sadness is still there, but you kind of reminisce. And people haven't been able to do that.

We did a child's funeral, and so many people couldn't come that would have come. And the children weren't at school, so it was a case of 'this person's died'. They did a special assembly online, but that was it. The family didn't get the goodbye, like all our families didn't, but I think they really could have done with seeing the full outpouring of love for their child.

And we also have done funerals for people that, unfortunately, you know, struggled with their mental health, and we have seen an increase in that as well. So that's been quite difficult. People taking their lives.

I'm just desperate for things to be normal. Every day is driven by Covid at the moment at work. We have Teams meetings every day at two o'clock, and they're driven by Covid – how much PPE, how many masks have we got, how many gloves? It will just be good to not have that conversation every day. It's constant. How many coffins? You've got masonry that couldn't get here; it comes over on a boat, masonry stone, so they weren't coming over. It would be nice just to have everything in its normal chain. No restrictions on how many coffins we can order, all of those things. I'm not trying to say we are hard done by because, you know, look at the NHS, they're going through it, so I'm not saying we're worse done by than them, but it will just be nice to be able to see our families, speak to them when they come in. I mean, often they'll hold your hand or they give you a hug, and it's been so difficult if someone's really breaking down and you can't just give them a hug.

I had Covid in November [2020]. We think I caught it from a colleague at work. They felt ill; I'd been with them that day. They went home, they had a test. Then I had a test. It was such a shame, because we'd come through all of the tough part of Covid. So, me, my husband and my two children locked down at home. I was poorly for about a week, but apart from that I do think I was quite lucky. I think I was lucky because I've seen how many people we've looked after. I don't have underlying conditions, but even I was shocked at how much it knocked me off my feet.

So many of my friends were furloughed or were working from home, and I found it quite difficult because they were constantly WhatsApping things like, 'Oh, I've done this cooking course online.' A lot of people said about new habits and hobbies. And people were saying, 'I don't know what to do this weekend, I've got nothing to do, I'm so bored.' And I was getting that from family as well. People were saying, 'Oh, let's do another quiz tonight,' and I was thinking, do you know what, Friday night I'm wiped out, I just want to sit on the sofa, just sleep.

But I'm happy to be a key worker. I'm proud of what we've done. I'm proud of everyone that I work with and anyone that's been a funeral director through it, because I think it has been unique. Yeah, just don't want to do it again.

*20 April 2021*

It has quietened down quite a lot, so that's odd because obviously we've been used to being at full speed for a long time. It's given us a chance to get all the staff through their second vaccination, so that's been really good. It's quieter than pre-pandemic. We haven't had anyone with Covid in for over four weeks. None at all. None at all in the whole area. The death rate hit an all-time low last month and has followed on this month, because I think obviously people had already passed away that had illnesses and things like that, people that were vulnerable. It really did hurt the most vulnerable people, didn't it?

The supply chains have sorted themselves out. We've had our masonry delivered now, the stones we were waiting for. But the coffins, they've decided now to only do certain sizes. We used to be able to put in any sizes we wanted, but they've decided to limit the sizes moving forward. They did that during Covid, and they've decided to stay with it. Obviously, it's made it a lot easier for them because they don't need to set their jigger to resize the coffins.

We watched Prince Philip's funeral [17 April 2021]. I was moved by it, because the Queen looked vulnerable and just normal, and we're used to seeing her look really regal, aren't we? It's interesting seeing the Queen sat on her own; obviously, we'd seen that from last April, that people were sat on their own, and it's really hard to see. But for the public, seeing the Queen on her own has really put it in the forefront of people's minds what it was like to go through a funeral during Covid times.

# Pradeep Bhardwaj

*I am a much better human being after this pandemic*

*14 March 2021*

I moved to the UK in the beginning of 2000. I hadn't even heard about Swindon, to be honest. When I was exploring opportunities I came across two of them: one was in London and the other one was in Swindon. I picked Lucent Bell Labs over London, and I made a few enquires, you know, whereabouts is this place Swindon? I have to say, I have no regrets at all; I was fortunate that I landed up here.

I'm an engineering graduate; mainly I specialise in mobile communications. I'm one of the global experts for 5G technology, which is being rolled out around the world. I had the privilege to be involved in a few historic milestones back in India; I was involved in the launch of their first public email service, India's first public electronic data interchange service and India's first public internet service.

In March [2020], I helped set up this group called Swindon Volunteers. We started in simple ways, like picking up medical prescriptions from the local pharmacy here in Wroughton, then delivering to elderly people in the town. Then, when the lockdown was announced, the schools were closed and a lot of children were relying on free school meals, but this was before they started giving the vouchers. They were still preparing the meals at the school, but then this difficulty parents had that, you know, somebody's got to pick up the school meals. So I used to go to the schools and pick up the meals and then deliver to the homes of the children. Then we started with this thing called shop and drop – elderly people can email Swindon Volunteers with their shopping list.

Then we launched this free hot meal service thing. So we used to prepare hot meals at the Patriot Arms in Chiseldon, which is a pub and restaurant. We had well over 150 volunteers who had signed up to the group, and everybody was very eager to help in any way they can. We had a small team of volunteers who would help with the cooking and packing the food. People would order by phone or WhatsApp or email or by Facebook. We would then give a shout out to our volunteers, who would come outside the Patriot Arms. Then the volunteers would drive around and deliver to the residents. We continued with that until August or so, when things started to improve.

We run lots of free kitchens. A lot of things in India – the Indian culture and the Hindu way of life – revolve around food. So, whether it's at festivals or at gatherings, food is considered to be a big, let us say, binding force that brings everyone together. If you are eating the same meal, you kind of become one family; think of it that way and food's a big unifying force. When we give these free meals, it is not necessarily to say that everybody who is benefiting from this is necessarily poor, that's definitely not the point. I think, no, it is more about bringing that feel-good factor. Who doesn't love a free hot meal, whether it is rich or poor? There were a lot of other people also providing free meals. The Biplob were doing that; Rokib was doing a lot. He is a good friend of mine.[34]

I have also been volunteering at STEAM, for the vaccination clinic. I was doing this as part of my Rotary Club. In fact, this

---

34 See earlier interview with Rokib Ali.

week, I had my break because they had lots of volunteers, which is a good thing – good to have a problem of plenty!

I believe in this thing that man is born for the society. Yes, I have a full-time job, but my real passion lies in the community world. For example, we set up the first Hindu temple in the town. If you don't mind, maybe I can give a very small background to that. In 2013, I got a call from Prospect Hospice that somebody from the Hindu faith wanted to have a priest to read from the Hindu scripture during his dying moments. And I really felt bad that I could not find one, because there was nobody available, and because they wanted somebody at very short notice. So that made me think hard that here is this person who has spent almost his entire life here, and we could not afford him the choice or the dignity to die properly. So that is when I started to work on this. Finally, after three long years, we managed to establish this area's first Hindu temple on 1 April 2016. That, I think, is my proudest moment, that is the biggest accomplishment in my life.

Our temple is in a warehouse; we have taken an office block in Cheney Industrial Estate. From outside it looks like a typical office block, but inside it feels very serene and people find peace straight away. In the temple hall we have a big altar, with a set of deities – we have some of the prominent forms of gods and goddesses. These deities have been specially made in India over a period of several months. Some are stone, some are metal, and they are immensely heavy; some you need four people to lift. Yes, very, very heavy and very beautiful. Some people get drawn just by the sight of the deities; they want to have that sight every day.

Normally, the temple is buzzing with activity all the time. It's people chatting and making noise and chanting and praying and singing. We used to have two or three hundred people crammed in that hall upstairs at different events. We have had in excess of a thousand people celebrating at a festival. We had to close the place because of lockdown. We organised a lot of events online, including Diwali, which is the festival of lights. Online, the experience may not be the same as you would typically have at a physical event, but online has the benefit that it has no boundaries, it does not know any borders. So that helped in that sense that certainly we could have, let us say, a different cross section of the community participating, which typically they would not have been able to come to the temple and attend. You have people either who are very elderly, or people, sometimes they don't have transport. Or sometimes people don't have the flexibility to go there at a particular time. Online, the beauty is you attend from anywhere. We are finding a lot of people, for example, they may have children, so they were not able to come in the evening on weekdays, but now they can attend online activities because it's not that onerous for them.

I think we have also realised the limitations of online events, and I think the result of that, moving forwards, is we would move to a new normal which would be a hybrid delivery, where we have physical as well as online events, so that we can have the best of both worlds.

When things started to improve, and again improvement is a relative word, we opened the temple. Obviously, we undertook all the safeguards and the preparations for reopening; we had all the social distancing stickers in place and thorough cleaning twice a day. It is very, very different. You can't mingle and we limited attendees to thirty, so we would have time slots. Last Thursday, we had a big Hindu festival, Lord Shiva's birthday, so we assigned people time slots of thirty minutes. People have to pre-register before coming. They would come in, obviously wearing masks, and they would sanitise their hands and their temperature would be recorded; we would take their consent for recording all these things, and take their name and contact number. Normally we don't put chairs – people sit on the carpet – but now we have chairs. So people sit on these chairs that are limited in numbers and spread apart. Chanting is not allowed in the new Covid protocol. It's a different world.

I think it is good to have career ambitions, but I think we don't spend that much time with the families. Now we are all being forced to spend all the time with the families, working from home. When you have these conference calls, kids and pets are jumping around you sometimes. It's a good thing and nobody bothers. I mean again, in the olden times, in the pre-pandemic times in the corporate circle, people wouldn't have appreciated that. But now it is fine. People say, 'That's fine if you have kids who want to join you in the call, who want to come and sit with you.' People actually encourage that, which is a wonderful thing. That never happened earlier; you should be in a very silent environment, no disturbance and whatnot. Now, sometimes on these conference calls you can see prayer going on in their house, people ringing bells and chanting, and that's absolutely fine.

I think, as human beings, we somehow lost our way. Making money became our highest priority. We became far too ambitious. We became busy in all the things that were not necessarily that important. We got our priorities wrong, and this was, kind of, a correction. So, as it happens, these corrections are normal, very natural. When markets are over-hyped we see corrections in the stock markets, and this is a correction in the market of humanity, if there is one.

People have this feeling that it can't happen to me, people sometimes have this overconfidence. I think what hits you hard is when somebody you know so very well gets Covid and, unfortunately, they don't come out of it. They die. Some of my very good friends are no more with us, and you develop a different perspective of life.

I am a much better human being after this pandemic. I am changed as a person. I think my priorities have changed now in life, how I approach things. I'm tilting the balance decisively in favour of all the things that I believe are right in life. Normally in the corporate world, when you are working you accumulate a lot of stress, stress of all kinds – stress of meeting targets, stress of completing a job, stress of getting a deal signed. So what we do is we overcompensate by partying hard in the evenings and by enjoying the weekend to the fullest. We do that all the time. On business trips, we work hard during the day, and it's a long day, believe me, but the evenings are equally long: we party. But I think what I have realised is there is also great joy in serving the community.

We may believe that sitting in a club or watching the cinema or having drinks in a pub, that these are the only things that give you pleasure and joy. That is not necessarily true. I know that there is a lot of satisfaction in volunteering. So, for me, one decisive change is that I really find true joy in volunteering, so it's not just that I'll put less emphasis on my professional side of things, but I will also place less emphasis on my entertainment and de-stress side of things. I don't necessarily have to party hard and drink hard to find that joy, to de-stress myself. I think the real satisfaction you get is not by winning a race or doing something big, the real satisfaction is when you can make the other person feel happy. You can't measure that joy. That is the most wonderful thing. I think helping a person who needs help is the best service you can render to God, and that is better than praying. The motto that we have at Swindon Hindu temple is, *Hands that help unconditionally are holier than the lips that pray.* We try to practise it every single day, and we all take great pride in that.

In every crisis, we should try to find an opportunity. How do we learn from it, and how do we move forward, so that we emerge better and stronger from that crisis? That is how the human race has evolved over these, you know, tens of thousands of years, so we should use this crisis as a huge opportunity to emerge stronger and make it a better world and find that right balance in everything we do. The right balance in our personal and professional lives, the right balance in our duties – duties towards family, duties towards society, duties towards nature, duties towards the world at large. So I think this is the right time; we should make a new start and find that right balance which can serve the people and the planet better. So, maybe, I think, on that note, I can stop!

*Afterword – one year later*

The pandemic has caused irreparable damage to our communities, and to our Hindu community in particular. What happened was we had six different break-ins at the temple, and as a result the lease from the council was terminated because the place was deemed unsafe. So we do not have a temple now, not as a direct consequence of the pandemic, but those break-ins happened because the pandemic forced us into a lockdown where people were not visiting the temple and it was not being opened on a regular basis. The bad elements in society, they made the most of that opportunity to burgle and break in. So, while everything is open back again now, we do not have a temple and the deities are simply stored at the moment.

It started as theft, for monetary gains, but after the first three instances of break-ins, when they broke into the temple area, then it turned into something else, because the way they desecrated the altar, the way they treated the idols of the gods and goddesses, the way they disrespected and vandalised the religious artefacts and items, that, without any iota of doubt, was clearly motivated by causing disrespect to the Hindu faith. Why would anybody throw an idol on the floor? They brought items from upstairs in the temple hall and threw them on the ground floor in the back warehouse area, and they had to walk maybe thirty or forty metres to do that carrying those items.

We are still trying to recover from this, and it's a challenge. When sadness prevails upon you for a long period it turns into disillusionment, and you tend to withdraw, you tend to give up, you tend to feel it's not worth it. But we have now taken new premises; we are going through the planning processes and formalities for acquiring those premises. We will have to undertake huge recommissioning work, refurbishment; tens of thousands of pounds to get back to where we were earlier, and still we would not be at the same place. I think it pushed our lives back by more than a decade, I would say. That is the story of human evolution, that we are presented with challenges and sometimes we can cope well, sometimes we cannot.

# Appendix
## *Timeline of lockdowns in England, 2020 to 2022*

*First national lockdown – March to June 2020*

On 23 March 2020, Boris Johnson announced the UK's first national lockdown. People could only leave their homes for strictly limited reasons, including shopping for essential items and one form of outdoor exercise each day. The police were given powers to enforce the rules. All non-essential shops closed, as did schools, except to children of key workers and vulnerable children.

*Minimal lockdown restrictions – July to September 2020*

Most lockdown restrictions were lifted on 4 July. Gatherings of up to thirty people were allowed, though the government recommended against more than six people meeting.

*Further restrictions – September to October 2020*

On 14 September, gatherings were legally restricted to six people, whether indoors or outdoors. A range of restrictions came to be imposed across England, with the government introducing a three-tier system on 14 October. While most of the country began on Tier 1, as time went by most areas came to be placed in the higher two tiers.

*Second national lockdown – November 2020*

On 5 November, a second national lockdown began.

*Resumption of tiered system – December 2020*

By the beginning of December, the second lockdown ended and the tiered system was re-introduced, with a fourth tier added. By 30 December, seventy-five per cent of the country was placed in Tier 4.

*Third national lockdown – January to March 2021*

A third lockdown was imposed from 6 January 2021.

*Leaving lockdown – from March 2021*

From 8 March 2021, England began a phased exit from lockdown, and the majority of restrictions ended by 19 July 2021. On 21 February 2022, the very last domestic restriction was lifted when people with Covid-19 were no longer required to self-isolate.

## Acknowledgements

When I began this project, we were in the middle of lockdown, so I could not wander around streets and parks, shops and places of worship, looking for potential interviewees. Instead, I had to take a new approach to writing an oral history: I put messages out on social media, got articles onto local news sites, wrote emails and sent out flyers to the convenience stores that remained open throughout the pandemic. I was concerned that it might be hard to find anyone to interview, let alone enough people to fill a book. I need not have worried. My first response was a reply on Facebook that simply said, 'Can my input just be a page of aghhh all in caps? It's all I have to be honest.' From an initial trickle of interest, it snowballed as people came forward to share their experiences. To all those who spoke to me – to all those I interviewed, not just those whose tales appear in print – I extend the greatest thanks and gratitude.

Thanks also to my readers at various stages of the manuscript, in particular Rachel Murphy, Rosemary Martindale and Sarah Byrne. And to my family - my husband, children and mum - for their love and support.

© Katie Ball

A. J. Stone was a residential social worker at a specialist community for disadvantaged, vulnerable and traumatised young people. She has a Masters in Creative Writing from the University of Oxford and is the author of several short stories and radio dramas. *Unlocked: Portraits of a Pandemic* is her first non-fiction book.